THE UNBELIEVERS

THE

UNBELIEVERS

The Evolution of
MODERN ATHEISM

S. T. JOSHI

59 John Glenn Drive
Amherst, New York 14228-2119

Published 2011 by Prometheus Books

Inquiries should be addressed to
Prometheus Books
59 John Glenn Drive
Amherst, New York 14228–2119
VOICE: 716–691–0133
FAX: 716–691–0137
WWW.PROMETHEUSBOOKS.COM

15 14 13 12 11 5 4 3 2 1

Library of Congress Cataloging-in-Publication Data

Joshi, S. T., 1958–
The unbelievers: the evolution of modern atheism / by S. T. Joshi.
p. cm.
Includes bibliographical references and index.
ISBN 978–1–61614–236–0 (pbk.)
1. Atheism. 2. Agnosticism. 3. Secularism. I. Title.

BL2747.3.J67 2011
211'.8—dc22

2010043636

Printed in the United States of America

CONTENTS

INTRODUCTION

In the absence of a full-scale and up-to-date history of atheism,[1] the following chapters are offered in the hope that they can serve as the nucleus for at least certain phases of that history. In the West, we might well commence with the shadowy figure of Diagoras the Atheist, a Greek thinker of the late fifth century BCE who was forced to flee Athens because he declared that there were no gods at all. His punishment is one that atheists, agnostics, secularists, and freethinkers of all stripes would face for the better part of the next two and a half millennia. We have no writings by Diagoras (who was also a lyric poet), and only the scantiest accounts of or anecdotes about him; but this proto-Voltaire appears to have taken great pleasure both in logical proofs against the existence of the Greek gods and in light-hearted mockery of the average Greek's credulous acceptance of implausible and paradoxical notions of deity.

The fact that Diagoras was a disciple of Democritus is perhaps no accident. Democritus was not an avowed atheist, but this cofounder (with the even more shadowy Leucippus, who may not have existed at all) of atomism was perhaps the most penetrating thinker in classical antiquity—Plato and Aristotle not excepted—and it is a tragedy of the first order that his voluminous work survives only in extensive fragments. As a materialist, Democritus pioneered the scientific approach to the problems of existence: he regarded both the mind and the soul as intimately related material parts of the body; he apparently denied the survival of the soul after death; he envisioned a crude theory of evolution by declaring that human beings arose out of water and mud. It is true that Democritus conceived his theories of the universe and of human life largely by deduction rather than by experiment, but the fact that, as W. K. C. Guthrie notes, "Democritus's biological work must have rivalled Aristotle's in comprehensiveness and attention to detail,"[2] makes us keenly regret that his work has almost entirely perished. Had it survived, the history of Western thought would have been substantially different.

Democritus's atomism was adopted by Epicurus (341–270 BCE), whose conception of the gods—they are beings of infinite material tenuity, dwelling in the *intermundia* (the spaces between the stars) contemplating their own perfection and having nothing to do with imperfect human beings—is as close to atheism as any thinker aside from Diagoras ever came in classical antiquity; indeed, the Epicureans were often accused of atheism by rival philosophical sects. Through the imperishable poetry of Lucretius's *De Rerum Natura*, the philosophy of Epicurus (which also survives only in fragments) ultimately reached the early modern period and was a significant intellectual influence on the Renaissance.

The advocates of religion point with a certain smug pride at the fact that many, perhaps all, of the leading scientific thinkers of the fifteenth through nineteenth centuries were Christians. To this claim a number of remarks can be made: first, few of them appear to have conducted their researches *because* they were Christian, and a number of them were clearly hostile to certain core elements of Christian dogma; second, as Richard Dawkins has pointed out, there was very little option for these thinkers, since the open profession of anything approaching even skepticism, let alone actual atheism or even agnosticism, would have quickly led to severe punishment, not excluding death; and, third and most important, regardless of their own views, it was the work of these scientists that laid the groundwork for the fully secular conception of the universe that became possible in the middle to late nineteenth century. The work of Copernicus, Galileo, Kepler, Newton, Laplace, and many others was central in the arduous task of thrusting God out of the universe: with their explanations in place, God suddenly had nothing to do—he could no longer be considered responsible for the revolution of the planets, the seemingly erratic appearance of comets, the very formation of the solar system and the universe—and these developments led inevitably to the formation of Deism, a halfway house to atheism in its assertion that God does indeed exist, but that all he did was get the universe started and then, like the Epicurean gods, sit back and admire his handiwork.

The emergence of religious skeptics in the later seventeenth and eighteenth centuries is striking; it becomes rare to find any thinker of note who does not harbor some doubts about many phases of religious orthodoxy. The mere fact that the empiricist philosopher John Locke was forced to write a slim and sadly unconvincing tract on *The Reasonableness of Christianity* (1695) suggests that there were any number of thinkers who no longer regarded Christianity as reasonable. In England,

David Hume was at the forefront of religious skeptics, but he was overwhelmed by the tidal wave of French *philosophes*—Montesquieu, Diderot, d'Alembert, Voltaire, Holbach, La Mettrie, Condorcet—several of whom were actual atheists and wrote pungently against the doctrinal, ethical, and political errors of the church. Even orthodox religionists were compelled to moderate their positions. The noted Anglican clergyman Conyers Middleton wrote a bold treatise, *A Free Inquiry into the Miraculous Powers* (1749), declaring that the "miracles" found in the scriptures must all be rejected as contrary to natural law.

It was in this period, too, that Voltaire and others, repelled by centuries of religious warfare, made fervent pleas for religious toleration—pleas that ultimately prevailed in much of the West, although at a curious cost. Since the main monotheistic religions—Christianity, Judaism, and Islam—all made *exclusive* claims to the truth about God, the notion that there could be any "tolerance" of opposing views becomes paradoxical, even heretical. Yet religious sects had very little choice in the matter: the continuing wars over points of doctrine—not to mention such abominations as the persecution of hundreds of thousands of "witches" and heretics, the forced conversion of Jews and Muslims to Christianity, and the various social and legal barriers against non-Christians—were becoming so intolerable to evolving standards of civilization that their abandonment was inevitable.

The upshot of these developments was momentous not merely in terms of intellectual history—where, it might now be said, the burden of proof began to shift to the pious to prove, or even to render plausible, a continued belief in God rather than to freethinkers to doubt or deny his existence—but in political history. In effect, the late eighteenth and much of the nineteenth centuries saw the definitive eviction of religion from positions of legal and political power in the West. The United States can take pride in being the first nation to enshrine a separation of church and state, while atheist France of the post-Revolutionary period became the first Western nation to abolish slavery. The Anglican church may have been nominally the established church of Great Britain, but its powers and privileges underwent a steady decline in the course of the nineteenth century. And the decline of the power of the Catholic church—once dominant throughout Europe in the guise of the Holy Roman Empire, but reduced by 1870 to a postage-stamp-sized principality engulfed in a newly resurgent Italy—is as cataclysmic as the fall of the Roman Empire itself. As W. E. H. Lecky states in his landmark treatise, *History of the Rise and Influence of the Spirit of Rationalism in Europe* (1865), "No human pen can write its epitaph, for no imagination can adequately realise its glories."[3]

Two intellectual movements represented a pinnacle in the formation of a fully secular view of life and the universe. The first was the publication of Charles Darwin's *Origin of Species* (1859), a treatise that provided an overwhelmingly convincing refutation of the final argument to which religionists had clung in defense of their worldview—the argument from design. It is no wonder that the theory of evolution continues to provoke a furor among the religious, for they appear to sense dimly that it constitutes the final piece of the puzzle that allows atheists to be, in Richard Dawkins's words, "intellectually fulfilled." It is no accident that one of Darwin's chief defenders, Thomas Henry Huxley, also became a leading agnostic philosopher of the age.

The second movement was no less significant. The "higher criticism"—the study of the historical origins of the Bible, as opposed to "lower criticism," which focused on textual analysis—was fostered by a succession of mostly German historians beginning in the late eighteenth century and centered around the University of Tübingen. It should be emphasized that few of these scholars were avowed atheists or even freethinkers—the one notable exception was David Friedrich Strauss, whose radical *Life of Jesus* (1835) was translated into English by George Eliot—but the effect of their work was no less revolutionary. For the first time, it became clear that the Bible was simply a somewhat haphazard collocation of tracts written over a very long period by a wide array of authors, containing material both historical and unhistorical, and rife with contradictions and paradoxes. The upshot of this work was to deal a deathblow to the notion that the Bible was somehow "inspired" by God; it became an all-too-human work that at best embodied the hopes and fears of its diverse authors. It is difficult to convey the significance of this intellectual cataclysm: while Christians may not have adhered to the Islamic belief that their scripture was somehow dictated by God, they nevertheless rarely doubted its direct inspiration by their deity, and the systematic obliteration of this conception left many of the faithful in a state of unnerved puzzlement. Toward the end of the century, a number of literary works focused on loss of faith through increasing awareness of its intellectual deficiencies; perhaps the most noteworthy was the bestselling novel *Robert Elsmere* (1888) by Mrs. Humphry Ward.

A third development may be worth noting here—the rise of the disciplines of psychology and anthropology. Such pioneering anthropological works as Edward Burnett Tylor's *Primitive Culture* (1871) and Sir James George Frazer's *The Golden Bough* (1890–1915) established with an impressive array of evidence that primitive human beings invariably invented gods, demons, and angels as a means of accounting for the bewildering array of natural phenomena that they were incapable of explaining rationalistically, so that the early growth and development of religion was a necessary but entirely human-created component of the progress of the species. Psychologists such as Havelock Ellis and Sigmund Freud began accounting for the continuing tenacity of religious belief as an outgrowth of wish-fulfillment, fear of death, indoctrination by parents and other authority figures, and other elements that have nothing to do with the truth or falsity of the belief in question. Once again, these discoveries brought religion down to earth by making it an all-too-human reaction to phenomena that had puzzled our ancestors and continue to puzzle us today.

The result, by the end of the nineteenth century, was inevitable: a wide and diverse array of thinkers began speaking out more and more forcefully against religion in general and (in the West) Christianity in particular—using not merely the tools of logical analysis, scientific discovery, and careful scrutiny of sacred texts, but also the perhaps more-effective weapons of satire, mockery, and ridicule. No longer was it necessary to postpone antireligious criticisms, even the mildest, to a period beyond one's death, as John Stuart Mill still felt the need to do with his *Three Essays on Religion* (1874). This was when Friedrich Nietzsche could write, toward the end of his career, such fulminations as *Twilight of the Idols* (a parody of the Wagnerian conception of the twilight of the gods) and *The Antichrist*; when Clarence Darrow, in a succession of public debates with religious figures, could argue vociferously against the existence of God, the immortality of the soul, and the reliance of morality upon religion; and, most pungently of all, when H. L. Mencken, in article after article in the *Baltimore Evening Sun* (subsequently syndicated in many other newspapers), could heap abuse upon the benighted

Tennesseeans who had passed an antievolution law and put the hapless John Thomas Scopes on trial in 1925. True, Mark Twain reserved many of his most ferocious tirades against religion to posthumous publication, whether it be such works of fiction as *The Mysterious Stranger* or such essays as "Reflections on Religion"; and H. P. Lovecraft—whose horror fiction, in spite of its citation of alien "gods" that ruled the cosmos, was atheistic to its core—was in his time not celebrated enough to find widespread publication for the antireligious tirades he embedded in essays and letters. But such figures were a minority. Bertrand Russell, the most distinguished philosopher of the twentieth century, was an atheist from his earliest days and made no secret of the fact; the revocation of his teaching assignment at the City College of New York in 1940 brought more disrepute upon the college, and upon American religious figures in general, than it did upon himself.

The Scopes trial was a landmark event in that it put an eventual halt (only temporarily, sad to say) to efforts to ban evolution from the public schools, and also caused religious fundamentalists to go underground in the United States for half a century. In England the situation was quite different: the Church of England, in spite of its established status, was losing adherents by the year; the "dissenting" churches (other Protestant sects) and Roman Catholicism weren't faring much better. The same could be said for much of Western Europe, where churchgoing became increasingly a formality that could easily be foregone. The interwar years were a period in which many intellectuals believed that religion might be on the way out; it might indeed have been for them, but the general populace appeared unwilling to face a purely secular future. World War II strengthened the forces of religion—not so much by the defeat of the Nazis, who were not atheists in any meaningful sense of the term, but by fears of Soviet and Chinese communism, which was seen by many as a baleful instance of atheistic totalitarianism. Even today, many religionists still use the specter of communism and socialism—despite their thorough intellectual, political, and economic demise in the past two decades—as a stick with which to beat atheists over the head. It was, let us recall, in the postwar period that the motto "In God We Trust" became affixed permanently and uniformly to the US currency, and when "under God" was inserted into the Pledge of Allegiance. Both insertions are so flagrantly in violation of the First Amendment's establishment clause that it is difficult to credit how they could have survived legal challenges in the past half century.

Yet the intellectual prospects for religion were not improving. Indeed, such theologians as Paul Tillich (*Dynamics of Faith*, 1957) and Hans Küng (*Does God Exist?* 1980) questioned some central tenets of Christian belief, such as the omnipotence of God and the reality of miracles, and many other religious persons began unconsciously adopting a nebulous, dogma-free faith that allowed them to evade intellectual scrutiny of positions that had, with the advance of human knowledge, become untenable. Leslie Stephen had already pointed to such a tendency as early as his trenchant essay "Are We Christians?" (1873), but it gained force even among prominent religious figures as the twentieth century came to a close. Many individuals found themselves disenchanted with mainline Christian denominations, adopting a tenuous belief in vaguely "spiritual" values or shedding faith altogether. The 1960s were a time of social ferment, with sexual liberation challenging the church's ferociously enforced dicta on every phase of sexual life, and with the Existentialists (most of them atheists or agnostics) and their partial inspiration, Nietzsche, gaining wide followings on college campuses. It was during this period that the liberalizing Vatican II council (1962–1965) occurred, as well as Madalyn Murray O'Hair's improbable campaign to ban sectarian prayer in American public schools, which reached a successful culmination in a Supreme Court verdict of 1963.

The past three or four decades have appeared to witness a rebirth of religion, but this rebirth has occurred in relatively narrow confines. The founding of the Moral Majority in 1978 was, in large part, a counterrevolution to the turmoil of the 1960s and early 1970s, when a certain class of Americans reached the limit of their endurance of what they perceived to be the moral laxity of American society as evidenced in the increasing sexual content of all aesthetic and entertainment products, from books and magazines to films and television. Fundamentalists now claim to constitute at least a quarter of the American populace, but their overall influence has been surprisingly weak: they have discovered that the First Amendment is stronger than any popular clamor that demands erection of the Ten Commandments on public ground or the reintroduction of prayer into public schools. Abortion remains legal, gays and women continue to make legal strides, banning the teaching of evolution (or the introduction of its stalking-horse, "intelligent design") rarely succeeds, and the politicians who lay lip service to the devout do little more than that, refusing to enact legislation that would advance their agenda. To such a degree does their frustration boil up that one of their tribunes, David Limbaugh (brother of Rush), could actually write a treatise in 2003 claiming that Christians were being "persecuted" in the United States![4]

But we should not let the noisy religious right in this country take our attention away from what is happening in the rest of the world. In most of the countries in Western Europe, religion has become such an irrelevancy that, for perhaps the first time in human history, it can plausibly be said that civilized societies are essentially nonreligious. This development exposes the intellectual weakness of assertions claiming that society and morals cannot function in the absence of religion: there is scarcely any doubt that the nations of Western Europe constitute thriving, culturally vibrant societies in which religion plays a relatively insignificant role; that their rates of crime, in particular of violent crime, are immensely lower than that of the pious United States should tell us much about the intersection of religion and antisocial behavior.

The rest of the world, perhaps, is not so happy, and religious conflicts continue to plague much of South America, Africa, and especially the Middle East and Asia. For the first time since the Renaissance, the nations of the West are facing the emergence of a militant form of Islam, and how we deal with this threat will define geopolitical stability for at least the coming generation. I will argue in this book that this threat is perhaps less significant than it appears on the surface, and that it may give way sooner than we think to liberalizing forces that have nothing to do with atheism or science, but have everything to do with the spread of communications technologies and notions of political, social, and intellectual freedom. Nevertheless, the radicalization of even a tiny number of Muslims now has the potential to put the entire world at risk.

Intellectually, however, at least in the West, the battle is, in my mind, over. Atheism has won. The intellectual classes are, if not explicitly atheistic, certainly nonreligious and in many cases antireligious. Very few cultural products—books, television shows, films, music—are based on religion or religious themes, and the great majority assume an atheistic worldview. The fact that, especially in America, the state of public education is so poor has created an unfortunate cleavage between the tiny band of intellectual elites and the vast mass of the ignorant and ill educated. For it does take a certain amount of knowledge—knowledge of science, knowledge of history, knowledge of language and literature, knowledge of fundamental philosophical conceptions—to grasp the intellectual issues at stake in the battle between religion and irreligion, and once those issues are grasped, the majority will come, regretfully or joyously, to the realization that religion simply has no credibility. It is an emperor without clothes and has been without clothes for the better part of two centuries.

The truth of these assertions is evident not so much in the surprising burst of bestselling atheist books of the past few years—Sam Harris's *The End of Faith* (2004), Richard Dawkins's *The God Delusion* (2006), and Christopher Hitchens's *God Is Not Great* (2007)—as in the peculiar defensiveness of those who seek to maintain the tattered attire of that naked emperor. I do not refer to such intellectual embarrassments as Dinesh D'Souza's *What's So Great about Christianity* (2007), a work by a right-wing political commentator who is so out of his depth in matters of philosophy and science that he presents a better case *against* religious belief than any atheist could. Even more respectable works—such as Robert Wright's *The Evolution of God* (2009) and Karen Armstrong's *The Case for God* (2009)—make very curious reading. Wright's ponderously long and simple-minded treatise goes into painstaking detail about the "evolution" of our conceptions of God, relating the progression of thought in the Judeo-Christian world toward a "better" (by which Wright apparently means more tolerant, less savage and primitive) idea of deity. Aside from his irritating tendency to present as startling revelations certain findings that have been known to scholars and even general readers for decades, Wright is remarkable in failing to attribute much of this supposed "advance" in religious thinking to the work of the irreligious; for it is, as I have suggested above, precisely they who have forced religions to give up some of their more preposterous dogmas and also to treat both their adherents and their opponents in a civilized manner that precludes burning at the stake, fines and imprisonment for "blasphemy," and the like. This same flaw besets Armstrong's misleadingly titled book, which is in no sense a defense of the notion of godhead but merely a detailed examination of the intellectual and cultural means by which successive generations, mostly in the West, have wrestled with the god idea. Neither book provides much comfort to the pious.

I have written this book in the hope that it might shed some light on the development of atheist thought over the past century and a half or so. It will quickly become evident that not all writers treated here were full-fledged atheists, although a good number were; but even those who were agnostics or secularists, or even quasi-religious in their own distinctive ways (such as Mark Twain), provided intellectual fodder for what has become a viable and challenging atheist vision of the universe and of human life. In some cases, where the figures in question are not as well known as they should be, I have provided a certain modicum of biographical information to place their thought in the context of their lives and their historical eras; in other cases, my focus is largely on the details of their thought as evinced in their writings. I have been careful to cite actual passages from their work, sometimes at length, to convey the flavor of their prose and the tendency of their thought. In cases where a given work is cited frequently within a chapter, I have provided full bibliographical information for the first citation; further citations appear under an abbreviation and are included in the text.

There will always be a question as to which figures should or should not be treated in a work of this sort, and I will confess that in some instances I have chosen some thinkers and rejected others chiefly because I do or do not share an intellectual sympathy with them. Such a figure as Robert G. Ingersoll, probably the most celebrated American freethinker of the nineteenth century, seems to me more interesting for his rhetorical gifts than for the intellectual substance of his work, so I have bypassed him here. The Existentialists, especially Camus and Sartre, are of considerable significance in the development of contemporary atheism, but their work is difficult to summarize in small compass; much the same could be said for such a recent thinker as Kai Neilsen. And the true history of modern atheism, as I have suggested above, really begins in the eighteenth century, with the French *philosophes* and the British and American Deists, including the Founding Fathers, but a treatment of their work requires far more space than I could devote to it here.

If the three bestselling atheist books of recent years tell us anything, it is that there are millions of individuals in the West who have been waiting eagerly for the definitive emergence of a bold, forthright atheism that challenges religious orthodoxy and the lingering, but unearned, respect that religion continues to demand in spite of its intellectual, social, political, and cultural failings. Certain tender-minded souls may lament this revitalized "warfare between reason and religion" and hope against hope for some "reconciliation" between the two factions; but, like many other conflicts, there is simply insufficient common ground to foster such a reconciliation. Reason and religion look at the world in such antipodally different ways that even matters of potential agreement (such as in certain phases of morality) are arrived at from such different directions that the agreement becomes ultimately superficial and transient. As some of our recent writers have asserted, the outcome of this conflict may go a long way in determining what kind of future humanity has—or whether it has a future.

Chapter 1

THOMAS HENRY HUXLEY: GLADIATOR-GENERAL FOR SCIENCE

Thomas Henry Huxley (1825–1895) was, even more than his great friend Charles Darwin, the face of British science in the latter half of the nineteenth century. A far more forceful and dynamic public speaker than the shy and retiring Darwin, Huxley rapidly embraced the theory of evolution and used it as a springboard for the establishment of a purely secular worldview. In pure philosophy, he is noted for coining the term *agnosticism* and for defending it—both as a philosophical principle and in its ethical ramifications—in a series of vigorous papers he wrote in the final decade of his life.

The most important fact about Huxley may be his birth above a butcher's shop in the town of Ealing, now a suburb of London. That he was born into a manifestly lower-middle-class family, with limited means and opportunities for education and economic advancement, at a time when English society was still highly stratified by class, may account for much of the aggressiveness he demonstrated in defending his scientific and philosophical views against his opponents. This is not to say that Huxley's hostility toward his perceived intellectual enemies was exclusively or even largely based on class; rather, it suggests that his determination to prevail in his chosen profession was in no small part founded upon his quest to transcend his socioeconomic origins and to prove that someone of his class could indeed excel in areas that had previously been reserved for his social betters. Huxley, indeed, could be said to have been instrumental in the transition of English science from an aristocracy of class to an aristocracy of intellect.

As the sixth and youngest child of an impecunious schoolteacher, Huxley had only two years of formal education—at Ealing School, where his father taught mathematics. He later looked back upon his boyhood:

"I see myself as a boy, whose education has been interrupted, and who, intellectually, was left, for some years, altogether to his own devices. At that time, I was a voracious and omnivorous reader; a dreamer and speculator of the first water, well endowed with that splendid courage in attacking any and every subject, which is the blessed compensation of youth and inexperience."[1] Elsewhere Huxley also recalled the general tenor of religious teaching during his childhood, when biblical literalism was unquestioned and the very existence of religious skepticism was almost unheard of:

> From dark allusions to "sceptics" and "infidels," I became aware of the existence of people who trusted in carnal reason; who audaciously doubted that the world was made in six natural days, or that the deluge was universal; perhaps even went so far as to question the literal accuracy of the story of Eve's temptation, or of Balaam's ass; and, from the horror of the tones in which they were mentioned, I should have been justified in drawing the conclusion that these rash men belonged to the criminal classes. ("Prologue" to *SC* 21)

Yet perhaps Huxley is guilty of underplaying the influence of religion upon his own temperament: although he does not ever seem to have been an orthodox believer, the influence of the Evangelical movement during his youth—a movement that strove to take religion out of the churches and to use it as a force for social betterment—may well have led Huxley, in later years, to do what he could to relieve the suffering of the poor through scientific inquiry and advance.

After taking some classes in anatomy at Sydenham College (1841–1842) and doing further study at Charing Cross Hospital (1842–1845), Huxley, seeking a way to make an income, decided to become an assistant surgeon on the HMS *Rattlesnake*; its four-year journey to Australia and the South Seas (1846–1850) was a kind of poor man's voyage of the *Beagle*, but it resulted both in Huxley's first scientific work—chiefly on corals and other invertebrates—as well as his acquaintance with Henrietta Anna Heathorn, whom he would marry in 1855 and with whom he would have eight children during a long and generally happy marriage.

Huxley's return to England in 1850 saw him plunged into the world of both science and philosophy. Not only was he—remarkably for someone without orthodox academic credentials—elected a Fellow of the Royal Society in 1851, but it was not long before he became acquainted with the leading thinkers of the age, including George Henry Lewes and Herbert Spencer. As he remarked in a letter, "Every thinking man I have met with is at heart in a state of doubt"[2] about religion. These doubts were, ultimately, only augmented by his encounter with Charles Darwin—a relation that became the seminal event of his intellectual life.

Huxley appears to have come into epistolary contact with Darwin in 1851 or 1852, and their first meeting occurred in 1856. Darwin was, of course, by this time already at work on the book, first titled *Natural Selection*, that became *The Origin of Species*; indeed, he had devised his theory of evolution in rough form as early as 1837. Huxley was already an up-and-coming figure in British science, specializing in paleontology. But, like his friend Charles Lyell (whose landmark treatise *The Principles of Geology* [1830] was one of the first to present a cogent account of the million-year history of the earth, in contrast to the creation story in Genesis), he was still so much under the sway of contemporary religious and scientific thinking that he refused to acknowledge the possibility of any transmutation of one species into another, in spite of the weighty evidence that Darwin had amassed; the notion that each species, especially humankind, had been the product of "special creation" was still so uniformly held that it required years for even so dynamic and iconoclastic a thinker as Huxley to wrap his mind around the idea. But he finally did so in the mid-1850s, to the great pleasure and relief of Darwin. Darwin, indeed, was himself asking for Huxley's advice on small points of biology and paleontology while preparing the final draft of *The Origin of Species*.

It was, in fact, Huxley who first proclaimed—in a lecture entitled "The Distinctive Characters of Man," given at the Royal Institution—the relation of man to the apes, and he did so in 1858, a year before the publication of Darwin's treatise. Displaying the brain of a baboon, a gorilla, and a human being, Huxley declared: "Now I am quite sure that if we had these three creatures fossilized or preserved in spirits for comparison and were quite unprejudiced judges we should at once admit that there is very little greater interval *as animals* between the *Gorilla* and the *Man* than exists between the *Gorilla* and the [baboon] *Cynocephalus*."[3] Even though Huxley went on to maintain the vast *cultural* gap between man and the apes, his lecture created a furor.

That furor was, of course, dwarfed by the emergence, in November

1859, of *The Origin of Species*. Darwin, indeed, had delayed the publication of his book for years precisely because of the intellectual turmoil he knew it would cause: temperamentally very unlike Huxley, he wished only to lead the quiet life of a gentleman scientist, and as the publication date of his book approached, he actually became ill and had to recuperate in a sanitarium. Huxley, for his part, wrote at least three separate reviews of the book, including a highly prominent one in the London *Times* (December 26, 1859). In these notices, he was not shy in pointing out the implications of the work upon religious orthodoxy; in one of them, he pungently noted, "Extinguished theologians lie about the cradle of every science as the strangled snakes beside that of Hercules."[4] Huxley had by this time already become so intimately associated with Darwin that many of the attacks on *The Origin of Species* took aim at the scientist who would become its most tireless defender.

The most celebrated contretemps—one that catapulted Huxley into a celebrity that today is accorded only to rock stars or sports figures—occurred at the meeting of the British Association for the Advancement of Science at Oxford in June 1860. The highly orthodox Samuel Wilberforce—an honorary vice-president of the association, a title he received as a consequence of his being the bishop of Oxford—attempted a feeble joke at Huxley's expense by publicly wondering whether the apes in his ancestry were on his grandfather's or his grandmother's side. When Huxley took the stage, he had a ready and devastating response, as he notes in a letter:

> If then, said I, the question is put to me would I rather have a miserable ape for a grandfather or a man highly endowed by nature and possessed of great means of influence and yet who employs these faculties and that influence for the mere purpose of introducing ridicule into a grave scientific discussion, I unhesitatingly affirm my preference for the ape.[5]

(The letter by Huxley is cited because there is no printed account of this part of the proceedings.) What this crushing response suggests, aside from Huxley's quick-wittedness, is that a good deal of his hostility to religion derived from what he believed were the unjust benefits and advantages that the Anglican clergy received as a result of the government's continued support of the Church of England. The mere fact that an

Anglican bishop who clearly had no grasp of science was permitted to deliver a speech in front of a serious scientific conference offended Huxley's notions of scientific rigor and professionalism.

As a minor footnote, Wilberforce did gain a bit of revenge by being inexplicably chosen by John Murray, Darwin's own publisher and the editor of the *Quarterly Review*, a leading intellectual journal of the period, to write a review of *The Origin of Species*! Huxley was astounded that Murray could have perpetrated such a gaffe; the review was, as everyone could have predicted, both hostile and ignorant.

Yet it was precisely because Darwin, in *The Origin of Species*, was so cagey in regard to *human* evolution that Huxley felt the need to step in. By this time, as he stated in a lecture that also caused an uproar, "I entertained no doubt of the origin of man from the same stock as the apes."[6] And so Huxley, in 1863, published *Evidence as to Man's Place in Nature*—eight years before Darwin addressed the same issue in *The Descent of Man* (1871). His biographer, Adrian Desmond, speaks with pardonable exaggeration when he writes, "Huxley was about to utter the greatest profanity since Copernicus moved the earth from the centre of the universe. He would move man from the centre of creation."[7] The book, a revision of a series of lectures given to a working-class audience, was an immediate success; it was read throughout the English-speaking world and was translated into several European languages. Its frontispiece—depicting a series of five skeletons, from primitive apedom to modern man, each becoming progressively more upright in stature but also clearly related in basic framework—has become iconic. But Huxley's nemesis, Samuel Wilberforce, was still being a pest. At the Oxford Diocesan Conference on November 25, 1864, he egged on the mild-mannered but highly conservative Tory leader Benjamin Disraeli into the celebrated comment: "Is man an ape or an angel? I, my lord, I am on the side of the angels. I repudiate with indignation and abhorrence those newfangled theories." But the time was rapidly passing when such ill-informed pronunciamentoes could check the growing skepticism of the age.

It was, indeed, around this time that Huxley began slowly turning his attention from pure science to the philosophical and religious implications of science. It was at a meeting of the Metaphysical Society on April 21, 1869, that he coined the term *agnosticism*. The meeting had been convened to discuss the very question of the existence of God, and Huxley claimed to be offended by "gnostics" on either side of the issue—both those religious fossils who continued to maintain biblical inerrancy and those who claimed to "know" that God did *not* exist. Huxley himself did not wish to be associated with the positivism of Auguste Comte, who had postulated a tripartite evolution of human thought, proceeding from the religious to the metaphysical to the positive (whereby thought, action, and morals would presumably be founded on science); Huxley dismissed Comte as a bad scientist and a covert religionist, referring to positivism as "Catholicism *minus* Christianity."[8] And there is some evidence that Huxley did not proceed all the way to atheism—even though it is eminently clear that his reliance on science left very little room for God to function—because he feared being linked to an unruly group of radical atheists who for decades had sought to convert the masses from Christianity to freethought: Huxley, having worked so hard to climb out of the lower-class prison of his birth, did not wish to fall back into it even on an intellectual level.

His solution was agnosticism. For Huxley the term had both intellectual and moral implications. From an intellectual perspective, he was simply seeking to distinguish himself from those who, in his judgment, asserted certainly about matters on which certainty was impossible:

> When I reached intellectual maturity and began to ask myself whether I was an atheist, a theist, or a pantheist; a materialist or an idealist; a Christian or a freethinker; I found that the more I learned and reflected, the less ready was the answer; until, at last, I came to the conclusion that I had neither art nor part with any of these denominations, except the last. The one thing in which most of these good people were agreed was the one thing in which I differed from them. They were quite sure they had attained a certain "gnosis,"—had, more or less successfully, solved the problem of existence; while I was quite sure I had not, and had a pretty strong conviction that the problem was insoluble. ("Agnosticism," *SC* 237–38)

The precise wording of that last sentence is critical: Huxley is maintaining, not only that *he himself* does not know the answers to certain questions about the nature of the universe, but that *everyone* must of necessity be so ignorant—chiefly because the human information-gathering process is insufficient to settle the questions at issue. Huxley is, of course, aware that a wide array of matters might be subject to agnosticism, but he also asserts in numerous essays that scientific advance has allowed certain matters to be settled with relative security, so that the probability of their being "true" is fairly high. But the existence of God, however unlikely such an entity may be in light of scientific advances that were explaining more and more phenomena by natural means, was not one of these.

It is at this point that the moral element enters. In responding to Henry Wace's offensive assertion, "It is, and it ought to be, an unpleasant thing for a man to have to say plainly that he does not believe in Jesus Christ" (see p. 31), Huxley responds in a manner that recalls his pungent rebuttal to Wilberforce:

> That "it ought to be" unpleasant for any man to say anything which he sincerely, and after due deliberation, believes, is to my mind, a proposition of the most profoundly immoral character. I verily believe that the great good which has been effected in the world by Christianity has been largely counteracted by the pestilent doctrine on which all the Churches have insisted, that honest disbelief in their more or less astonishing creeds is a moral offence, indeed a sin of the deepest dye, deserving and involving the same future retribution as murder and robbery. If we could only see, in one view, the torrents of hypocrisy and cruelty, the lies, the slaughter, the violations of every obligation of humanity, which have flowed from this source along the course of the history of Christian nations, our worst imaginations of Hell would pale beside the vision. ("Agnosticism," *SC* 240–41)

Elsewhere Huxley is careful to note that his agnosticism extends well beyond merely the question of the existence of God or other religious issues:

> I do not care to speak of anything as "unknowable." What I am sure about is that there are many topics about which I know nothing; and which, so far as I can see, are out of reach of my faculties. But whether these things are knowable by any one else is exactly one of those matters which is beyond my knowledge, though I may have a tolerably strong opinion as to the probabilities of the case. Relatively to myself, I am quite sure that the region of uncertainty—the nebulous country in which words play the part of realities—is far more extensive than I could wish. ("Agnosticism and Christianity," *SC* 311–12)

That first sentence is of some interest in suggesting one possible source for Huxley's agnosticism—or, at least, a source for the term and its basic thrust. Around 1860 he read Henry Mansel's *The Limits of Religion* (1858). Mansel, a professor of philosophy at Oxford and later dean of St. Paul's, was certainly not an agnostic; indeed, his treatise, which asserted that the finite minds of human beings could never establish direct contact with God, and that therefore there are no grounds to question the divine inspiration of the Bible (a priceless instance of circular reasoning), was designed to shore up religious belief in an age of skepticism. But throughout his work, Mansel used the word "Unknowable" in reference to God—a practice that the religious skeptic Herbert Spencer adopted with very different implications in such treatises as *First Principles* (1862). It is possible that these works laid the groundwork for Huxley's adoption of both the term *agnosticism* and its central conception.

It was only late in life that Huxley took up the cudgels on behalf of science against religion. Many essays he wrote during the last decade of his life—those that exhaustively expound his views on the principles of agnosticism and such central religious questions as biblical inerrancy, the divinity of Jesus Christ, and the interplay of religion and morals—were the direct products of controversies in which Huxley engaged with enthusiasm and vigor, and several features of their argumentation cannot be fully understood without an understanding of the polemical background out of which they emerged. As a result, however, the essays are at times limited by the intellectual battles Huxley chose to fight, and they do not always explicate his views in as much detail as one would wish. Most of his essays on the subject were reprinted in two volumes of his collected essays (1893–1894), *Science and Hebrew Tradition* and *Science and Christian Tradition*, but of course he could not reprint the essays by his opponents to which he was replying, so they are at times difficult to understand or contextualize.

There were, in essence, two controversies in which Huxley engaged—in part a result of his own aggressiveness in his chosen role (as he stated in a letter of 1887) as "gladiator-general for Science,"[9] and in part a result of deliberate taunts aimed at him by his opponents. The first concerned the veracity of the creation story in Genesis—that is, whether the account of the creation of the world as recorded in the two chapters of Genesis accords with present-day science or not. (Let it pass that there are actually two mutually inconsistent accounts of creation that have been bunglingly fused together; one states that animals were created before man, the other that man was created before animals.) From our perspective, it may appear that this controversy scarcely deserves the name, as no one today outside of the most rabid fundamentalists would even choose to debate the matter. But in Huxley's day, the issue was far from settled. We have seen that in his boyhood, the literal inerrancy of the Bible was assumed by a broad section of the public, including the educated classes. As late as 1864, in part as a response to *The Origin of Species*—although perhaps more in response to another work, the blandly titled *Essays and Reviews* (1859), in which a number of scholars and theologians were so bold as to doubt the stories of "miracles" recorded in the Bible—a petition drawn up by the redoubtable Samuel Wilberforce declared that "the whole Canonical Scriptures" were the "literal Word of God";[10] it was signed by half the clergy in England.

Granted, by the 1880s, this view had, as a result of scientific progress as well as advances in the study of the Bible itself, forced a number of liberal clergymen to withdraw into obfuscatory ambiguity, but the defenders of biblical inerrancy were numerous and loud. One of these was William Ewart Gladstone (1809–1898), who, as head of the Liberal Party, was prime minister on four separate occasions. In his old age, he came to regard science (which included the scientific theology of the Higher Criticism) as a grave threat to religion and morals, and he was not slow to wage a rearguard attack whenever the opportunity presented itself.

One such opportunity occurred when the French Protestant theologian Albert Réville's *Prolégomène de l'histoire des religions* (1881) was translated into English as *Prolegomena to the History of Religions* (1884). In an article entitled "Dawn of Creation and of Worship" (*Nineteenth Century*, November 1885), Gladstone took offense at what he took to be Réville's a priori dismissal of the possibility that primitive peoples (i.e., the Jews) could have been the recipients of a divine revelation that explicated the origin of the universe to them. Gladstone bluntly asserts such a revelation, going on to say that, since the details of that revelation (i.e., the creation story) fully accord with what is now known both of cosmology and of the origin and development of life on earth, not only is the creation story true, but—and this is a clever twist on Réville's own presuppositions—because it was made to peoples acknowledged as "primitive" and therefore largely in ignorance of natural science, they could only have arrived at it through divine intervention!

The details of Gladstone's long and meandering article need not be traced, especially when he goes off on odd tangents such as asserting—as he did in several previous treatises, such as *Studies on Homer and the Homeric Age* (1858)—that the Homeric poems reveal significant relations to the Hebrew scriptures, a view that Gladstone was, then and now, alone in espousing. The crux of his argument, at least as far as Huxley was concerned, was his attempt to reconcile the account in Genesis of the successive emergence of animal life on earth with what was then known by biologists and paleontologists. Gladstone writes:

> Looking largely at the latter portion of the narrative [i.e., chapter 1 of Genesis], which describes the creation of living organisms, . . . there is a grand fourfold division, set forth in an orderly succession of times as follows: on the fifth day
>
> 1. The water-population;
> 2. The air-population;
>
>   and, on the sixth day,
> 3. The land-population of animals;
> 4. The land-population consummated in man.[11]

It was probably an error for Gladstone to go so deeply into the details of Genesis in an attempt to maintain its harmony with contemporary science, but he was well aware of the Latin adage *falsus in uno, falsus in omnibus* (false in one thing, false in everything): if the Bible could be shown to be in error even on the most insignificant point, its claim to inerrancy must necessarily collapse, and *no* statement—even such central matters as the divinity and resurrection of Jesus—could withstand scrutiny and skepticism. So everything had to be defended.

Huxley, however, was in no mood to accommodate Gladstone on this point. Knowing that Réville was a theologian and not a scientist, Huxley, in the article "The Interpreters of Genesis and the Interpreters of Nature" (*Nineteenth Century*, December 1885), responded vehemently by defending his own turf: "Important questions of natural science—respecting which neither of the combatants professes to speak as an expert—are involved in the controversy; and I think it is desirable that the public should know what it is that natural science really has to say on these topics, to the best belief of one who has been a diligent student of natural science for the last forty years."[12] After dissecting Gladstone's fourfold order of the creation of animals, Huxley concludes that "the facts which demolish his whole argument are of the commonest notoriety" (*H* 144). In particular, the idea that the air-population could have preceded the land-population is preposterous, since it was Huxley himself who, decades earlier, had first established the evolution of birds from primitive reptiles.

Huxley himself is perhaps at fault in this phase of the debate also, since of course the extraordinarily complex history of the actual evolution of animal life on earth cannot possibly be simplified to the "creation" of one broad swath of creatures followed by another. He in some sense compounds his error by asserting an alternate order—"Land and air-population" followed by "Water-population" (*H* 148)—that, as he rightly claims, contradicts Gladstone's order, although it too is an immense oversimplification; but all that Huxley needed to do was to show that Gladstone's (i.e., Genesis's) sequence was wrong even in one particular: once that is established, the claim that Genesis can be "reconciled" with natural science falls to the ground.

In his response, "Proem to Genesis" (*Nineteenth Century*, January 1886), Gladstone accepted the opening Huxley afforded him and presented a revised order for animals: the sequence is now (1) fishes, (2) birds, (3) mammals, and (4) man. Somehow Gladstone manages to convince himself that this sequence can now be found in Genesis, even though in his previous article he had maintained (correctly) a quite different sequence. He actually gives the game away by asserting that Genesis appears to be in error only in regard to the relative order of birds and "beasts,"[13] and then he augments his difficulties by asserting that Genesis is apparently concerned only with "then living species" (*P* 9), so that inconvenient extinct species like dinosaurs don't come into play. Indeed, according to Gladstone, Genesis fails to mention reptiles at all because "they were deemed . . . secondary and insignificant" (*P* 14)!

Gladstone had left so many openings that Huxley could scarcely wait to reply. In "Mr. Gladstone and Genesis" (*Nineteenth Century*, February 1886), he demolishes Gladstone on several fronts. First is the matter of reptiles: Huxley proves by numerous citations (especially to the mention of "creeping things" in Gen. 1:24) that the creation story *does* take account of reptiles, so that, however low the poor reptiles have fallen, they have to be accounted for somehow. And Huxley rightly points out that Gladstone's new fourfold order is "rather more inconsistent with Genesis than its fourfold predecessor" (*H* 175). In the end he delivers an epitaph to the creation story:

> My belief . . . is, and long has been, that the pentateuchal story of the creation is simply a myth. I suppose it to be an hypothesis respecting the origin of the universe which some ancient thinker found himself able to reconcile with his knowledge, or what he thought was knowledge, of the nature of things, and therefore assumed to be true. As such, I hold it to be not merely an interesting, but a venerable, monument of a stage in the mental progress of mankind; and I find it difficult to suppose that any one who is acquainted with the cosmogonies of other nations—and especially with those of the Egyptians and the Babylonians, with whom the Israelites were in such frequent and intimate communication—should consider it to possess either more, or less, scientific importance than may be allotted to these. (*H* 180–81)

It appears that this article—to which was appended some further remarks by Henry Drummond, a theological writer associated with the Evangelical movement who flatly declared that there was no science in the Bible—as well as a belated response by Réville himself, "'Dawn of Creation'—An Answer to Mr. Gladstone" (*Nineteenth Century*, January 1886), finally shut Gladstone up. He appears to have realized—in spite of his assertion, in his second article, that Genesis was intended to give "moral, and not scientific, instruction" and that the text of Genesis cannot "in all points be sustained" (*P* 8, 16)—that he had talked himself into a corner and that the best policy was silence. But that silence, as we shall see, was not permanent.

Huxley, for his part, went on to write a long, two-part article, "The Evolution of Theology" (*Nineteenth Century*, March and April 1886), that sought to trace the progression of early Jewish thinking as found in the Old Testament, specifically in relation to the notion of Sheol (the Jewish hell), the anthropomorphism of God, and other issues. The article is relatively nonpolemical. Somewhat less so is "An Episcopal Trilogy" (*Nineteenth Century*, November 1887), a review of *The Advance of Science*, a series of sermons by three Anglican bishops; I will have more to say on this essay presently.

But two years later, Huxley was, out of the blue, attacked by Henry Wace, principal of King's College, Cambridge (1883–1897) and dean of Canterbury (1903–1924). In the *Official Report of the Church Congress Held at Manchester* (1888), Wace directly addressed the growing skepticism of the age, painting it as a threat to morality. He took particular aim at agnosticism, which he interpreted as merely a cowardly brand of atheism:

> But if this be so, for a man to urge, as an escape from this article of belief [i.e., that God exists], that he has no means of a scientific knowledge of the unseen world, or of the future, is irrelevant. His difference from Christians lies not in the fact that he has no knowledge of these things, but that he does not believe the authority on which they are stated. He may prefer to call himself an Agnostic; but his real name is an older one—he is an infidel; that is to say, an unbeliever. The word infidel, perhaps, carries an unpleasant significance. Perhaps it is right that it should. It is, and it ought to be, an unpleasant thing for a man to have to say plainly that he does not believe in Jesus Christ. (Quoted in *AS* 210)

This was just the kind of thing to make Huxley see red, and it led to the writing of his three great papers, "Agnosticism" (*Nineteenth Century*, February 1889), "Agnosticism: A Rejoinder" (*Nineteenth Century*, April 1889), and "Agnosticism and Christianity" (*Nineteenth Century*, June 1889).

Yet in spite of the obnoxious manner in which Wace has expressed his views, there appears to be a core of truth in them: it is fairly evident that Huxley, whatever his professed views, *acted* as if no god existed, and to that degree he could rightly be called an atheist. The entirety of his belief system rested upon the working hypothesis that no god envisioned by any scriptures of the human race had any likelihood of existence and that science—especially the theory of evolution, which, in its elimination of the last redoubt of Christian theology, the argument from design, made a fully secular conception of the universe viable for the first time in human history—was the sole arbiter of truth and accounted for phenomena far better than any conceivable religious system. As he himself asserted, evolution "excludes creation and all other kinds of supernatural intervention."[14] In this sense, Huxley's repeated denials that he was an atheist or unbeliever come off as a bit forced.

Nevertheless, his papers on agnosticism are the pinnacles of his polemical writing on religion. In "Agnosticism" he pungently discusses what it means to be an "infidel": to a Muslim, a Christian is a "dog of an infidel" (*AS* 234). And as for the idea that the agnostic "does not believe the authority" on which the central pillars of the Christian faith are founded, Huxley turns this idea around to Wace's discomfiture: do even Protestant theologians believe every statement in the Bible? It is here that Huxley, not for the first time or the last, unearths the story of the Gadarene swine.

This tale—found in all three of the Synoptic Gospels, although with some significant variations—records how Jesus, coming upon a man (or perhaps two men) afflicted with madness, was convinced that the insanity was a product of demonic possession, so he engaged in some kind of hocus-pocus ("Come forth, thou unclean spirit, out of the man," Mark 5:8) that ejected the demons (whose "name is Legion: for we are many," Mark 5:9) and thrust the various devils into the bodies of swine feeding "nigh unto the mountains" (Mark 5:11), with the result that the swine "ran violently down a steep place into the sea, (they were about two thousand;) and were choked in the sea" (Mark 5:13). This story appears to have exercised Huxley, for he not only cites it repeatedly but bluntly asserts that "I venture to doubt whether, at this present moment, any Protestant theologian, who has a reputation to lose, will say that he believes the Gadarene story" (*AS* 220).

But Huxley realizes that there is a broader point to be made here. He actually maintains that the story *may* be true ("For anything I can absolutely prove to the contrary, there may be spiritual things capable of the same transmigration, with like effects" [*AS* 227]), but the likelihood of its being true—given all that we now know of the sciences of biology, physics, chemistry, and psychology—is very slim:

> It seems to me that this is just one of the cases in which the canon of credibility and testimony, which I have ventured to lay down, has full force. So that, with the most entire respect for many (by no means for all) of our witnesses for the truth of demonology, ancient and modern, I conceive their evidence on this particular matter to be ridiculously insufficient to warrant their conclusion. (*AS* 227)

The crux of Huxley's discussion is that "miracles" of this sort have a very high threshold of proof to surmount, and the great majority of them cannot reach that level. Indeed, he asserts in "Agnosticism: A Rejoinder" that the "difficulties in the way of arriving at a sure conclusion" as to a number of points in the Synoptic Gospels "are insuperable" (*AS* 285), although he is amused to note that, in a response to his article, Wace actually went ahead and asserted his belief in the Gadarene story. An earlier paper by Huxley is of relevance here. In "The Value of Witness to the Miraculous" (*Nineteenth Century*, March 1889), he carefully dissects a purported first-hand account of a "miracle" as recorded in a work by the ninth-century courtier Einhard (or Eginhard). Showing to his satisfaction that the story—involving miraculous cures effected by touching the bones of some ancient Christian martyrs—is incredible, Huxley asks pointedly:

> If, therefore, you refuse to believe that "Wiggo" was cast out of the possessed girl on Eginhard's authority, with what justice can you profess to believe that the legion of devils were cast out of the man among the tombs of the Gadarenes? And if, on the other hand, you accept Eginhard's evidence, why do you laugh at the supposed efficacy of relics and the saint-worship of the modern Romanists? . . . If the evidence of Eginhard is insufficient to lead reasonable men to believe in the miracles he relates, a fortiori the evidence afforded by the Gospels and the Acts must be so. (*AS* 185–86)

"Agnosticism: A Rejoinder" is largely a response to Wace's assertion that

> The main question at issue, in a word, is one which Professor Huxley has chosen to leave entirely on one side—whether, namely, allowing for the utmost uncertainty on other points of the criticism to which he appeals, there is any reasonable doubt that the Lord's Prayer and the Sermon on the Mount afford a true account of our Lord's essential belief and cardinal teaching. (Quoted in *AS* 272)

Huxley is not prepared to back down on these points either. He states bluntly that neither the Lord's Prayer nor the Sermon on the Mount are found in the Gospel of Mark, which is widely acknowledged to be the earliest of the Gospels, and that the versions of the Sermon as found in

Matthew and Luke are widely different, leading one to have serious doubts as to whether they are veridical reports of Jesus' actual utterances. Huxley addresses the greatest "miracle" in the Bible: the resurrection of Jesus after his crucifixion. Can this account be accepted? There is no need to dwell in detail on Huxley's arguments, although at one point he appears to suggest that Jesus may have still been alive when taken down from the cross, since he was crucified for only six hours ("that any one should die after only six hours' crucifixion could not have been at all in accordance with Pilate's large experience of the effects of that method of punishment" [*AS* 280]). But Huxley does not elaborate upon this point, going on to say that Paul's testimony on the matter is worthless and concluding with his remark about the "insuperable" difficulties in the Gospels. In all this discussion, Huxley is keen on saying that he is not "denying" Jesus, only the testimony on which the claims for his life and actions are based.

In "Agnosticism and Christianity," Huxley returns to the Gadarene story, stating that its very existence is clear evidence that the Bible as a whole presupposes the existence of hell, demons, sorcery, demonic possession, and other such phenomena on which science has now cast grave doubt. What is the solution? A believer could simply dismiss some of these accounts as "allegory," but there is a great danger in this proceeding:

> The allegory pit is too commodious, is ready to swallow up so much more than one wants to put into it. If the story of the temptation is an allegory; if the early recognition of Jesus as the Son of God by the demons is an allegory; if the plain declaration of the writer of the first Epistle of John (iii. 8), "To this end was the Son of God manifested, that He might destroy the works of the devil," is allegorical, then the Pauline version of the Fall may be allegorical, and still more the words of consecration of the Eucharist, or the promise of the second coming; in fact, there is not a dogma of ecclesiastical Christianity the scriptural basis of which may not be whittled away by a similar process. (*AS* 324)

Huxley has keenly identified the central difficulty of Christian belief: a literal acceptance of the Bible entails immense difficulties because so many of its stories are, by current understanding, incredible, but an attempt to brush these stories under the rug presents the possibility that *all* the Bible stories can be brushed under the rug, leaving the believer with nothing.

Huxley elaborates upon this point in the trenchant essay "The Lights of the Church and the Lights of Science" (*Nineteenth Century*, July 1890). He states bluntly that "Christian theology must stand or fall with the historical trustworthiness of the Jewish Scriptures" (*H* 207), by which he means the Old Testament. Asserting that the scriptures have been attacked both on their historicity (by the Higher Criticism) and on their scientific errors, Huxley focuses on one specific event—the Flood. Two generations earlier, Charles Lyell had to tread very carefully on this matter in *The Principles of Geology* (1830); even so, Lyell was faced with "social ostracism" (*H* 216) because his book, even if only by implication, questioned the historicity of the Flood and of Noah's ark. Today, even theologians have given up literal belief in the Flood. But this caving in on what appears to be a central element of the early history of the earth, as conceived by Judaism and Christianity, poses problems of its own: by abandoning the idea of a universal deluge, "the references to the Flood in the New Testament are unintelligible" (*H* 220). For after all, didn't Jesus himself declare: "They did eat, they drank, they married wives, they were given in marriage, until the day that Noe [Noah] entered into the ark, and the flood came, and destroyed them all" (Luke 17:27)? Manifestly, Jesus had a literal belief in a universal deluge; therefore, the attempt to "save" the historicity of Genesis by asserting that it was referring merely to a "partial" or localized flood cannot stand. Huxley concludes by declaring flatly that both the Flood and the creation story are "pure fiction" (*H* 234).

It was at this point that Gladstone reentered the debate. In a ponderous book, *The Impregnable Rock of Holy Scripture* (1890), he attempted valiantly to assert the historicity of the entire Bible: the advance of science, in his view, does not "disintegrate or undermine the basis of belief."[15] Referring specifically to Huxley's essay, he strove to bring geology, hydraulics, and other sciences to bear in claiming that the Flood could still be believed in. Probably Huxley would not have troubled with Gladstone on this point, since the latter's reasoning was so obviously absurd; but Gladstone made the mistake of raising once again the vexing question of the Gadarene swine, and that was more than Huxley could tolerate.

Gladstone wanted to assert that keeping swine in Gadara was in fact an illegal act for Jews, given their prohibition from eating the flesh of pigs; accordingly, Jesus' killing of the swine by inciting them to jump over the cliff was not, as Huxley had suggested, a wanton act of property destruction. In "The Keepers of the Herd of Swine" (*Nineteenth Century*, December 1890), Huxley responded that Gadara was in fact a Gentile city, probably occupied by Greeks. Gladstone then countered, in "Professor Huxley and the Swine-Miracle" (*Nineteenth Century*, February 1891), with an array of seemingly impressive citations to ancient and modern authorities that Gadara was in fact a Jewish city.

The discussion at this point became merely a contest to see who could marshal the most impressive evidence—but it turns out that both combatants were wrong, although Gladstone perhaps a bit more so. A modern biblical scholar, John McRay, noting that the texts of the Synoptic Gospels disagree over the actual spelling of the name (Gadara in Matthew, Gerasa in Mark and Luke) and that there are several other variant readings, including Gergesa, concludes:

> Gerasa, modern Jerash, can hardly be the location of the miracle story because it is 37 miles SE of the Sea of Galilee—too much of a run for the pigs. Gadara, which is to be identified with modern Um Qeis, is also too far away, 5 miles SE of the sea. This leaves Gergesa, modern El Koursi, on the E bank of the sea as the only reasonable possibility, if any credence is to be given to the geographical statements of the gospels.[16]

And that, I hope, settles that.

For all the pedantry of this phase of the debate, both combatants knew that vital issues were involved. Gladstone, in his final article, stated plainly that "the excision on moral grounds of this narrative [i.e., the Gadarene story] from the Synoptic Gospels affects their credit as a whole."[17] For his part, Huxley, in a final paper, "Illustrations of Mr. Gladstone's Controversial Methods" (*Nineteenth Century*, March 1891), while acknowledging that "Mr. Gladstone and I might be better occupied than in fighting over the Gadarene pigs" (*AS* 414), declared what is at stake: "We are at a parting of the ways. Whether the twentieth century shall see a recrudescence of the superstitions of mediaeval papistry, or whether it shall witness the severance of the living body of the ethical ideal of prophetic Israel from the carcase, foul with savage superstitions and cankered with false philosophy, to which the theologians have bound it, turns upon their final judgment of the Gadarene tale" (*H* 417).

On random occasions Huxley broached another central issue in the broader debate of the conflict of religion and science—the role of science in the formation of ethics, and specifically what role science will play if religion ceases to be the source of morality. Huxley's discussions on this subject are not as cohesive and forthright as one would like, in part because, as with so many of his other screeds on religion, they are the product of polemical debate. Consider the essay "Science and Morals" (*Fortnightly Review*, November 1886). Here Huxley is keen on defending himself against accusations by W. S. Lilly, a literary and religious scholar and a convert to Roman Catholicism, that he was a materialist. The crux of Lilly's argument is that the prevalence of morals—or, in his judgment, what passes for them—based purely on secular reasoning, without a religious foundation, will inevitably lead increasingly to the degradation of society. In his response, Huxley never comes fully to terms with this assertion, merely stating that science is no more responsible for the "diseased" (*EE* 144) state of society than philosophy . . . or theology.

Somewhat more relevant is "Agnosticism and Christianity." Here Huxley states—although he makes no attempt to prove—that the development of morals is separate from the truth or falsity of any given religion:

> Even if the creeds, from the so-called "Apostles," to the so-called "Athanasian," were swept into oblivion; and even if the human race should arrive at the conclusion that, whether a bishop washes a cup or leaves it unwashed, is not a matter of the least consequence, it will get on very well. The causes which have led to the development of morality in mankind, which have guided or impelled us all the way from the savage to the civilised state, will not cease to operate because a number of ecclesiastical hypotheses turn out to be baseless. (*AS* 316)

This is all well and good, but I think Huxley is failing to make an important point. His praise for what he believes to be the core of Judeo-Christian teaching is unremitting and no doubt heartfelt:

> All that is best in the ethics of the modern world, in so far as it has not grown out of Greek thought, or Barbarian manhood, is the direct

> development of the ethics of old Israel. There is no code of legislation, ancient or modern, at once so just and so merciful, so tender to the weak and poor, as the Jewish law; and, if the Gospels are to be trusted, Jesus of Nazareth himself declared that he taught nothing but that which lay implicitly, or explicitly, in the religious and ethical system of his people. (*AS* 315)

This assertion is itself problematical, since the "ethics of old Israel" advocated such things as stoning for adultery, capital punishment for practicing homosexuals or for sabbath violators, and other such elements that surely cannot serve as the basis for present-day law or morals. But even if Huxley is right, he ignores the fact that the toppling of Judeo-Christian *metaphysics*—specifically, the notion of divinity of Jesus, not to mention the entire creation story that Jesus manifestly accepted as a literal event—renders Judeo-Christian *ethics* merely one option among many, no more or less to be preferred (depending on one's temperament) than the ethics espoused by Confucius, David Hume, or the Marquis de Sade. The *authority* of the Judeo-Christian ethical system falls to the ground, and it was this that so concerned the theologians of Huxley's (and our) day.

But if Huxley's reasoning on religion and ethics leaves something to be desired, he made important declarations regarding another significant issue—the "ethics" of evolution. I am referring specifically to the doctrine that has come to be called Social Darwinism, a perversion of the theory of evolution that states that the "survival of the fittest" (a phrase never uttered by Darwin) not only constitutes the actual workings of evolution, especially in human society, but is the way human society *should* operate. In the essays "Evolution and Ethics" (1893) and the "Prolegomena" to *Evolution and Ethics* (1894), Huxley takes strong issue with this view, a view that had been expounded vigorously by his own friend and colleague, Herbert Spencer, among others. In these essays, Huxley declares that the brute "struggle for existence" has been mitigated, if not entirely set aside, by the advance of civilization. In a civilized society, the "ethical process" replaces the "cosmic process" (*EE* 81):

> The practice of that which is ethically best—what we call goodness or virtue—involves a course of conduct which, in all respects, is opposed to that which leads to success in the cosmic struggle for existence. In place of ruthless self-assertion it demands self-restraint; in place of

> thrusting aside, or treading down, all competitors, it requires that the individual shall not merely respect, but shall help his fellows; its influence is directed, not so much to the survival of the fittest, as to the fitting of as many as possible to survive. It repudiates the gladiatorial theory of existence. (*EE* 82)

Huxley may actually be in error here: he would have been grateful to hear of recent assertions by evolutionary biologists that the practice of altruism in primitive societies may well have contributed to their survival. In any event, nobler words were rarely uttered by Huxley, and it is unfortunate that they were spoken so late in his life. Once again, his impoverished upbringing, during which he no doubt witnessed the searing effects of poverty and malnutrition at first hand, rendered him more rather than less sympathetic to his economic inferiors, and he saw in civilization a means for rectifying the injustices that the "struggle for existence" engenders. But in the end, it comes down to a matter of basic human feeling:

> It strikes me that men who are accustomed to contemplate the active or passive extirpation of the weak, the unfortunate, and the superfluous; who justify that conduct on the ground that it has the sanction of the cosmic process, and is the only way of ensuring the progress of the race; who, if they are consistent, must rank medicine among the black arts and count the physician a mischievous preserver of the unfit; on whose matrimonial undertakings the principles of the stud have the chief influence; whose whole lives, therefore, are an education in the noble art of suppressing natural affection and sympathy, are not likely to have any large stock of these commodities left. ("Prolegomena," *EE* 37)

Thomas Henry Huxley was far more than merely "Darwin's bulldog"—a nickname bestowed upon him in derision, but one that he came to embrace. He was far more than a popularizer of science; he made lasting scientific contributions himself. I have already cited his discovery that birds evolved from primitive reptiles. Huxley was also the first to establish that Neanderthal man was a separate species from *Homo sapiens* and not a "missing link" between man and the apes. His writings on religion, agnosticism, and related issues, even if many of them grew out of polemical debates, perhaps had more influence than those of anyone else in his generation on the demise of biblical inerrancy, the fashioning of a secular view of life, and the establishment of science as the chief arbiter of empirical truth. His adherence to agnosticism, and his disinclination to proceed all the way to atheism, were no doubt based on sound principle, but by the end of his life he had made the adoption of atheism as a working hypothesis far more intellectually viable than it had been in the generations that preceded him.

Chapter 2

Leslie Stephen: A Logician Dissects Theology

Leslie Stephen (1832–1904), although perhaps best known today as the querulous and demanding father of Virginia Woolf, whom she portrayed somewhat harshly in the character of Mr. Ramsay in her novel *To the Lighthouse* (1927), was one of the towering British intellectuals of his period. He would deserve to be remembered for no other reason than for his editing of the immense reference work *Dictionary of National Biography* (1885–1891), for his pioneering treatise, *History of English Thought in the Eighteenth Century* (1876), and for his numerous critical and biographical essays on British and European writers; but he is now coming to be admired for advocating a vigorous and intellectually cogent brand of agnosticism in a series of essays from as early as 1868 up to the time of his death. Many of his essays trenchantly take religious orthodoxy to task, including such prominent religious thinkers of the day as Edward Pusey, Matthew Arnold, and John Henry Newman, and his refutation of some of the central defenses for religious belief in an age of science paved the way for the agnosticism or outright atheism of such later thinkers as Bertrand Russell and of his own daughter, Virginia Woolf, whose philosophical and religious outlook was more affected by her father's writings than she sometimes acknowledged.

Stephen was born on November 28, 1832, in a suburb of London. His father, James Stephen, was a longtime civil servant and a fervent member of the Evangelical movement, an offshoot of Anglicanism that emphasized a personal connection with Jesus and the moral rehabilitation of society. Under this influence, James Stephen helped to write the bill that outlawed slavery in the United Kingdom. (Leslie Stephen's grandfather, Jem Stephen, had married the sister of William Wilberforce, a clergyman who had led the movement toward the abolition of slavery in England.) Leslie was no doubt imbued with Evangelicalism during his childhood, but he does not appear to have been a particularly devout believer. Late in life he commented on the evolution of his skepticism:

> When I ceased to accept the teaching of my youth, it was not so much a process of giving up beliefs as of discovering that I had never really believed. The contrast between the genuine convictions that guide and govern our conduct, and the professions which we were taught to repeat in church, when once realised, was too glaring. One belonged to the world of realities and the other to the world of dreams.[1]

The contrast between the beliefs that one merely talks about and those that actually govern one's conduct would become a central issue in Stephen's agnostic writings.

Stephen attended Eton (1842–1846) and, after several years of private tutoring, entered Trinity Hall, Cambridge, in 1850, initially studying mathematics. He became an enthusiast of healthful living, spending much of his time to competitive rowing; later in life he would become a devotee of Alpine mountain climbing and write much on the subject. In 1854, he won a fellowship at Cambridge that would allow him to teach, but it required him to take holy orders. In contrast to Oxford, however, where John Henry Newman and others were leading a fervent renewal of religious belief that would come to be called the Oxford Movement, religion was not strongly emphasized at Cambridge, and Stephen took holy orders the next year largely as a means of advancing his career. By the late 1850s, he had begun to read philosophy, especially the work of the positivist Auguste Comte, and it was largely through this influence, rather than that of the advancing scientific thought of the day as embodied in Darwin's *Origin of Species* (1859), that Stephen's skepticism developed. Accordingly, in 1862 he announced that he could no longer conduct chapel services and therefore felt compelled to resign his fellowship.

This decision sheds further light on the nature and evolution of Stephen's shedding of religious belief. His early biographer, F. W. Maitland, cites a college friend (without naming him) as remarking:

> When I first went up [to Trinity Hall], Stephen was a clergyman and took his part in the clerical services in chapel. I was a grieved witness to the misery endured by my friend during the time when doubt as to the truth of revealed religion according to the orthodox view gradually increased, until he made up his mind that his views were incompatible with his continuing to be a clergyman of the Church of England. The pain he suffered was very acute, as was sure to be the case when a highly sensitive and loving nature like his had to pass through such a crisis of life, and was made doubly so because he knew what grief his determination would cause to some of his family who were nearest and dearest to him.[2]

This passage puts a somewhat different complexion on Stephen's own assertions that his disbelief was a largely intellectual matter unencumbered with emotional trauma, but no doubt he was well aware that his giving up holy orders would cause great distress to his family, in particular to his devout father.

Stephen decided to pursue a career in journalism in London. Through the influence of his brother, James Fitzjames Stephen (later to become a prominent lawyer and judge), he began writing for such leading intellectual journals as the *Saturday Review*, the *Pall Mall Gazette*, and the *Cornhill Magazine*. His increasingly skeptical writings on religion, however, could find a haven only in such periodicals as *Fraser's Magazine* and the *Fortnightly Review*, edited by the secularists James Anthony Froude and John Morley, respectively. In 1871 he became editor of *Cornhill*, publishing in it many substantial literary essays that would later be collected in *Hours in a Library* (1874–1876) and *Studies of a Biographer* (1898). His early agnostic articles were collected in *Essays on Freethinking and Plainspeaking* (1873), although the volume attracted little attention at the time.

In 1867, Stephen had married Harriet ("Minny") Thackeray, daughter of the novelist William Makepeace Thackeray. Minnie died in 1875, leaving Stephen (who was indeed of a "highly sensitive" nature) shattered. After a long courtship, he married Julia Duckworth (a young widow with three children) in 1878. They would have four children: Vanessa, Thoby, Virginia, and Adrian. It was during this period that Stephen wrote his landmark treatise, *History of English Thought in the Eighteenth Century*, an exhaustive study of the British deists and their influence. Stephen materially assisted in the resurrection of the reputation of these thinkers, who had fallen into obscurity and disrepute. Although removed as editor of the *Cornhill* in 1882, he continued to work prolifically, even a bit frenetically, especially when a publisher, George Smith, commissioned him to edit the enormous reference series *Dictionary of National Biography*, a work that remained standard for more than a century, until its recent wholesale revision (2004).

Along with his critical and biographical essays, Stephen wrote monographs on Samuel Johnson (1878), Alexander Pope (1880), Jonathan Swift (1882), George Eliot (1902), and Thomas Hobbes (1904) for the prestigious English Men of Letters series. His later writings on religion were gathered in *An Agnostic's Apology and Other Essays* (1893), although a number of essays remain uncollected. His later treatise, *The English Utilitarians* (3 volumes, 1900), was an impressive philosophical study of Jeremy Bentham, John Stuart Mill, and their disciples. Stephen's later life, however, was saddened by the death of his wife Julia in 1895, and during his final years, he put increasing demands on his children to care for his needs. Stephen, although liberal in many facets of his thought, remained curiously conservative as far as women's place in society was concerned: he was opposed to woman suffrage and did not believe women to be the intellectual equals of men. But his careful education of his two daughters would bear rich fruit, both in the novelist Virginia Woolf and in the painter Vanessa Bell.

Stephen's evolution from a fairly orthodox faith to full-fledged agnosticism was gradual, if his published writings are any gauge. In "The Broad Church" (1870), one of his first essays on religion, he asserted, "The greatest danger to which we are exposed at the present moment is not that people find the old faiths failing them, but that they begin to doubt that there is anywhere such a thing to be found as faith in anything."[3] This suggests that Stephen still believed that faith in something—whether it be a religious dogma or a series of moral stances—is conceivable and desirable. In another early essay, "The Religious Difficulty" (*Fraser's Magazine*, May 1870), Stephen still advocated Bible teaching to children,[4] even though he was no doubt well aware that such teaching can easily lead to indoctrination so that subsequent attempts to gauge the metaphysical and moral claims of the Bible become difficult. Even in this essay, Stephen went on to say, "The Church, in short, acquires a very great and real influence by having entrusted to it the management of the chief system of national education; and it is the sense that such an influence really exists which gives the chief bitterness to the struggle between secularists and denominationalists."[5]

Stephen was, however, well aware that Christianity in general, and Anglicanism in particular, was increasingly under attack, and that it had become, as early as the 1870s, a minority view among the intellectual classes. He himself stated plainly that he was an "agnostic," adding somewhat frustratingly that "for reasons which I need not here discuss I do not consider myself to be an atheist."[6] It is possible that Stephen simply did not wish to declare *publicly* that he was an atheist, given that certain social and legal disabilities still existed in England for those who openly professed atheism; certainly, his agnosticism seems to leave little room for even the mathematical possibility of a god, and he is likely to be the sort of agnostic who, as Bertrand Russell later remarked, "is, for practical purposes, at one with the atheists."[7]

Stephen took note of the widespread prevalence of atheism in Europe ("Religion as a Fine Art" [1872], *E* 43f.). In the trenchant essay "Are We Christians?" (1873), Stephen addresses the German skeptic David Friedrich Strauss's claim that intellectuals must abandon Christianity entirely. In mulling over Strauss's query, "Are we still Christians?" Stephen writes:

> The "we" of whom he speaks belong to the class—a class, he adds, no longer to be counted by thousands—to whom the old faith and the old Church can no longer offer a weatherproof refuge. The majority even of this class would be content to lop off the decayed bough, trusting that there is yet vital power in the trunk. But there is a minority, and it is in their name that Strauss speaks, who think that, in giving up the old supernaturalism, they must also take final leave of the worship to which it alone could give enduring power over the souls of men. . . . The attempts to effect a compromise between Christianity and Rationalism are nothing but a lamentable waste of human ingenuity. (*E* 110–11)

That final statement is still a reflection of Strauss's view and not necessarily of Stephen's, but in the course of his career, it becomes plain that he was more and more inclined to adopt it himself.

Stephen recognized that Christians were on the defensive. There were those who, rather than saying that the Bible was true, asserted merely that "its falsehood cannot be mathematically demonstrated" ("The Broad Church," *E* 10). Others claimed that religion was a kind of "fine art," but even a religion conceived in this fashion cannot be "entirely divorced from reality" ("Religion as a Fine Art" [1872], *E* 62). One of the main enemies of religion, as Stephen knew, was science; he defended the findings of science, where they could be definitively ascertained, against religious obscurantism. He admitted that he was present at the celebrated meeting of the British Association at Oxford when Thomas Henry Huxley made his vigorous defense of Darwin's theory of evolution against the attacks of Bishop Samuel Wilberforce:

> It was one incident in a remarkable outburst of intellectual activity. The old controversy between scientific and ecclesiastical champions was passing into a new phase. Darwin's teaching had not only provided a fresh method, but suggested applications of scientific principles which widened and deepened the significance of the warfare. A "new reformation," as Huxley afterwards called it, was beginning, and the intellectual issues to be decided were certainly not less important than those which had presented themselves to Erasmus and Luther.[8]

Stephen disavowed A. J. Balfour's assertion—an anticipation of the views of Stephen Jay Gould—that theology and science rest "upon separate bases," asserting, "Every theological system includes at least a large mass of purely scientific statements," which can and should be criticized by the rules of science. Theologians err, in Stephen's view, when they speak dogmatically about issues on which there is no sound knowledge. Theology, in many particulars, is merely "bad science."[9]

What, then, is there left to believe? One would think that the essay "The Religion of All Sensible Men" (1880) would provide an answer, but Stephen dances around the subject. He begins by postulating the query: "What form of belief will satisfy at once the philosophic thought and the popular impulses of the time? How is it to attract at once the thinkers, whose sole aim is the extension of our narrow circle of intellectual daylight, and the poor and ignorant, who are moved only by the power of the creed to grasp their imaginations and stimulate their emotions?"[10] Expressed in this way, it is not surprising that Stephen was unable to come up with a coherent answer. The best he can say is that the evolution of a new and sounder religion—or the evolution of a worldview not based upon religion at all—will be a long and slow process, since "You can't change a man's thoughts about things as you can change the books in his library" (*AA* 376).

One of the cleverest of Stephen's strategies against his religious opponents was to undercut their ground by declaring that they themselves had unwittingly lapsed into agnosticism. Stephen knew that dogma—unequivocal statements about the nature of entity, which were offered without proof and must be accepted without question—was central to religion, but it was exactly in regard to certain central dogmas of Christianity that science and philosophy had had their most corrosive effects. The result, in many cases, was that the devout resorted to a deliberate vagueness in doctrine, so that disproof becomes difficult. As Stephen stated in "The Broad Church":

> The Atonement is spiritualised till it becomes difficult to attach any definite meaning to it whatever. The authority of the Bible becomes more difficult to define and to distinguish from the authority of any other good book. Everlasting punishment is put out of the way by the aid of judicious metaphysical distinctions. The sharp edges of old-fashioned doctrine are rounded off till the whole outline of the creed is materially altered. (*E* 31)

"Are We Christians?" makes the same argument in even more pungent form. There are those, Stephen maintains, who now espouse something called "unsectarian Christianity" as a means of both escaping from the strictures of science and the battle of various sects and denominations, but this really amounts to "scepticism in a gushing instead of a cynical form" (*E* 119). He goes on to say: "Unsectarian Christianity can no more exist than there can be a triangle which is neither scalene nor isosceles nor equilateral. All Christians might conceivably be converted to one sect; but if you strip off from the common creed all the matters which are in dispute between them, the residuum is at most the old-fashioned deism, if, indeed, it amounts to that" (*E* 119). He concludes devastatingly:

> The doctrine, turn it how you will, is essentially sceptical . . . for it amounts to saying that the doctrines which were the very life-blood of

> the old creeds which once stirred men's hearts to flame, are to be respectfully and civilly shelved, and that morality can do very well without them. It is the product of intellectual indolence, though not of actual intellectual revolt. We have not the courage to say that the Christian doctrines are false, but we are lazy enough to treat them as irrelevant. (*E* 122)

"An Agnostic's Apology" (1876) points to the paradoxes in the position of theists (whom Stephen names Gnostics [those who know], in contrast to agnostics), who on the one hand maintain that "God is knowable" (*AA* 3) but then turn around and say that many of his acts are a "mystery" to limited human minds: "You say, as we say, that the natural man can know nothing of the Divine nature. That is Agnosticism. Our fundamental principle is not only granted, but asserted" (*AA* 8).

"The Scepticism of Believers" (1877) declares pithily that "faith often means belief in my nonsense; and credulity, the belief in the nonsense of somebody else" (*AA* 43). It is deists and skeptics who have "forced" (*AA* 66) theists to modify their views and to abandon some of the harsher aspects of their faith. One of these is religious persecution. In the essay "Poisonous Opinions" (1883), Stephen addresses the issue of whether it is ever morally right to persecute beliefs in the name of religious orthodoxy. Stephen concludes that such persecution, when directed toward scientific facts (such as Darwin's theory of evolution, assuming it has been proven to the point where it can be declared, for all practical purposes, a fact), is both unwise and ineffective: these facts are not independent entities but form a complex network intertwined with other facts. As civilization advances, persecution becomes anachronistic and inefficient; it constitutes a futile attempt to return to a prior stage of human society. In disputing the view that religious toleration is "opposed to the 'principle of authority'" (*AA* 295), Stephen retorts: "Toleration is, in fact, opposed to any authority which does not rest upon the only possible ground of rational authority—the gradual agreement of inquirers free from all irrelevant bias, and therefore from the bias of sheer terror of the evils inflicted by persons of different opinion" (*AA* 296).

Many of Stephen's essays are extraordinarily acute analyses of the views of a wide range of religious thinkers ranging from the sixteenth to the nineteenth centuries. Some essays reveal a dry wit that underscores their religious iconoclasm. In a lengthy and seemingly reverential essay on the tortured Christian Blaise Pascal, Stephen concludes that Pascal "was a sincere, a humble, and even an abject believer precisely because he was a thorough-going sceptic."[11] An essay on Jonathan Edwards, the fire-and-brimstone preacher of eighteenth-century America, is similar. Seeing Edwards as the link between Puritan theocracy and the transcendentalism of Emerson, Stephen appears to treat Edwards with respect, although his scorn of Edwards's belief in hell (a doctrine that, in another essay, he refers to as "inconceivably repulsive in its more intense forms" ["Dreams and Realities" (1878), *AA* 96]) and other dogmas is evident. He makes the further point that this belief in hell cannot be restricted merely to religious fundamentalists like Edwards but is a central tenet of mainline Protestantism and Catholicism as well.

In "Mr. Maurice's Theology" (1874), Stephen treats the religious philosophy of the mild-mannered thinker Frederick Denison Maurice. F. W. Maitland quotes Stephen's remark that "I was for a time a disciple of Maurice,"[12] which makes Stephen's condemnation of Maurice's thought all the more interesting. In essence, Stephen criticizes Maurice for advocating a Christianity whose dogmatic structure has been deliberately obscured. He provides examples of Maurice's equivocations: "The Bible is inspired; but 'every other book is part of the same divine institution.' Miracles are wrought by the divine power; but all the ordinary operations of nature testify to the same hand." This leads to the following conclusion:

> He is trying to reconcile two radically incompatible tendencies. Every formula is worthless in itself, and then appears to be of infinite value when rightly interpreted. His Deity is the infinite and incomprehensible being who dazzles the inner eye of the mystic, and then the definite or anthropomorphic god of Christian dispensation and of Jewish mythology. To meet the philosopher this theology expands without bounds; to meet the ordinary British Christian it confines itself within the historical limits.[13]

"Matthew Arnold and the Church of England" (1870) takes the great British critic (and author of *Literature and Dogma*, 1873) to task. Arnold had asserted that "all who believe in right reason, culture, and enlightenment should endeavour to maintain the Church of England as a national institution."[14] Why? Because Dissenters (the British term for members of other Protestant sects outside the Church of England) tended to promote strife, jealousy, and other reprehensible things. But Stephen retorted that this could be said of Protestants as a whole. Dissenting sects, in Stephen's view, were a natural consequence of an established church. Arnold wanted the Church of England to remain united with the state, but Stephen maintained that the Church was now just another sect—so why should it have this kind of undue influence?

Stephen's favorite whipping-boy was John Henry Newman, the devout Oxford theologian who had progressed from an ardent "high church" Anglicanism to full-fledged Catholicism, becoming a cardinal in his later years. Two essays—"Newman's Theory of Belief" (1877) and "Cardinal Newman's Scepticism" (1891)—address Newman's views, and several other essays refer to him in passing. Stephen's general view is that Newman espouses skepticism without realizing it. In "Newman's Theory of Belief," Stephen maintains that Newman never makes an attempt to defend his religion (whether it be Anglicanism or Catholicism) by direct argument; instead, he adopts a historical point of view, referring to the "development" of Christianity over the centuries. Summarizing Newman's views, Stephen writes: "If we assume that creeds live in proportion to the amount of truth which they contain, the plainest facts written on the very surface of history will tell us which are the truest" (*AA* 188). The very fact that Christianity has endured so long is, in Newman's view, a testament that it contains some kind of "truth." But Stephen points out that this argument is a highly dangerous one for the religious thinker to rely on; for if pushed to its logical extreme, it shows that Christianity is in fact in decline as a "vital" force (among the intelligentsia, at any rate), and that it is therefore yielding to agnosticism or actual atheism as the dominant creed of the present and future. As Stephen remarked in the essay "Belief and Conduct" (1888), the fact that Christianity has lasted for two thousand years suggests that it has had some kind of "utility"; but its recent decay suggests that "the belief will not work"[15] anymore, at least for a widespread segment of the population.

"Cardinal Newman's Scepticism" points out that Newman's views of the Bible (found in some of the papers in *Tracts for the Times*)—including such views as that the Bible is not one book but "a great number of writings, of various persons, living at various times, put together into one, and assuming its existing form as if casually and by accident," and that it does not contain any discussion of some of the central tenets of Christian belief, such as infant baptism—"may be as good a persuasive to scepticism as to belief."[16] The only way Newman could get around the difficulties posed by the actual text of the Bible is to appeal to the "authority" of the church—specifically, the Catholic church, which he saw was the only institution that could trace its lineage in an unbroken chain back to the time of Jesus. But, as Stephen points out, there are two kinds of authority: one based on scientific or historical evidence and one based on coercion. It is only the latter kind that the Catholic church can espouse, especially as embodied in the notion of papal infallibility, which Newman had by this time embraced. This "authority" can only lead to persecution.

Some of Stephen's most valuable essays are those that make the case—albeit tentatively and hesitantly—that religion and morality are not indissolubly linked and that morality must stand independently of religion if society is to advance. This was a remarkably bold stance on Stephen's part, for the religious basis of morality was one of the final areas on which the devout could base their case for the "utility" of religion, and few thinkers could conceive of an ethical system that did not rely on religion in some fashion or other. One of Stephen's first forays into this subject was "The Scepticism of Believers" (1877), in which he maintains that the agnostic "wishes . . . to place morality on a scientific basis" (*AA* 71). Moral laws have, historically, been arrived at inductively, rather than by an appeal to authority. Morality, in fact, cannot be (and has not been) founded upon theology, but upon "a knowledge of the concrete constitution of human nature and society" (*AA* 78).

Stephen's central essay on the subject is "Belief and Conduct" (1888). Here he asks plainly: Is religion useful, all apart from its truth? Is it essential to morality? In discussing the theologian William Paley's belief that "the essence of virtue consists in obedience to an external sanction," Stephen asks a series of increasingly awkward questions:

> Let us look for a moment at Paley's logic. Why should I not lie? Because liars will be damned. How do you know that? By a divine revelation made by the founder of my religion. How do you know that it was a divine revelation? Because I can prove that certain miraculous events

> happened in Palestine eighteen centuries ago. Upon this showing the pyramid is balanced upon its apex, and morality in most precarious equilibrium; its very existence is made to depend upon the evidence of a particular set of events at a particular period of history. (*B* 373)

In fact, morality (in the West) was not *caused* by a belief in Christianity, because neither the history of Christianity nor the moral doctrines actually found in the Bible are conducive to a moral life. Why has Christianity not made people—even professed believers—behave in a more moral manner than, as history shows, they actually do? What, in fact, are the actual implications of Christian morality? Are they not a series of incoherencies and paradoxes?

> I am—according to that mythology—an infinitesimal agent in a world governed by unlimited power working upon inscrutable principles. If I am good, I must give the glory to the being who has bestowed his grace upon me and refused it to my neighbour; if I am bad, I may plead that I was tempted by supernatural malice and cunning. I may be forgiven because somebody else has suffered, and punished by a suffering which has no proportion to my offence or relation to my reform. (*B* 388)

Stephen concludes resoundingly: "Of all the illusions patronised by philosophers, there is none more baseless, as it seems to me, than the notion that morality is dependent upon speculative opinions. The facts of human nature lie below the theories" (*B* 388).

The totality of Leslie Stephen's writings on religion is an impressive achievement. His most recent biographer, Noel Annan, has written, "There has never been much doubt that, second only to Arnold, Leslie Stephen was the outstanding critic of late Victorian times,"[17] although Annan was referring exclusively to his literary criticism; but a good case can be made that Stephen's essays on religion were critical in paving the way from the somewhat tentative agnosticism of Thomas Henry Huxley to the open defiance of Christianity found in many early twentieth-century thinkers, from Bertrand Russell to H. L. Mencken. Stephen, learned in the sciences as well as in literature and philosophy, was able to integrate the findings of contemporary science and to grasp their implications for religious belief. His carefully argued essays, devastating in their exposure of the logical fallacies of his opponents but expressed with a studied politeness that eschews all forms of cheap cynicism or polemic, exercised a profound influence in showing how agnosticism was not only an intellectually cogent but a morally sound stance. His broaching of the notion of a morality independent of religion was far ahead of his time, and as a whole, his writings still have much to teach us in regard to proper role of the intellectual when facing the conflict between the dogmas of religion and the necessarily tentative findings of science and history.

Chapter 3

John Stuart Mill: Theism and Its Discontents

One of the towering intellects of the nineteenth century, John Stuart Mill (1806–1873) distinguished himself in a number of disciplines, including philosophical logic, political economy, ethics, and feminism. Although best known today by the slim but immensely influential treatise *On Liberty* (1859), Mill in his own time was known as a leading proponent of the philosophical school known as *utilitarianism*, with its central theory of "the greatest happiness of the greatest number"—a school that today continues to have widespread support among philosophers. Mill's early advocacy of equal rights for women, including woman suffrage, helped lay the groundwork that ultimately led to the overthrow of legal, social, and political barriers for women in both England and the United States.

Religion was, on the surface, only a side issue with Mill, as evidenced by the late and posthumously published *Three Essays on Religion* (1874). But several recent studies have argued convincingly that his lifelong thoughts about the existence and nature of God, the afterlife, and the place of religion in society lay just below the surface of much of his work on ethics and politics. In the course of his career, Mill dissected a number of central tenets of religion and helped establish the intellectual cogency of such issues as the free discussion of religion, the separation of church and state, and the development of a secular ethic.

Mill told his own life in his *Autobiography* (1873), one of the most poignant documents of the nineteenth century. Although written with the impeccable precision, reserve, and fluency that marked his entire work, the *Autobiography* exhibits the remarkable early life of a man whose upbringing seemed destined to single him out from the mass of humanity. Mill was born in London on May 20, 1806, one of the nine children of the Scottish philosopher and historian James Mill (1773–1836), who appeared determined to test his ideas on education in the living laboratory of his own son. Accordingly, John was taught the rudiments of Greek at the age of three and Latin at eight; he was also fed heavy doses of ancient literature, mathematics, modern European history, and English poetry. Philosophical logic was learned at the age of twelve, and John first read Jeremy Bentham—who, along with his own father, had devised a rudimentary theory of utilitarianism—at about the age of fifteen. The Mill family in fact spent several summers with Bentham at Ford Abbey in Devonshire in the 1810s. Mill testifies eloquently to the overwhelming impact of Bentham's philosophy on his developing intellect:

> The Benthamic standard of "the greatest happiness" was that which I had always been taught to apply; I was even familiar with an abstract discussion of it, forming an episode in an unpublished dialogue on Government, written by my father on the Platonic model. Yet in the first pages of Bentham it burst upon me with all the force of novelty. . . . The feeling rushed upon me, that all previous moralists were superseded, and that here indeed was the commencement of a new era in thought.[1]

In regard to Mill's early religious outlook, the second chapter of his autobiography is of the highest importance. Once again, his father's views were central to the views he himself came to adopt. Mill notes that his father "remained in a state of perplexity, until, doubtless after many struggles, he yielded to the conviction that, concerning the origin of things, nothing whatever can be known. This is the only correct statement of his opinion; for dogmatic atheism he looked upon as absurd; as most of those, whom the world has considered Atheists, have always done" (*AM* 27). As a result, James Mill refused to indoctrinate his son into religious belief, although he "took care that I should be acquainted with what had been thought by mankind on these impenetrable problems" (*A* 29). The result is striking:

> I am thus one of the very few examples, in this country, of one who has, not thrown off religious belief, but never had it: I grew up in a negative state with regard to it. I looked upon the modern exactly as I did upon

> the ancient religion, as something which in no way concerned me. It did not seem to me more strange that English people should believe what I did not, than that the men I read of in Herodotus should have done so. (*AM* 29)

This lack of religious training did have, in Mill's mind, one drawback: "In giving me an opinion contrary to that of the world, my father thought it necessary to give it as one which could not prudently be avowed to the world" (*AM* 29). Mill continues, "The great advance in liberty of discussion, which is one of the most important differences between the present time and that of my childhood, has greatly altered the moralities of this question" (*AM* 30); but, if so, it is curious that Mill did not make efforts to publish his *Three Essays on Religion* in his lifetime.

James Mill, who was a high functionary in the quasi-governmental entity, the East India Company, felt that college would do little to foster his son's education, so in 1823 he found a place for him in the company as a clerk. Mill continued in his employment at the East India Company until 1858, himself rising up the ranks to become head of the office of India Correspondence. Mill was not, however, devoid of the intellectual stimulation that college brings: beginning as early as 1822, he became a member of several informal debating societies, including the Utilitarian Society (which Mill himself named and formed) and the London Debating Society. It was here that he became acquainted with a number of his lifelong friends, including George Grote (later the author of a celebrated *History of Greece*), John Austin, and several others. Mill had begun publishing brief essays and letters in newspapers and magazines as early as 1822.

But in 1826 Mill suffered a "crisis" in his intellectual and emotional life. It is worth citing his own description of it in his *Autobiography*:

> I was in a dull state of nerves, such as everybody is occasionally liable to; unsusceptible to enjoyment or pleasurable excitement; one of those moods when what is pleasure at other times, becomes insipid or indifferent; the state, I should think, in which converts to Methodism usually are, when smitten by their first "conviction of sin." In this frame of mind it occurred to me to put the question directly to myself: "Suppose that all your objects in life were realized; that all the changes in institutions and opinions which you are looking forward to, could be com-

> pletely effected at this very instant: would this be a great joy and happiness to you?" And an irrepressible self-consciousness distinctly answered, "No!" At this my heart sank within me: the whole foundation on which my life was constructed fell down. All my happiness was to have been found in the continual pursuit of this end. The end had ceased to charm, and how could there ever again be any interest in the means? I seemed to have nothing left to live for. (*AM* 87)

This remarkable testament suggests that James Mill's relentless education of his son had the serious drawback of stunting Mill's social and emotional life. It is sad to read that, during his youth, "I had ample leisure in every day to amuse myself; but as I had no boy companions, and the animal need of physical activity was satisfied by walking, my amusements, which were mostly solitary, were in general of a quiet, if not a bookish turn" (*AM* 25). Clearly, James Mill had attempted to make his son a kind of "thinking machine"; Mill in fact notes, "For passionate emotions of all sorts, and for everything which has been said or written in exaltation of them, he professed the greatest contempt" (*AM* 33).

Mill emerged from this nearly suicidal state in an unusual way. Having by chance picked up the memoirs of the French writer Jean-François Marmontel, he came upon Marmontel's touching account of the death of his father. "A vivid conception of the scene and its feelings came over me, and I was moved to tears. From this moment my burthen grew lighter. The oppression of the thought that all feeling was dead within me, was gone. I was no longer hopeless: I was not a stock or a stone" (*AM* 91). Shortly thereafter, Mill discovered the poetry of Wordsworth and Coleridge (with both of whom he later established contact), finding in their Romanticism the elevation of human feeling that he sought. But it was not simply the revival of his emotions that he found so vital at this critical turning point; as Alan P. F. Sell notes, "the poems made him sensitive to the feelings of others, and by so doing became a spur in his quest for social reform."[2]

Mill, indeed, at this juncture began deviating from orthodox utilitarian doctrine, which similarly downplayed the emotions and regarded happiness as a purely rational choice. The evolution of his own version of utilitarianism takes far greater account of human feelings than the work of Bentham or James Mill and thereby gains added intellectual cogency by basing its reasoning on the full human being.

Another climactic moment in Mill's life was his acquaintance with Harriet Taylor in 1830. At that time a twenty-two-year-old woman married to John Taylor, a London merchant, Harriet became for Mill "the most admirable person I had ever known" (*AM* 119). Although even some of Mill's friends and supporters expressed puzzlement at the glowing terms with which he spoke of Harriet, it is clear that his words were inspired by deep affection, as well as by an admiration of her "intellectual gifts," which Mill states "did but minister to a moral character at once the noblest and the best balanced which I have ever met with in life" (*AM* 121). Although John and Harriet were intent on observing the proprieties as far as they could, there is some evidence that their continual association was looked upon with disfavor by friends and colleagues—as well as by Mill's own parents. In spite of their intellectual and emotional bond, there could be no thought of divorce for Harriet. After nearly two decades, the matter was settled for them by John Taylor's death in 1849. Two years later, they married. Their union evidently led to an estrangement with Mill's mother, and it is believed that this is the chief reason Mill does not so much as mention her in his *Autobiography*.

There is no reason to doubt Mill's statements that much of the work he wrote during this period was heavily influenced by Harriet's input. Clearly she had much to offer on questions of ethics and politics from her unique perspective as a sharp-witted and emotionally engaged woman. Mill's first major work, *A System of Logic* (1843), which established his credentials as a radical empiricist, probably owes little to Harriet, but such later works as *Principles of Political Economy* (1849) and, most notably, *On Liberty* probably do contain substantial traces of her thinking. In regard to the latter work, Mill states that "The 'Liberty' was more directly and literally our joint production than anything else which bears my name, for there was not a sentence of it that was not several times gone through by us together, turned over in many ways, and carefully weeded of any faults, either of thought or expression, that we detected in it" (*AM* 161).

Regrettably, Harriet's death in 1858, after only seven years of marriage, cast a shadow over the rest of Mill's life. Mill, of course, continued to write, producing such works as *Considerations on Representative Government* (1861) and *Utilitarianism* (1863). In 1865, this otherwise reclusive scholar was persuaded to run for a seat in Parliament. Mill, although largely an intellectual comfortable within the confines of his study, always regarded his work as having direct practical applications. Both he and his father had been involved in the passage of the Reform Act of 1832, which introduced numerous reforms that reduced corruption in Parliament, particularly by the elimination of "rotten boroughs" and the broadening of the suffrage (although it explicitly banned woman suffrage). But by the 1860s, it was apparent that further reforms were necessary, and Mill was persuaded to run to add his voice to the actual deliberations of the next reform bill. It is highly significant that among the several conditions Mill laid down before he agreed to run is the following: "On one subject only, my religious opinions, I announced from the beginning that I would answer no questions" (*AM* 181). Then (as, sadly, now, at least in the United States), the affirmation of atheism or even agnosticism was considered so severe a political liability that it would essentially bar a candidate from success at the polls.

Mill won a seat in Parliament and led the campaign for the Reform Act of 1867, which radically expanded (male) suffrage; in fact, the bill was passed largely as a means of warding off an even broader granting of the suffrage. But Mill's parliamentary career came to an abrupt end in 1868—and the main cause was, interestingly, religion. His donation of a small amount of money to the reelection campaign of the notorious atheist Charles Bradlaugh was used by his political opponents to turn the voters against him, and he was defeated. Retiring to Avignon, France, Mill put the finishing touches on both *The Subjection of Women* (1869) and his *Autobiography* (1873), the latter of which had been begun as early as 1854. There is something fitting in the fact that, in 1872, he served as the (secular) godfather of the son of his friend in Parliament, Lord John Russell. This child would grow up to become Bertrand Russell, who, more than anyone, carried on Mill's work in philosophical logic, ethics, and political freedom.

Mill's three essays on religion—"Nature," "Utility of Religion," and "Theism," the last being as long as the other two combined—were written over a long period. The first two were drafted between 1850 and 1858, the third between 1868 and 1870. Whatever the reasons for Mill's disinclination to publish these essays, there is no question of their cogency in attacking, and perhaps destroying, several major pillars of religious thought, particularly as regards the existence of God, the characteristics of God even if he is assumed to exist, the probability of immortality, and the role of religion in the formation and functioning of a viable moral system.

It is worth beginning with the essay "Theism," as it presents Mill's most wide-ranging arguments on the subject; the other two essays deal with more limited facets of the question. The first part of the essay deals with four of the principal "proofs" that theologians have adduced in support of the existence of a deity. But before he engages in the analysis of these "proofs," Mill outlines his methodology:

> It is indispensable that the subject of religion should from time to time be reviewed as a strictly scientific question, and that its evidences should be tested by the same scientific methods, and on the same principles as those of any of the speculative conclusions drawn by physical science. It being granted then that the legitimate conclusions of science are entitled to prevail over all opinions, however widely held, which conflict with them, and that the canons of scientific evidence which the successes and failures of two thousand years have established, are applicable to all subjects on which knowledge is attainable, let us proceed to consider what place there is for religious beliefs on the platform of science; what evidences they can appeal to, such as science can recognize, and what foundation there is for the doctrines of religion, considered as scientific theorems.[3]

Alan P. F. Sell, citing this very passage, delivers a strong criticism: "The position begs the huge question that the methods of science, construed as Mill construes it—that is, naturalistically and empirically—are competent to weigh religious claims. Nowhere does Mill defend his stance; he simply announces it and expects his readers to take it on trust."[4] But Sell has read "Theism" very carelessly and, perhaps, tendentiously. The fact is that Mill *does* justify his stance in the very next section of the essay by maintaining that it was the advance of science that led to the establishment of monotheism over polytheism in the first place. He asserts plausibly that polytheism is a more "natural" view of the world than monotheism, given that primitive "animism" (which assumed that all entities were governed by individual gods) was the foundation of polytheistic belief. It was only when, in Mill's estimation, science established that Nature was a "unified whole" (*T* 133) did the notion of a monotheistic creator-god become plausible. Whatever the historicity of Mill's anthropology of religion here, it is evident that he believes theism is indeed a direct outgrowth of science: "The reason, then, why Monotheism may be accepted as the representative of Theism in the abstract, is not so much because it is the Theism of all the more improved portions of the human race, as because it is the only theism which can claim for itself any footing on scientific ground" (*T* 133). Mill also implies, without explicitly stating it, that many fundamental tenets of monotheism and of religious belief in general are in fact based on appeals to science: the very claim that God created the universe is a scientific claim and can therefore be legitimately assessed based on the most up-to-date findings of science. Moreover, most of the arguments in "Theism" are not scientific arguments but those based on philosophical logic, of exactly the sort utilized by Thomas Aquinas and other defenders of "natural religion."

Mill first treats the notion of a First Cause. The argument he addresses is as follows: "Everything that we know (it is argued) had a cause, and owed its existence to that cause. How then can it be but that the world, which is but a name for the aggregate of all that we know, has a cause to which it is indebted for its existence?" (*T* 142). Mill's discussion of this "proof" is quite complex and at points vitiated by subsequent scientific discovery. It rests upon the purportedly eternal existence of what he calls Matter and Force (what today would be called *energy*). Mill never attempts to prove that these entities are in fact eternal, but merely assumes it. Nevertheless, his conclusion—"Theism, therefore, in so far as it rests on the necessity of a First Cause, has no support from experience" (*T* 150)—appears sound. Bertrand Russell would later deliver a much more crushing refutation of the First Cause argument, and today it is rarely evoked by theologians.

The second "proof" discussed by Mill is the "argument from the general consent of mankind." Surprisingly, Mill does not address one obvious refutation of this argument: that belief in God is not, in fact, "universal" anymore, therefore it cannot be likened to some kind of "instinct" like breathing. Perhaps Mill was deterred by the fact that the number of explicitly avowed atheists was (because of continuing legal punishments dealt to those who purportedly engaged in "blasphemy" or in "insulting" the Christian religion) still relatively small, so that it could (implausibly) be suggested that these few benighted souls were so morally and intellectually corrupt that they could not see the obvious existence of God. What Mill does state is that this argument is merely an appeal to authority—in this case, the authority is not one single (and presumably intellectually eminent) human being, but the great mass of humanity. Mill continues that this argument is dubious because, even if is assumed that all or most human beings actually do have some belief in God, that belief is so variable that it is impossible to imagine that all human beings are believing in the same god. Consider the animistic beliefs of primitive tribes:

> The religious belief of savages is not belief in the God of Natural Theology, but a mere modification of this crude generalization which ascribes life, consciousness and will to all natural powers of which they cannot perceive the source or control the operation. And the divinities believed in are as numerous as those powers. Each river, fountain or tree has a divinity of its own. To see in this blunder of primitive ignorance the hand of the Supreme Being implanting in his creatures an instinctive knowledge of his existence, is a poor compliment to the Deity. (*T* 157–58)

Although this essay was written just prior to Edward Burnett Tylor's exhaustive treatment of primitive religion in the landmark anthropological treatise *Primitive Culture* (1871), Mill was clearly drawing upon prior anthropological work to suggest that notions of godhead are almost as numerous and variable as the individuals who hold them.

The third "proof" of the existence of God is "the argument from consciousness." This is simply the argument that there is some "inward light" (*T* 162) that leads us inexorably to believe in God. Mill, rightly tracing this idea to the logic of Descartes, makes the obvious counterargument that it is impossible to know that such a belief is not the product of delusion. In effect, such a belief is nothing more than "a *naif* expression of the tendency of the human mind to believe what is agreeable to it" (*T* 166).

The fourth argument—"the argument from marks of design in nature"—is treated by Mill more exhaustively than the others, because he believes it has the greatest plausibility of the four he is discussing. The argument, which he asserts is "wholly grounded on experience," goes as follows:

> Certain qualities, it is alleged, are found to be characteristic of such things as are made by an intelligent mind for a purpose. The order of Nature, or some considerable parts of it, exhibit these qualities in a remarkable degree. We are entitled, from this great similarity of effects, to infer similarity in the cause, and to believe that things which it is beyond the power of man to make, but which resemble the works of man in all but power, must have been made by Intelligence, armed with a power greater than human. (*T* 167)

The best-known proponent of this argument was William Paley, who put forth a celebrated analogy: If one found a watch on a deserted island, one would naturally assume that it had been created by a watchmaker. But Mill destroys this argument in one sentence: "If I found a watch on an apparently desolate island, I should indeed infer that it had been left there by a human being; but the inference would not be from marks of design, but because I already knew by direct experience that watches are made by men" (*T* 168). But the poorness of this particular analogy should not prejudice us from assessing it carefully. Mill in fact presents a better-reasoned case for the argument from design:

> The circumstances in which it is alleged that the world resembles the works of man are not circumstances taken at random, but are particular instances of a circumstance which experience shows to have a real connection with an intelligent origin, the fact of conspiring to an end. The argument therefore is not one of mere analogy. As mere analogy it has its weight, but it is more than analogy. It surpasses analogy exactly as induction surpasses it. It is an inductive argument. (*T* 169–70)

At this point, Mill brings in, as a counterweight, the still relatively new doctrine of the theory of evolution, which he explicitly refers to (in quotation marks) as "'the survival of the fittest'" (*T* 172). After stating the theory (which, it is now widely acknowledged, did indeed overthrow the argument from design—which is no doubt why it continues to be vilified by the pious), Mill writes: "It must be acknowledged that there is something very startling, and *prima facie* improbable in this hypothetical history of Nature" (*T* 173). It is not clear how thoroughly Mill was educated in science: his account of his early readings shows that they were largely in the realms of philosophy, history, and belles lettres. It is evident that he did not fully understand the ramifications of the theory of evolution, and perhaps no one at this time—only a decade or so after the theory's promulgation in *The Origin of Species* (1859)—could have done so. The best Mill can say is that "the theory if admitted would be in no way whatever inconsistent with Creation. But it must be acknowledged that it would greatly attenuate the evidence for it" (*T* 174). Mill's final conclusion in regard to the argument from design is as follows: "I think it must be allowed that, in the present state of our knowledge, the adaptations in Nature afford a large balance of probability in favour of creation by intelligence" (*T* 174).

Some of Mill's secular colleagues were taken aback at this apparent gesture of letting God in by the back door after so many devastating rebuttals to standard arguments for his existence, but Mill does not afford much comfort to religionists in his discussion of what he takes to be the attributes of his deity, which forms the next section of "Theism." Here Mill immediately rejects the notion of a god who is both omnipotent and benevolent. The omnipotence of God is, in particular, a hypothesis that must be abandoned. Mill assumes that the universe is infinite and that therefore matter and force (i.e., energy) could not have been *created* by God: "There is in Nature no reason whatever to suppose that either Matter or Force, or any of their properties, were made by the Being who was the author of the collocations by which the world is adapted to what we consider as its purposes; or that he has power to alter any of those properties" (*T* 178). Mill is, in other words, putting forth the argument—held by a wide array of thinkers from classical antiquity to the present—that God could only manipulate the materials already in existence and that his power to do so is necessarily finite. Mill notes that there are abundant defects in Nature, both cosmic and human, making it unlikely that an omnipotent god could not have done better with the existing materials:

> The human body, for example, is one of the most striking instances of artful and ingenious contrivance which nature offers, but we may well ask whether so complicated a machine could not have been made to last longer, and not to get so easily and frequently out of order. We may ask why the human race should have been so constituted as to grovel in wretchedness and degradation for countless ages before a small portion

> of it was enabled to lift itself into the very imperfect state of intelligence, goodness and happiness which we enjoy. (*T* 181–82)

This argument is also venerable and can be traced at least to Lucretius's pungent one-sentence utterance "*Tanta stat praedita culpa*" ([The universe] stands endowed with so many flaws) (*De Rerum Natura* 5.199).

It is at this point that we should turn our attention to the essay on "Nature," for here Mill most vividly and even bitterly makes the case for the nonomnipotence of God. On its face, this essay would seem to have little to do with religion, as it begins with a discussion of two of the central meanings of the term *nature* (first as referring to all entities, and second as being distinguished from art or [human] artifice), but Mill gravitates to the notion that Nature cannot be a model for emulation by human beings, because it is both vicious and destructive:

> A single hurricane destroys the hopes of a season; a flight of locusts, or an inundation, desolates a district; a trifling chemical change in an edible root starves a million of people. The waves of the sea, like banditti seize and appropriate the wealth of the rich and the little all of the poor with the same accompaniments of stripping, wounding, and killing as their human antitypes. Everything in short, which the worst men commit either against life or property is perpetuated on a larger scale by natural agents. Nature has Noyades more fatal than those of Carrier; her explosions of fire damp are as destructive as human artillery; her plague and cholera far surpass the poison cups of the Borgias. Even the love of "order" which is thought to be a following of the ways of Nature, is in fact a contradiction of them. All which people are accustomed to deprecate as "disorder" and its consequences, is precisely a counterpart of Nature's ways. Anarchy and the Reign of Terror are overmatched in injustice, ruin, and death, by a hurricane and a pestilence. (*T* 30–31)

Mill has been criticized for presenting a one-sided view of nature as purely destructive—so different from the benevolence of nature found in the poetry of Wordsworth, which he admired—but of course it is to his purpose to do so: he is here addressing one of the most vexing of theological issues, the problem of evil. Why, in short, is there so much evil (whether "natural" as depicted above or "human" evil as embodied in supposed "sins") if God is believed to be both omnipotent and benevolent? Mill is right to berate the "sophistry" of theologians who would gloss over the sufferings of the world merely to maintain the academic theological point of God's simultaneous omnipotence and benevolence. His own argument was anticipated by David Hume in a laconic passage in *Dialogues concerning Natural Religion* (1779): "If he [God] is willing to prevent evil, but not able? then is he impotent. If he is able, but not willing? then is he malevolent. Is he both able and willing? whence then is evil?"[5] This question remains unanswerable by orthodox Christian theology, and Mill's own solution—that, to save the mere existence of God, it is better to give up his omnipotence than his benevolence—is surely the least unpalatable that could be offered.

Returning to the essay on theism, let us see how Mill elaborates on his notion of the probable attributes of a god of limited power: "It does appear that granting the existence of design, there is a preponderance of evidence that the Creator desired the pleasure of his creatures" (*T* 191). He can come to this conclusion because pleasure (for human beings) does exist in the world, and in a multitude of forms. (This very notion is predicated on Mill's utilitarianism, whereby "happiness" is strictly defined as pleasure, whether it be active pleasure or the elimination or absence of pain.) But from the mere existence of pain in the world, it cannot be asserted that "the single end and aim of Creation was the happiness of his creatures":

> If the motive of the Deity for creating sentient beings was the happiness of the beings he created, his purpose, in our corner of the universe at least, must be pronounced, taking past ages and all countries and races into account, to have been thus far an ignominious failure; and if God had no purpose but our happiness and that of other living creatures it is not credible that he would have called them into existence with the prospect of being so completely baffled. (*T* 192)

And so, once again, we are forced once again to assume a deity whose powers are limited.

Mill continues his essay on theism with a discussion of the issue of immortality. He begins by asserting that the very notion of the immortality of the soul becomes problematic, because the soul has been misconceived as a unitary substance rather than what it actually is—a "bundle of attributes, the attributes of feeling, thinking, reasoning, believing, willing, &c." (*T* 197). It is therefore not immediately obvious how this bundle of attributes could survive the extinction of the body to which it appears so intimately wedded. However, Mill is not as inexorably hostile to the notion of immortality as one might imagine him to be. He flatly asserts: "There is . . . in science, no evidence against the immortality of the soul but that negative evidence, which consists in the absence of evidence in its favour. And even the negative evidence is not so strong as negative evidence often is" (*T* 201). Mill, however, has little difficulty in dispensing with some of the theoretical arguments put forth in support of immortality: "We are told that the desire of immortality is one of our instincts, and that there is no instinct which has not corresponding to it a real object fitted to satisfy it" (*T* 204). On this point Mill could have cited the argument that many others, including H. L. Mencken, advanced—that, as a matter of fact, the "instinct" is not universal and that there are any number of people who have no desire for immortality—but Mill takes the argument on its face and presents a refutation on its own principles:

> Granting that wherever there is an instinct there exists something such as that instinct demands, can it be affirmed that this something exists in boundless quantity, or sufficient to satisfy the infinite craving of human desires? What is called the desire of eternal life is simply the desire of life; and does there not exist that which this desire calls for? Is there not life? And is not the instinct, if it be an instinct, gratified by the possession and preservation of life? To suppose that the desire of life guarantees to us personally the reality of life through all eternity, is like supposing that the desire of food assures us that we shall always have as much as we can eat through our whole lives and as much longer as we can conceive our lives to be protracted to. (*T* 205)

Turning to specific arguments on immortality offered by natural theology, Mill makes pretty much the same rebuttal, this one enlivened by dry wit:

> One thing . . . is quite certain in respect to God's government of the world; that he either could not, or would not, grant to us every thing

> we wish. We wish for life, and he has granted some life: that we wish (or some of us wish) for a boundless extent of life and that it is not granted, is no exception to the ordinary modes of his government. Many a man would like to be a Croesus or an Augustus Caesar, but has his wishes gratified only to the moderate extent of a pound a week or the Secretaryship of his Trades Union. There is, therefore, no assurance whatever of a life after death, on grounds of natural religion. (*T* 209–10)

Mill devotes a chapter to the plausibility of there being a revelation from God (in the form of the Bible or other scriptures), which involves an analysis of the likelihood of miracles. His conclusion—"miracles have no claim whatever to the character of historical facts and are wholly invalid as evidences of any revelation" (*T* 239)—is pretty much along the lines that David Hume had offered a century earlier.

What evoked the greatest controversy, especially among Mill's secularist colleagues, was the final chapter of the essay on theism, entitled "General Result." After waging so exhaustive a battle against the standard arguments of theology, it was startling for Mill to assert once again (based on his misunderstanding of Darwin) that "the indication given by such evidence as there is, points to the creation, not indeed of the universe, but of the present order of it by an Intelligent Mind, whose power over the materials was not absolute, whose love for his creatures was not his sole actuating inducement, but who nevertheless desired their good" (*T* 243). This would be bad enough, but Mill maintained that the current state of knowledge even allows for the "hope" of the immortality of the soul: "it appears to me that the indulgence of hope with regard to the government of the universe and the destiny of man after death, while we recognize as a clear truth that we have no ground for more than a hope, is legitimate and philosophically defensible" (*T* 249). This bizarre conclusion—which simultaneously asserted that the "hope" is not particularly likely but is nonetheless "defensible"—was not of a sort to satisfy critics on either side of the issue. Alan Millar has noted: "It is one thing to be hopeful about what for all we know might be the case when we think there is at least some chance that it may be so. It is another to indulge hope where we have no reason to think there is such a chance."[6]

Several reasons have been put forth for why Mill would somehow try to please both theists and nontheists in this way. Perhaps the most plausible is his inveterate tendency to try to find something good in even the weakest of arguments, and his attempts—most notably as a practical politician—to look for common ground even among the most widely discordant views. A provocative comment made in passing in the essay "Puseyism" (1842) may be worth citing: "We not only esteem it a more healthful exercise of the mind to employ itself in learning from an enemy, than in inveighing against him; but, we believe, that the extirpation of what is erroneous in any system of belief is in no way so much promoted as by extricating from it, and incorporating into our own system, whatever in it is true."[7] Whether Mill, indeed, ever "incorporated" any belief in immortality into his own philosophy is to be doubted; but perhaps he was guided by a desire not to rob his readers—most of whom no doubt did believe in it—entirely of this comforting belief.

In many ways, "Utility of Religion" is the most provocative of the *Three Essays on Religion*, for here Mill not only addresses the central issue of the interaction of religion and morality but also puts forth his own substitute religion, the "Religion of Humanity" (*T* 109). The first topic was one to which Mill had long been fascinated, and he was resolute in asserting that there is no necessary connection between morality and religion. As early as 1823, in a series of letters on "Free Discussion" (i.e., of religion), he bluntly asserted: "Even if (which God forbid) all sense of religion were to die away among men, there would still remain abundant motives to ensure good conduct in this life" (*CW* 22.17). Mill does not elaborate on the point in these letters, but he does so in "Utility of Religion" and other documents. The essay as a whole treats the subject of religion's "usefulness" all apart from its supposed truth. Mill acknowledges that this very issue came to the fore only when religion's "truth had in a great measure ceased to convince" (*T* 70). Although he states that it is "perfectly conceivable that religion may be morally useful without being intellectually sustainable" (*T* 73–74), the bulk of his essay presents a strong refutation of this claim.

Mill begins by stating the truism that good morals must be inculcated into the people and, as a practical matter, that such instruction is currently in the hands of religious authorities, chiefly in the form of state schools controlled by the Church of England. Mill also speaks of the indoctrination of children into religious belief. But he states that these forces, which did once lead (although with some unfortunate side effects) to good conduct in individuals, are now weakening. In particular, Christianity's constant use of the threat of hell to enforce morality has now become very weak: "Rewards and punishments postponed to that distance of time, and never seen by the eye, are not calculated, even when infinite and eternal, to have, on ordinary minds, a very powerful effect in opposition to strong temptation" (*T* 89). What is more, it is obvious that the morals recommended by religion were obeyed, not because they were religious, but because they were good morals all apart from their endorsement by any system of theism. Therefore, the separation of morals from theism will simply leave them still viable as self-standing principles.

Finally, there are various dangers in attributing morality to supernatural forces. In the first place, it seems quite unnecessary: "Are not moral truths strong enough in their own evidence, at all events to retain the belief of mankind when once they have acquired it?" (*T* 97). But there is a further danger:

> There is a very real evil consequent on ascribing a supernatural origin to the received maxims of morality. That origin consecrates the whole of them, and protects them from being discussed or criticized. So that if among the moral doctrines received as a part of religion, there be any which are imperfect—which were either erroneous from the first, or not properly limited and guarded in the expression, or which, unexceptionable once, are no longer suited to the changes that have taken place in human relations (and it is my firm belief that in so-called christian [*sic*] morality, instances of all these kinds are to be found) these doctrines are considered equally binding on the conscience with the noblest, most permanent and most universal precepts of Christ. Wherever morality is supposed to be of supernatural origin, morality is stereotyped; as law is, for the same reason, among believers in the Koran. (*T* 99)

This striking anticipation of one of the central tenets of Nietzsche's *On the Genealogy of Morals* leads Mill to reject supernaturalism as a basis for morals. In its place, he propounds the Religion of Humanity.

This conception was, at least in its rudiments, derived from Mill's early absorption of the work of Auguste Comte. Comte had proposed that human thought had evolved in three stages—the religious, the metaphysical, and the positive. The positive rests upon science and presents a secularized religion somewhat along the lines that Mill advocated decades later. Mill, however, eventually broke from Comte—as evidenced by his late treatise, *Auguste Comte and Positivism* (1865)—because he felt that the details of Comte's "religion" had elements of authoritarianism and even irrationalism that he found repugnant. His own "Religion of Humanity" may strike us as a bit vague and abstract, but it is evident that he himself saw it as a viable alternative to religions whose fallacies had become too obvious to ignore.

Exactly what Mill actually meant by the "Religion of Humanity" is not always clear. In "Utility of Religion" he notes that "the sense of unity with mankind, and a deep feeling for the general good, may be cultivated into a sentiment and a principle capable of fulfilling every important function of religion and itself justly entitled to the name" (*T* 110). Mill believed that his religion was particularly unselfish, in contrast to the manner of some adherents of Christianity, who were so concerned with personal salvation that they regarded this as the highest good, as opposed to actual concern for their family, neighbors, and society. The only advantage of supernatural religions, in Mill's eyes, over his own religion is "the prospect they hold out to the individual of a life after death" (*T* 118). In contrast to what he says in "Theism," Mill here maintains that such a belief should be extirpated and would be extirpated if the Religion of Humanity became prevalent:

> If the Religion of Humanity were as sedulously cultivated as the supernatural religions are (and there is no difficulty in conceiving that it might be much more so), all who had received the customary amount of moral cultivation would up to the hour of death live ideally in the life of those who are to follow them: and though doubtless they would often willingly survive as individuals for a much longer period than the present duration of life, it appears to me probable that after a length of time different in different persons, they would have had enough of existence, and would gladly lie down and take their eternal rest. (*T* 119–20)

Mill even goes so far as to say that, with the passage of time, "not annihilation but immortality may be the burdensome idea" (*T* 122).

It may well be that the Religion of Humanity was a pipe-dream on Mill's part, although there is no evidence that he ever thought it could be inculcated on a wide scale, at least not in the foreseeable future. It is not entirely clear what influence Mill's views had on the subsequent development of secular humanism, but there is no doubt that he strongly anticipated this movement and put forth a theoretically viable counterpart to religion that was free of the crippling defects to which conventional religion was increasingly liable.

As noted, one of Mill's earliest published writings, a series of three letters on "Free Discussion" (1823), advocated freedom of discussion of religion in the interest both of truth and of intellectual freedom. Here he presents strong arguments that, if such freedom of discussion is not allowed, then the government becomes a de facto arbiter of all intellectual advance, and thereby becomes despotic (see *CW* 22.11). Mill develops these points in *On Liberty*, relying here on the principle of fallibility. Since it is impossible for us to know, prior to engaging in a discussion, which opinion is true and which is false, it is dangerous to entrust the government with the power to suppress what it believes to be falsehood; for that purported falsehood may turn out to be the truth. In any event, truth can be ascertained only by the full airing of views on all sides; in the absence of such an airing, even a true belief can become stale and lifeless. Mill went so far as to state that Christianity itself, at least as the majority of its supposed believers adhered to it, had become just such a "dead belief."[8]

On this basis Mill expressed his lifelong opposition to the Church of England. An established church, being supported by and indistinguishable from the government, has no incentive to develop and remain vital:

> The Establishment, in its present state, is no corrective, but the great promoter of sectarianism; being itself, both in the exclusiveness of its tenets, and in the spirit of the majority of its clergy, a thoroughly sectarian institution. Its very essence is subscription to articles, and the bond of union which holds its members together is a dead creed, not a living spirit.[9]

It is a bit surprising that Mill did not address the issue of religion's role in suppressing women's rights. In his late treatise, *The Subjection of Women* (1869), which he admitted was deeply informed by discussions he had had with his wife, Christianity is scarcely mentioned. This is in stark contrast to the atheist Elizabeth Cady Stanton, who in the fiery tract

Bible and Church Degrade Women (1885) wrote that "the Church has done more to degrade woman than all other adverse influences put together" and that "the whole tone of Church teaching in regard to woman is, to the last degree, contemptuous and degrading."[10] In only one passage does Mill address the issue:

> We are told that Paul said, "Wives, obey your husbands:" but he also said, "Slaves, obey your masters." It was not St. Paul's business, nor was it consistent with his object, the propagation of Christianity, to incite any one to rebellion against existing laws. The apostle's acceptance of all social institutions as he found them, is no more to be construed as a disapproval of attempts to improve them at the proper time, than his declaration, "The powers that be are ordained of God," gives his sanction to military despotism.[11]

This is a most curious "defense." In the first place, many other passages in the Bible endorse the "subjection" of women (one can go back to the Tenth Commandment—"Thou shalt not covet . . . thy neighbor's wife" [Exod. 20:17], which plainly makes a wife the property of her husband); in the second place, it is an odd strategy to excuse Paul's remark on women (which is one of the mildest among many others he uttered) by also excusing his condoning of slavery. It remains a curiosity why Mill did not more forcefully press the role of Christianity in the continued oppression of women. Perhaps he felt it would detract from the thrust of his argument, which was to advocate remedial measures for women, and for society as a whole—a plan that might have been confounded if too much blame were put on Christianity or any other social forces for past derelictions.

John Stuart Mill's searching investigations of the scientific plausibility of religion, of the role of religion in forming morality, and on the precise place of a church within a state that purports to grant freedom to its citizens left a lasting legacy. Political partisans on both the right and the left draw upon his hallowed name as a source of their views; such thinkers in the empiricist tradition as Bertrand Russell and A. J. Ayer have continued his inquiries into philosophical logic; and both religionists and secularists have been compelled to address the points he had raised in his *Three Essays on Religion* and other writings. In attempting to carve out a middle ground between dogmatic religion and unequivocal atheism, he perhaps inevitably failed to please either side; but his writings, based on a lifetime of reading and thinking on the weightiest subjects in human thought, remain indispensable in their judicial weighing of the merits and defects of all the issues they treat.

Chapter 4

Friedrich Nietzsche: Prophet of the Superman

Friedrich Nietzsche (1844–1900) is one of the most difficult thinkers for the philosophically uninitiated to grasp—not because, as with Wittgenstein, his work is laced with highly technical terms and conceptions derived from philosophical logic, but because many of his major treatises are written in a poetical, and polemical, vein that relies little on step-by-step proofs but instead seeks to convince by means of the witchery of words. Nietzsche is as much a creative artist as a philosopher—but this is not in any way to suggest, as has frequently been done, that he is an irrationalist who advocates no sound reasons for his basic philosophical principles. Nietzsche is difficult precisely because he is, by his own account, an iconoclast—"*Overthrowing idols* (my word for 'ideals')—that comes closer to being part of my craft"[1]—who challenges his readers at the very foundations of their belief systems. His purpose is to inspire thought at the deepest levels; even if one ultimately rejects his conclusions, one will have done so after a thorough investigation of the bases for one's own assumptions and presuppositions.

Nietzsche's poetical manner of utterance, which requires intense contextualization and an open-minded sympathy with his philosophical goals and approach, has led to his being perhaps the most widely misinterpreted and misunderstood philosopher of the past two centuries. Both during and after World War I, he was held responsible for the aggression of the German army and government, in spite of the fact that throughout his work, he repeatedly ridicules German culture and war mongering. Later he was accused of anti-Semitism and of inspiring the Nazis with his conception of the "superman," an egregious misconstrual that the Nazis themselves did much to foster. Still more recently, his provocative utterance "God is dead" has been seized as a banner by both the religious and the antireligious. To clarify all these misinterpretations within the space of a single chapter may be a hopeless task, but some light can be shed on various essential conceptions.

It may well be true, as one scholar has maintained, that "the major premise of Nietzsche's philosophy is atheism."[2] If Nietzsche himself is to be believed, there never seems to have been a time when he accepted the standard dogmas of the Christian religion: "'God,' 'immortality of the soul,' 'redemption,' 'beyond'—without exception, concepts to which I never devoted any attention, or time; not even as a child. Perhaps I have never been childlike enough for them?" (*EH* 236). There is virtually no actual argumentation against these concepts in Nietzsche's work; it is as if he could hardly trouble himself to refute such obvious falsehoods. His early study of classical thought (the only job he ever held was that of professor of classical studies at the University of Basel from 1869 to 1879) led him to a profound study of ancient thought and religion, and his first book, *The Birth of Tragedy* (1872), vaunted Dionysus (god of wine and inspirer of madness and ecstasy, and hence, for Nietzsche, of animal vitality and instinct) in contrast to the arid rationalism symbolized by Apollo. Decades before E. R. Dodds placed the scholarly imprimatur on the thesis in *The Greeks and the Irrational* (1951), Nietzsche recognized that the Greeks were not the one-dimensional rationalists that centuries of tendentious scholarship had portrayed them to be.

The central conception in Nietzsche's thought is what he frequently termed a "saying Yes to life." By this is meant a fusion of mind and body, Apollo and Dionysus, to generate a sense of robust health and the quest for self-mastery, self-perfection, even self-overcoming in the real world. Nietzsche realized that his first book already embodied this conception in rudimentary form:

> I was the first to see the real opposition: the degenerating instinct that turns against life with subterranean vengefulness (Christianity, the philosophy of Schopenhauer, in a certain sense already the philosophy of Plato, and of all idealism as typical forms) versus a formula for the highest affirmation, born of fullness, of overfullness, a Yes-saying without reservation, even to suffering, even to guilt, even to everything that is questionable and strange in existence. (*EH* 272)

The relation with Arthur Schopenhauer is worth pursuing briefly. Schopenhauer's philosophy is of prodigious complexity, but at its essence it advocated the notion that human desires, embodied in his catchphrase "the will to live," could never be fulfilled in the real world, and any attempt to do so would only lead to futility and neurosis. Hence Schopenhauer's profound pessimism, most famously embodied in a posthumously assembled collection of essays, *Studies in Pessimism* (1890). Nietzsche was initially attracted to Schopenhauer's ideas but quickly rejected them, substituting his "will to power" for the "will to live." "Will to power" should not be interpreted in any trivial political (much less militaristic) sense; instead, it embodies Nietzsche's belief that at least a small segment of the human populace had the inner strength to grasp all that life had to offer, and so to become supermen.

The concept of the superman is perhaps the most misunderstood conception in Nietzsche's thought. His most sensitive interpreter, Walter Kaufmann, makes a good case that the term *Übermensch* should be translated as "overman," because at its root is the notion of overcoming (*Überwindung*)—overcoming of obstacles, including those obstacles imposed by one's own mind, character, and upbringing. What exact traits the superman or overman should embody is difficult to elucidate in small compass; perhaps Kaufmann's summary, distilled from the whole of Nietzsche's writings, is as close as we can come: "He has overcome his animal nature, organized the chaos of his passions, sublimated his impulses, and given style to his character—or, as Nietzsche said of Goethe: 'he disciplined himself to wholeness, he *created* himself' and became 'the man of tolerance, not from weakness but from strength,' 'a spirit who has *become free*.'"[3]

In past historical ages, this ideal was (very approximately) embodied in hereditary aristocracies: "The knightly-aristocratic value judgments presupposed a powerful physicality, a flourishing, abundant, even overflowing health, together with that which serves to preserve it: war, adventure, hunting, dancing, war games, and in general all that involves vigorous, free, joyful activity."[4] One should not be misled into thinking that the superman's traits are purely physical, as our subsequent discussion will make clear. It is, however, at this point that Nietzsche utters one of his most controversial statements:

> One cannot fail to see at the bottom of all these noble races the beast of prey, the splendid *blond beast* prowling avidly in search of spoil and victory; this hidden core needs to erupt from time to time, the animal has to get out again and go back to the wilderness: the Roman, Arabian, Germanic, Japanese nobility, the Homeric heroes, the Scandinavian Vikings—they all shared this need. (*GM* 40–41)

The phrase "blond beast" was quickly adopted by the Nazis to advocate Aryan supremacy, but it should be plain that, in the few times this phrase is mentioned, Nietzsche does not restrict it to Aryans, and that his superman conception emphatically applies to individuals and not races. Indeed, in its literal sense, the term refers simply to the lion as the king of beasts, and even metaphorically the phrase has no racial connotations.

One begins to sense the bases for Nietzsche's hostility and scorn of Christianity. Those bases are almost entirely moral—or, perhaps more broadly, sociocultural. For Christianity, as it evolved after the death of Jesus (who, to Nietzsche's mind, was the only true "Christian"), represents a triumph of the weak over the strong—"weak" and "strong" interpreted, as always, not in a crudely physical manner but in the widest possible sense, as encompassing both mental and physical vigor. The point is made emphatically in Nietzsche's last published work, *The Antichrist* (1888):

> What is good?—All that heightens the feeling of power, the will to power, power itself in man.
>
> What is bad?—All that proceeds from weakness.
>
> What is happiness?—The feeling that power *increases*—that a resistance is overcome.
>
> *Not* contentment, but more power; *not* peace at all, but war; *not* virtue, but proficiency (virtue in the Renaissance style, virtù, virtue free of moralic acid).
>
> The weak and ill-constituted shall perish: first principle of *our* philanthropy. And one shall help them to do so.
>
> What is more harmful than any vice?—Active sympathy for the ill-constituted and weak—Christianity.[5]

Once again, this passage is easily open to misinterpretation. When Nietzsche later remarks that Christianity has "taken the side of everything weak, base, ill-constituted" (*AC* 117), he is quick to note that one phase of this formulation is Christianity's attack on intellectual inquiry: "It has depraved the reason even of the intellectually strongest natures by teaching men to feel the supreme values of intellectuality as sinful, as misleading, as *temptations*" (*AC* 118). And again: "Christianity also stands in opposition to all *intellectual* well-constitutedness . . . it takes the side of everything idiotic" (*AC* 169). The prototypical example of this is the story of Eve's plucking the apple from the tree of knowledge, the moral of which is: "Thou shalt *not* know" (*AC* 164).

Christianity has been called the religion of pity, but pity, in Nietzsche's view, "stands in antithesis to the tonic emotions which enhance the energy of the feeling of life: it has a depressive effect. One loses force when one pities" (*AC* 118). This notion is an explicit attack on Schopenhauer, who, convinced that human life was wretched, recommended an all-embracing pity as our only source of consolation. As he writes in "On the Sufferings of the World": "The best consolation in misfortune or affliction of any kind will be the thought of other people who are in a still worse plight than yourself; and this is a form of consolation open to every one. . . . The conviction that the world and man is something that had better not have been is of a kind to fill us with indulgence towards one another."[6] It can easily be seen how this sickly philosophy would have driven Nietzsche to distraction. For him this attitude was the denial of all vitality, all nobility of life that is within reach on this earth.

Some commentators have seen in this hostility to pity an adherence to the crude "survival of the fittest" ideology of the Social Darwinists of the time. Probably this is something of an oversimplification, although it is undeniable that the general tenor of Nietzsche's thought points to some degree in this direction. The whole issue of Nietzsche's attitude to Darwin is worth extended study. Here we can note that Nietzsche's general acceptance of the theory of evolution led to his disavowal of any fundamental or metaphysical distinction between human being and animal, but in *The Antichrist*, Nietzsche denies that humanity is by any means the summit of evolution: "Man is absolutely not the crown of creation: every creature stands beside him at the same stage of perfection" (*AC* 124). All this leads to the delightful witticism in *Thus Spake Zarathustra* (1887): "Once you were apes, and even now man is more of an ape than any ape."[7]

In all his writings, but particularly in *The Antichrist*, Nietzsche engages in a wholesale revision of our understanding of the past two thousand or three thousand years of Western history, suggesting that Christianity has effected a "revaluation of all values" for the worse—the weak are held superior to the good, the base superior to the noble. Nietzsche's task, then, becomes a counterrevaluation where the moral values he advocates can once again reign supreme.

How was this revaluation effected by the Christians? They first did so by perverting the religions that went before them. For Nietzsche, the Old Testament propounded a vigorous, pitiless god that embodied the life-affirming values of the ancient Israelites. (It should be understood that Nietzsche is not acknowledging any belief in the God of the Old Testament but is merely making a sociological assessment of the kind of gods that a given people chooses for itself.) As he declares in *On the Genealogy of Morals* (1887): "All honor to the Old Testament! I find in it great human beings, a heroic landscape, and something of the very rarest quality in the world, the incomparable naïveté of the *strong heart*; what is more, I find a people" (*GM* 144). The ancient Greek religion was also to Nietzsche's liking:

> That the conception of gods *in itself* need not lead to the degradation of the imagination that we had to consider briefly, that there are *nobler* uses for the invention of gods than for the self-crucifixion and self-violation of man in which Europe over the past millennia achieved its distinctive mastery—that is fortunately revealed even by a mere glance at the *Greek gods*, those reflections of noble and autocratic men, in whom *the animal* in man felt deified and did *not* lacerate itself, did *not* rage against itself! For the longest time these Greeks used their gods precisely so as to ward off the "bad conscience," so as to be able to rejoice in their freedom of soul—the very opposite of the use to which Christianity put its God. (*GM* 93–94)

Nietzsche's attitude to Jesus is interesting and complex. He admits to a grudging admiration for Jesus' ability to *live* the doctrines he practiced—and he may have been the only one ever to do so. Jesus' life and actions were a revolt against the already corrupt Jewish church, which had by his day become dominated by a priestly caste. For Jesus, sanctity is entirely embodied in *practice:*

> Precisely the opposite of all contending, of all feeling oneself in struggle has here become instinct: the incapacity for resistance here becomes morality ("resist not evil!": the profoundest saying of the Gospel, its key in a certain sense), blessedness in peace, in gentleness, in the *inability* for enmity. What are the "glad tidings"? True life, eternal life is found—it is not promised, it is here, it is *within you:* as life lived in love, in love without deduction or exclusion, without distance. Everyone is a child of God—Jesus definitely claims nothing for himself alone—as a child of God everyone is equal to everyone else. (*AC* 141)

Nietzsche may not be historically sound in denying that Jesus had any belief in the afterlife, but it serves his purpose to maintain that the Christianity of Jesus can only be maintained by *living* it.

What did Paul—the real founder of Christianity as it is known in the West, in Nietzsche's judgment—do? He and other early disciples of Jesus began by appropriating the Old Testament to their purposes, pulling it "from under the feet of the Jews with the assertion that it contained nothing but Christian teaching and *belonged* to the Christians as the *true* people of Israel, the Jews being only usurpers."[8] Much more significantly, Paul "shifted the centre of gravity of that entire existence *beyond* this existence—in the *lie* of the 'resurrected' Jesus" (*AC* 155). In other words, Paul transferred all the "blessings" of existence to a (mythical) future life. "The great lie of personal immortality destroys all rationality, all naturalness of instinct" (*AC* 155) because it is a flat denial of the "saying Yes to life" in *this* world. Christianity becomes a religion that looks toward death (and beyond) for its ultimate fulfillment. The God of the New Testament is "pitiable, absurd, harmful, not merely an error but a *crime against life*" (*AC* 163–64).

Yet this the only step that could have been taken by a powerless and tiny sect such as the Christians were in the years after Jesus' death; for this was the only way in which the Christians could gain revenge upon their masters, the Romans. Here Nietzsche applies his conception of *ressentiment*—always written in French, and meaning much more than simple "resentment." The notion expresses the sense of envy and impotent hatred embodied in a weak and powerless class or caste against their intellectual and physical betters. For the Christians of the early first century CE, *ressentiment* could not be expressed in physical resistance—the Romans could hardly be troubled to crush them—but in a feeble eschatalogical triumph that depicted themselves as enjoying everlasting bliss in heaven while the Romans and other enemies were condemned to hell.

Nietzsche also maintains that the conflict of the early Christians (whom he sometimes refers to as Jews) and the Romans is also a prototypical conflict of plebeian versus noble:

> For the Romans were the strong and noble, and nobody stronger and nobler has yet existed on earth or even been dreamed of: every remnant of them, every inscription gives delight, if only one divines *what* it was that was there at work. The Jews, on the contrary, were the priestly nation of *ressentiment par excellence*, in whom there dwelt an unequaled popular-moral genius: one only has to compare similarly gifted nations—the Chinese or the Germans, for instance—with the Jews, to sense which is of the first and which of the fifth rank. (*GM* 53)

But lest one assume that Nietzsche is indulging in anti-Semitism (an odd trait for one who repeatedly expressed admiration for the ancient Israelites and, moreover, broke with his early idol and mentor Richard Wagner in part over the latter's increasingly crude and unrestrained anti-Semitism), Nietzsche goes on to identify the "three Jews" and "one Jewess"—"Jesus of Nazareth, the fisherman Peter, the rug weaver Paul, and the mother of the aforementioned Jesus, named Mary" (*GM* 53)—who, by some miracle, overthrew the Roman Empire.

How this occurred is a source of constant wonderment to Nietzsche—as it was to Edward Gibbon, whose ideas on the subject Nietzsche may in part have borrowed. Christianity was, indeed, the "vampire of the *Imperium Romanum*" (*AC* 180), and the Christians worked secretly to corrupt Rome from within:

> These stealthy vermin which, shrouded in night, fog and ambiguity, crept up to every individual and sucked seriousness for *real* things, the instinct for *realities* of any kind, out of him [the Roman], this cowardly, womanish and honeyed crew gradually alienated the "souls" of

> this tremendous structure [the Roman Empire]—those precious, those manly-noble natures who found their own cause, their own seriousness, their own pride in the cause of Rome. This underhanded bigotry, conventicle secrecy, gloomy concepts such as Hell, such as the sacrifice of the innocent, such as the *unio mystica* [mystical union] in blood-drinking, above all the slowly stirred-up fire of revengefulness, of Chandala revengefulness—*that* is what became master of Rome. (*AC* 180–81)

Here all the contrasts that course through Nietzsche's work—saying Yes to life as opposed to saying No; the pride of nobility as opposed to the skulking craftiness of the plebeian (as symbolized by the Chandala—the lowest caste of Hindu society, here used metaphorically for low-born Christians)—come to the fore. The trick was accomplished in particular by the advocacy of a moral and legal *equality*:

> The poison of the doctrine "*equal* rights for all"—this has been more thoroughly sowed by Christianity than by anything else; from the most secret recesses of base instincts, Christianity has waged a war to the death against every feeling of reverence and distance between man and man, against, that is, the *precondition* of every elevation, every increase in culture—it has forged out of the *ressentiment* of the masses its *chief weapon* against *us*, against everything noble, joyful, high-spirited on earth, against our happiness on earth. (*AC* 156)

Nietzsche's hostility to the principle of democracy was unremitting, and—given his advocacy of such doctrines as the overman—it is scarcely surprising that it would be.

The triumph of Christianity had, in Nietzsche's view, the inevitable result of putting unprecedented power in the hands of priests:

> The priest had, with precision and pedantry, right down to the imposts large and small which had to be paid to him (—not forgetting the tastiest pieces of meat: for the priest is a beefeater), formulated once and for all *what he intends to have*, "what the will of God is." . . . From now on all things of life, at birth, marriage, sickness, death, not to speak of "sacrifice" (meal-times), there appears the holy parasite to *denaturize* them—in his language to "sanctify" them. (*AC* 138)

Even after the church was deprived of its control of the government and the courts, it still, down to the present day, controls or seeks to control as many other aspects of political and social life as it can. The result is a "priestly tyranny" (*AC* 155).

At this point Nietzsche, in various works beginning with *Beyond Good and Evil* (1886), introduces his fundamental distinction between "master-morality" (*Herrenmoral*) and "slave-morality" (*Sklavenmoral*). Although, in *On the Genealogy of Morals*, Nietzsche attributes the "*slave revolt in morality*" (*GM* 34) to the Jews, it is plain that he is referring to the early Christians, since he goes on to refer to "that revolt which has a history of two thousand years behind it and which we no longer see because it—has been victorious" (*GM* 34). What slave-morality objects to most of all is anything different from itself—it is by nature intolerant and dogmatic:

> While every noble morality develops from a triumphant affirmation of itself, slave morality from the outset says No to what is "outside," what is "different," what is "not itself"; and *this* No is its creative deed. This inversion of the value-positing eye—this *need* to direct one's view outward instead of back to oneself—is of the essence of *ressentiment*: in order to exist, slave morality always first needs a hostile external world; it needs, physiologically speaking, external stimuli in order to act at all—its action is fundamentally reaction. (*GM* 36–37)

Elsewhere Nietzsche asserts that the slave-morality of Christianity found the tolerance and lack of faith of their Roman masters deeply offensive:[9] the Romans rarely intruded on the religious traditions of the groups or territories it conquered, except in those few instances (as, ultimately, in regard to the Christians themselves) when they felt that a political or military threat to their rule was in the offing.

Western Europeans have no one to blame but themselves for the catastrophic triumph of Christianity. Why have the "strong races of northern Europe" (*AC* 128) not repudiated Christianity?

> They ought to have felt *compelled* to have done with such a sickly and decrepit product of *décadence*. But there lies a curse on them for not having had done with it: they have taken up sickness, old age, contradiction to all their instincts—since then they have failed to *create* a God! Almost two millennia and not a single new God! But still, and as if

> existing by right, like an ultimate and maximum of the God-creating force, of the *creator spiritus* in man, this pitiable God of Christian monotono-theism [*sic*]! (*AC* 128–29)

Christianity has done nothing but "*worsen the European race*":

> Stand all valuations *on their head—that* is what they had to do. And break the strong, sickly o'er great hopes, cast suspicion on the joy in beauty, bend everything haughty, manly, conquering, domineering, all the instincts characteristic of the highest and best-turned-out type of "man," into unsureness, agony of conscience, self-destruction—indeed, invert all love of the earthly and of dominion over the earth into hatred of the earth and the earthly—*that* is the task the church posed for itself and had to pose, until in its estimation "becoming unworldly," "unsensual," and "higher men" were fused into a single feeling. (*BG* 75)

Nietzsche does take brief note of Islam, and it is no surprise that he speaks of it with moderate praise: "If Islam despises Christianity, it is a thousand times right to do so: Islam presupposes *men*" (*AC* 183).

If it is countered that European explorations and conquests in the Renaissance and Early Modern periods, often done under the banner of religion, belie Nietzsche's view of Christianity as a weak and inward-looking religion, he would probably assert that these conquests were the product of the native vigor of the "European races"—the descendants of either the German barbarians or the Romans themselves. He also maintains that the Renaissance was a fleeting period of the "*revaluation of Christian values*"—"the attempt, undertaken with every expedient, with every instinct, with genius of every kind, to bring about the victory of the opposing values, the *noble* values" (*AC* 184). Nietzsche could point both to the artistic impulse of the Renaissance, which consciously harked back to the ideals of pagan antiquity, and to the radical scientific developments that ultimately overthrew Christian dogma. But the dynamism of the Renaissance was confounded by the German theologian Martin Luther, who "*restored the Church*" (*AC* 185) in the very act of attacking it—and the result was another two or three centuries of religious warfare.

It is in this precise context, I believe, that Nietzsche's "God is dead" utterance should be interpreted. The phrase occurs in the course of a parable in the work entitled *Die Fröhliche Wissenschaft*, which has been variously translated as *The Gay Science* or *Joyful Wisdom*, although perhaps *Cheerful Scholarship* would be the most accurate or literal rendition, lame as it sounds. The parable is too lengthy to quote in full, but it begins with a "madman" who (like Diogenes the Cynic) runs into the marketplace in the bright morning hours, holding a lantern and crying, "I seek God! I seek God!" But as he is ridiculed by the crowd, he concludes: "Whither is God? . . . I will tell you. *We have killed him*—you and I. All of us are his murderers." And he goes on to say: "Gods, too, decompose. God is dead. God remains dead. And we have killed him."[10]

To state that God is dead is, however, to suggest that God was once alive. Now Nietzsche is not likely ever to have believed that *any* god—not even Dionysus or Zarathustra ("the most Yes-saying of all spirits" [*EH* 305]), whom he put forward as alternatives to the Christian deity—had any real existence. The remark, then, is an analysis of the state of religious belief in Western Europe in the late nineteenth century. Nietzsche was well aware that very few Christians actually *live* their faith: "Christians have never put into practice the acts Jesus prescribed for them."[11] To say, then, that "God is dead" is to suggest that Christianity is a dead letter even among its purported believers. And because the "madman" in the parable goes on to remark, "I have come too early . . . my time is not yet. This tremendous event [the death of God] is still on its way, still wandering" (*GS* 182), one gains the impression—an impression confirmed by the conclusion of *The Antichrist*—that Nietzsche is the "madman" who has come to kill off Christianity once and for all, replacing it with his own Dionysian/Zarathustran religion of the superman.

What, then, are the chief reasons for Nietzsche's indictment of Christianity? First of all, it has inculcated the notion of *sin*—a means of keeping its followers sick (by its repudiation of natural instincts, ranging from sex to intellectual inquiry) and, simultaneously, of keeping priests in control of the bodies and souls of its victims: "Man shall *not* look around him, he shall look down into himself; he shall *not* look prudently and cautiously into things in order to learn, he shall not look at all: he shall *suffer*. . . . And he shall suffer in such a way that he has need of the priest at all times" (*AC* 165). Second, there is the pernicious doctrine of "equality of souls before God" (*AC* 186), which proves to be nothing but a "*pretext* for the *rancune* [spite] of all the base-minded" (*AC* 186). Finally, there is the "parasitism" of the church,

> its ideal of green-sickness, of 'holiness' draining away all blood, all love, all hope for life; the Beyond as the will to deny reality of every kind; the Cross as the badge of recognition for the most subterranean conspiracy there has ever been—a conspiracy against health, beauty, well-constitutedness, bravery, intellect, *benevolence* of soul, *against life itself*. (*AC* 186)

It should be emphasized that Nietzsche's condemnation of religion goes well beyond the "sickly" faith of Christianity. In a number of important passages, he condemns the very act of belief: "One should not let oneself be misled: great intellects are sceptics. . . . The vigour of a mind, its *freedom* through strength and superior strength, is *proved* by scepticism" (*AC* 172). The need for "faith" is itself a sign of weakness. Faith, after all, nowadays "means not *wanting* to know what is true" (*AC* 169); as a result, to become a believer is merely to turn oneself into the adheent of a quasi-political party—and "the party man necessarily becomes a liar" (*AC* 173).

It is perhaps difficult for contemporary readers to wrap their minds around Nietzsche's radical conceptions. We have ourselves been (as he would have termed it) so infected with Christian morality that we are hindered from grasping the perspective from which he is writing. And our culture's relentless inculcation of the dogma of democracy (entailing, in many instances, an illegitimate extension of the principle of equality before the law to the point of hostility to all excellence or distinction) makes many of us inherently hostile to the very principle of the superman as Nietzsche articulated it. Whether Nietzsche is right or wrong in any given facet of his historical reconstruction of Christianity's triumph over Europe, his view is nonetheless a bracing one. Nietzsche himself hoped to effect a "revaluation of all values" (*AC* 187) that would reverse the earlier revaluation that Christianity had engendered; how much he succeeded is an open question. But his assertion that putting aside Christian metaphysics necessitates an analogous repudiation of Christian ethics is something that deserves deep consideration.

Chapter 5

Mark Twain: God's Fool

The conventional portrait of Mark Twain (1835–1910) as a cynical mocker of religion—especially in the late works of his "dark" period, notably *The Mysterious Stranger*—envisions him as a nineteenth-century American offshoot of Voltaire, whose work is enlivened with the same stinging wit, iconoclastic fervor, and irreverent banter as that of his French counterpart, and who masked his deeply felt indignation at religious obscurantism and hypocrisy under a scintillating barrage of raillery and satire.

In recent years, however, some Twain scholars, distressed by the prevalence of this image and disagreeing with those who have maintained that Twain may actually have become a full-fledged atheist, or at the very least an agnostic, toward the end of his life, have been strenuously putting forth a different picture of Twain—a picture of a man who was deeply engaged in both religious doctrine and religious practice, who never renounced faith in God, who maintained deeply abiding friendships with prominent clergymen, and whose burning hatred of injustice and cruelty was fundamentally religious in nature. One scholar has even gone so far as to maintain that the conventional portrait of Twain is the product of an antireligious bias among academicians.[1] While we will find that this revisionist portrayal is not without its merits (and, in fact, is not necessarily in conflict with the image of Twain as a religious satirist), it seems on the whole a highly tendentious argument designed to whitewash Twain and to brush some of his more pungent lampoonings of religion—and specifically Christianity—under the rug. In any case, the keenness and, at times, the vitriol of Twain's criticism of religion make him at the very least a dubious ally of the devout. With friends like Twain, religion doesn't need any enemies.

There is, of course, no question of Samuel Langhorne Clemens's saturation in the Christian religion from an early age. He was raised as a Presbyterian and no doubt accepted the stern precepts of the Westminster Catechism, although there is evidence that his own father, Marshall Clemens, was not a full believer.[2] His mother, Jane Clemens, was unquestionably devout, but her broad-minded and undogmatic faith stressed the role of religion in relieving social ills and injustices, and there is no doubt that the mature Twain's devotion to these same principles was initially a result of his mother's influence. Sam attended church and Sunday school faithfully as a boy, and his letters and other writings are filled with vivid memories of church services. Twain's writings also display his thorough familiarity with the central texts of the Bible.

By age fourteen, Twain had already become something of a skeptic. Around 1858, when he was a pilot on a riverboat on the Mississippi, he was enraptured by Thomas Paine's *The Age of Reason*—which displayed exactly the same fury at the cavernous gap between religious doctrine and religious practice that Twain himself would later emphasize. Twain would also later read that monumental polemic, Andrew D. White's *A History of the Warfare of Science with Theology in Christendom* (1896).

Twain's views on religion were markedly influenced by his marriage to Olivia (Livy) Langdon, of Elmira, New York. The Langdons were liberal Presbyterians opposed to slavery and devoted to the social gospel. It does appear that, under Livy's influence, Twain became more religiously observant; it was also at this time that he became friends with the Beecher family (especially Thomas Beecher, a longtime pastor in Elmira) and with Joseph Twichell, pastor of the Asylum Church in Hartford, Connecticut. But Twain told both Livy and Twichell that he frankly disbelieved in the divine inspiration of the Bible, so it is hardly accurate to say that their influence inclined Twain toward greater religious orthodoxy.

It has been maintained that Twain's "animus was not so much against religion as it was against the institutions that controlled the religious spirit. His virulent attacks are upon the hypocrites who appropriate the language of religion to achieve an irreligious end."[3] We will find that this is a serious misconstrual of Twain's views, especially as they evolved toward the end of his life, but some of his earlier writings do focus on these matters. "About Smells" (1870) pointedly criticizes a fastidious pastor who did not wish working-class people (who might not have bathed recently) to occupy the pews of their wealthier neighbors. "The

Indignity Put upon the Remains of George Holland by the Rev. Mr. Sabine" (1871) takes to task another clergyman who refused to preside over the funeral of an actor—a member of a profession in very low social and moral standing at the time. "The Revised Catechism" (1871) suggests that money has become the core of the American religion (a point made also in his collaborative novel, *The Gilded Age* [1873]). Even the much later squib, "Letter from the Recording Angel" (c. 1885), pungently skewers the niggardly charity of a wealthy acquaintance of purportedly pious demeanor.

But it would be a serious error to think that Twain is criticizing merely the hypocrisy of those whose professed belief in Christianity should make them advocates, rather than opponents, of justice, mercy, and kindness. A series of three untitled statements of belief, written in the 1880s, does indeed begin with the resounding statement, "I believe in God the Almighty";[4] but it quickly proceeds with *disbelief* in the divine inspiration of the Bible ("it not only was not written by God, but was not even written by remarkably capable *men*" [*WM* 145]), in special providences (the interference of God in human affairs), in eternal punishment (one of Twain's *bêtes noires*), and in a religiously based morality.

Several of these points are worth elaborating. Twain had actually accepted a belief in special providences early as a young boy and acknowledged the doctrine as late as 1878.[5] But the statements of the 1880s definitively reject the notion—as does "Letter from the Recording Angel," which tartly displays the self-serving nature of prayers for God's intervention in human affairs.

Twain's blunt assertion that "the world's moral laws are the outcome of the world's experience" (*WM* 144) puts the lie to Harold K. Bush's claim that "the insistence today that a person can indeed be quite 'ethical' even if that person is not 'religious' might have baffled many Americans of the Gilded Age," and that "throughout Twain's life he was 'ethically' a Christian."[6] In fact, it becomes eminently clear that Twain found Christian ethics fundamentally lacking—not merely because they were observed more in word than in action, but because they were, in their very essence, unsound. The harshly critical essay "Bible Teaching and Religious Practice" (1890) lays bare the fact that the Christian church itself has historically engaged in outrageous moral practices—the ownership of slaves, the persecution of supposed "witches"—and done so because its own scripture unequivocally endorses these practices. It was only the civilizing influence of Western society that forced the church to modify its behavior. In this whole issue, Twain appears to have been influenced by a number of British intellectuals—from W. E. H. Lecky to Herbert Spencer to Leslie Stephen—who were working toward a self-supporting theory of morals not tied to religion but based upon the overall good of society and the individuals who compose it.

The doctrines of hell and eternal punishment angered Twain more violently than any other feature of Christian dogma. He may have erred in attributing the doctrines specifically to Jesus—although he is correct in asserting that the Hebrew scriptures contain few if any hints of a hell where the wicked are consigned for all eternity, and Twain is also correct in maintaining that Jesus' statements in the Synoptic Gospels are rife with references to fire and brimstone. Twain could not ascertain the *purpose* of eternal punishment: it could not possibly be done to rectify the behavior of sinners, for they are not given any opportunity to redeem themselves, and punishment for any other reason is merely a product of hatred and vengeance, something that no morally upright person could attribute to God. As it is, by the 1880s, Twain was already coming to doubt the very existence of an afterlife. Late in life he definitively rejected it:

> I have long ago lost my belief in immortality—also my interest in it. . . . I have sampled this life and it is sufficient. . . . Annihilation has no terrors for me, because I have already tried it before I was born. . . . There was a peace, a serenity, an absence of all sense of responsibility, an absence of worry, an absence of care, grief, perplexity; and the presence of a deep content and unbroken satisfaction in that hundred million years of holiday which I look back upon with a tender longing and with a grateful desire to resume, when the opportunity comes.[7]

It is likely that Twain's skepticism, during the 1880s and 1890s, developed from two distinct causes: his acceptance of the theory of evolution and his absorption of some of the central theses of the "higher criticism" of the Bible. William E. Phipps writes that Twain "was one of the first noted Americans to accept Darwin's theory of evolution . . . Darwin's views so interested him that he owned thirteen of his books. Marginal notes in his copy of Darwin's *The Descent of Man* show that he read that book carefully."[8] Twain's views on Darwin are exhibited in amusing fashion in two satirical pieces, "The Character of Man" (1885) and "Man's Place in the Animal World" (1896). Both essays firmly place humanity within the spectrum of sentient life on this planet, but the latter wittily declares that Darwin is wrong on one point: it is not that the human race has *ascended* from the "lower" animals, but has in fact declined. For it is only the human being who is greedy, vengeful, and hypocritical: "He is the only one that inflicts pain for the pleasure of doing it" (*WM* 156). He is the only one who enslaves, who is a patriot, who is religious (and this is put forth as a criticism), who is intolerant of others' beliefs. A pendant to these two pieces, "'Was the World Made for Man?'" (1903), reveals Twain's absorption of contemporary geology: if the world is at least one hundred million years old, as geologists such as Sir Charles Lyell have asserted, why is it that God created humanity so late in the game?

The effect of the "higher criticism" was believed by many in the nineteenth century to be even more of a threat to orthodoxy than evolution or other scientific advances.[9] If the Bible was not God's word, how could it be trusted as a guide to doctrine and conduct? Twain reflects these doubts in numerous writings, perhaps never more piquantly than in the satire "The Second Advent" (1881). Here, Twain brings the story of the Virgin Birth up to date, laying bare how implausible it would be to believe, merely on the basis of the woman's own testimony and of the "angel" whom she claims to have visited her, that a virgin could have borne a child from God. A much later piece, "As Concerns Interpreting the Deity" (1905), may actually be a satire of the higher criticism in its bogus citations of scholars who have attempted to decipher the Rosetta Stone.

One issue that tormented Twain throughout his life was the origin of evil. How could God let evil—whether it take the form of "natural" evils (earthquakes, floods, pestilence) or "moral" evils (human greed, depravity, cruelty)—exist? Why is God himself not responsible for these evils, if he created them or created human beings and other creatures who, in performing "evil" actions, are merely obeying the dictates of their nature? Twain emphasizes these points in another pungent satire, "Little Bessie" (1907 or 1908). However implausible it may be to envision a three-year-old asking the difficult questions that come out of

Bessie's mouth, Twain's point—expressed through the words of an "innocent" who has not been indoctrinated in the acceptance of such an irrational dogma—is emphatically made. "Thoughts of God" (written in the early 1900s) lays out the conundrum more straightforwardly: If a man invented such a thing as a fly whose spreading of disease among human beings is productive of so much evil, we would certainly condemn him as inexpressibly wicked; so why do we not similarly condemn God? Twain points repeatedly to the irresolvable paradox of assuming a god who is both omnipotent and benevolent. In such a situation, God could relieve all suffering at once. If he cannot do so, he is not omnipotent; if he refuses to do so, he is not benevolent.

One might even apply one of the most celebrated of Twain's bon mots—"I am God's fool"—to this general idea. The statement occurred in a letter to William Dean Howells, first cited in Albert Bigelow Paine's biography of Twain; in full, it runs as follows: "Ah, well, I am a great and sublime fool. But then I am God's fool, and all his work must be contemplated with respect."[10] If Twain wished to convey any serious idea behind this largely whimsical utterance, it is the idea that the God as conventionally envisioned by Christians must take responsibility for all the actions in the universe, both good and bad.

The standard counterargument against evil—at least "moral evil," that which is theoretically under our control—is that God has granted us free will, so that any "sins" we commit become our own responsibility. To this Twain replied bluntly: free will is a myth and an illusion. This is the thrust of the philosophical dialogue *What Is Man?* (1906). It may well be true that Twain, in asserting that all human actions without exception are the product of "outside influences," is espousing an "inverted Calvinism" inspired by his Presbyterian upbringing. As William Pellowe has written:

> In the place . . . of the Calvinistic Deity who foreordained some souls to happiness and heaven, and foredoomed others to lives of sin and the punishment of hell, Twain had put a machine which determined everything which happened on the earth and above it, in the individual's life and in society, thereby being the cause of joy and woe, of respectability and crime, of diseases and war.[11]

But the stance also reveals Twain's thorough absorption of contemporary science and philosophy, which was making it more and more evident that our acts are very largely the result of antecedent and circumambient acts on the part of others and that the standard notion of free will as an uncaused or self-caused action is both inconceivable and paradoxical. Twain also provides, in this long dialogue, a compelling argument against the conventional notion of altruism: no action, however seemingly self-sacrificing, is done save as a salve to one's own psychological discomfort. However benevolent and selfless a given act may appear, its prime motivation is the assuaging of our own conscience. "In *all* cases without exception we are absolutely indifferent to another's pain until his sufferings make us uncomfortable" (*WM* 38). This essay is, in many ways, even more subversive of Christian ethics than many of his other writings, for an acceptance of Twain's doctrine renders any moral approval or disapproval a logical impossibility: putatively "good" actions (as when someone refrains from indiscriminate killing) are so judged merely because they conduce to physical comfort, not because of any intrinsic virtue in them.

Twain's most unrestrained attack upon religion is the late essay "Reflections on Religion" (1906), which, like *The Mysterious Stranger*, *Letters from the Earth*, and several other documents,[12] was decreed by Twain to be published only after his death. H. L. Mencken criticized Twain for what he took to be a certain pusillanimity in this regard, both as regards these posthumously published pieces and as regards *What Is Man?* which Twain, in a prefatory note to the (anonymous) 1906 edition, admitted he had been working on for twenty-five years. Mencken wrote:

> Mark knew his countrymen. He knew their intense suspicion of ideas, their blind hatred of heterodoxy, their bitter way of dealing with dissenters. He knew how, their pruderies outraged, they would turn upon even the gaudiest hero and roll him in the mud. And knowing, he was afraid. He "dreaded the disapproval of the people around him." And part of that dread, I suspect, was peculiarly internal. In brief, Mark himself was also an American, and he shared the national horror of the unorthodox. His own speculations always half appalled him. He was not only afraid to utter what he believed; he was even a bit timorous about *believing* what he believed.[13]

These late treatises were written during a particularly difficult period in Twain's life, as he was beset by tragedies both professional (the failure of a business enterprise that led to bankruptcy) and, more significantly, personal (the death of his daughter Susy in 1896, his wife Livy in 1904, and his daughter Jean in 1909). It would, however, be an insult both to Twain's intellect and to his artistic sensibility to argue that it was merely these personal crises that led him to something akin to pessimism and misanthropy. There is very little in these late writings that is not foreshadowed in his earlier work. "Reflections on Religion" does make some spectacularly provocative claims—the Bible reveals God to be "overcharged with evil impulses far beyond the human limit"; the Bible itself "is perhaps the most damnatory biography that exists in print anywhere" (*WM* 191)—but these barbs are supported by arguments that systematically destroy the very pillars of Christian dogma: God is not a god of mercy; Jesus consigned the great majority of human beings to everlasting punishment; the God of the New Testament is *worse* than the God of the Old Testament, precisely because of this doctrine of hell; the Bible is not even original in its depiction of the Virgin Birth, a feature found in many other scriptures; Christians are perpetually persecuting others (especially Jews) and fighting wars. This criticism goes far beyond merely the criticism of Christian "institutions." And Twain was no doubt thinking of himself when he wrote: "No Protestant child ever comes clean from association with the Bible" (*WM* 201).

Nevertheless, "Reflections on Religion" does appear to present a more civilized God in contrast to the hideous God of the Old and New Testaments, and this portrayal may be Twain's final word on his own conception of deity:

> Let us now consider the real God, the genuine God, the great God, the sublime and supreme God, the authentic Creator of the real universe, whose remotenesses are visited by comets only—comets unto which incredibly distant Neptune is merely an outpost, a Sandy Hook to homeward-bound spectres of the deeps of space that have not glimpsed it before for generations—a universe not made with hands and suited to an astronomical nursery, but spread abroad through the illimitable reaches of space by the flat of the real God just mentioned; that God of unthinkable grandeur and majesty, by comparison with whom all the

> other gods whose myriads infest the feeble imaginations of men are as a swarm of gnats scattered and lost in the infinitudes of the empty sky. (*WM* 203)

All this is a trifle vague, suggesting a deist god, or perhaps even an Epicurean one. (Twain goes on to say, "We cannot conceive of His interesting Himself in the affairs of the microscopic human race" [*WM* 203].) Twain also remarks that this god cannot be said to be a "moral being" by our own conceptions of morality ("Do we know that He is just, charitable, kindly, gentle, merciful, compassionate? No" [*WM* 204]), and that we cannot know whether he listens to or answers our prayers. It is not entirely clear what use such a god would be, but Twain seems sincere in acknowledging the existence of such an entity.

The Mysterious Stranger is certainly one of the darkest tales of Twain's entire career. The text is now a bit of a mess, given the revelations of textual tampering by the work's first editor, Albert Bigelow Paine. But the antireligious thrust of the work—especially in its concluding lecture by Satan, who has descended upon a medieval village to disrupt the naive piety of the villagers—is unmistakable, providing a grand summation of Twain's lifelong indictment of God:

> Strange, indeed, that you should not have suspected that your universe and its contents were only dreams, visions, fiction! Strange, because they are so frankly and hysterically insane—like all dreams: a God who could make good children as easily as bad, yet preferred to make bad ones; who could have made every one of them happy, yet never made a single happy one; who made them prize their bitter life, yet stingily cut it short; who gave his angels eternal happiness unearned, yet required his other children to earn it; who gave his angels painless lives, yet cursed his other children with biting miseries and maladies of mind and body; who mouths justice and invented hell—mouths mercy and invented hell—mouths Golden Rules, and forgiveness multiplied by seventy times seven, and invented hell; who frowns upon crimes, yet commits them all; who created man without invitation, then tries to shuffle the responsibility for man's acts upon man, instead of honorably placing it where it belongs, upon himself; and finally, with altogether divine obtuseness, invites the poor, abused slave to worship him![14]

When Satan says, "It is true . . . there is no God," we should not conclude that Twain is finally acknowledging full-fledged atheism, for he goes on to say that there is also "no universe, no human race, no earthly life, no heaven, no hell. It is all a dream—a grotesque and foolish dream."[15]

Letters from the Earth is one of the last works to emerge from Twain's pen. The scene opens in Heaven: God has just created the universe out of nothing. A bit later (as celestial time goes) he creates the earth. Satan—still an archangel at this point—decides to go down to this seemingly insignificant planet to "see how the Human-Race experiment was coming along."[16] There follow eleven letters by Satan, written to St. Michael and St. Gabriel, about the state of things on earth. This premise allows abundant room for the pungent satire on human morals and institutions that was Twain's forte. At times the text can become surprisingly racy, as in Satan's puzzlement over God's punishment of Onan (who is generally thought to have been a masturbator) and against Jeroboam, who for various derelictions was punished as follows (in the King James Version): "Thefore, behold, I will bring evil upon the house of Jeroboam, and will cut off from Jeroboam him that pisseth against the wall" (1 Kings 14:10). To this Satan remarks:

> Protestant parents still keep the Bible handy in the house, so that the children can study it, and one of the first things the little boys and girls learn is to be righteous and holy and not piss against the wall. They study those passages more than they study any others, except those which incite to masturbation. Those they hunt out and study in private. No Protestant child exists who does not masturbate. That art is the earliest accomplishment his religion confers upon him. Also the earliest her religion confers upon her. (*LE* 51)

No wonder Twain's daughter Clara did not allow the publication of this work until 1962!

So did Mark Twain remain a believer even at the end of his life? The question is unanswerable, not least because it is not clear what exactly constituted a "believer" in his day—or, for that matter, in ours. While it certainly may be an exaggeration to say, as Maxwell Geismar did, that Twain was an "eloquent and outraged atheist,"[17] it seems to me that, especially in his later years, Twain was as close to being an agnostic as it is possible to be without actually stating any definite doubt of God's existence. Even if Twain acknowledged the existence of a deity, it was in no sense the Christian deity—for Twain had already discarded such indispensable doctrines as heaven and hell, the Trinity (a doctrine he always regarded as incomprehensible), the religious basis of morality, the Virgin Birth, and so forth. One of his last utterances, "Things a Scotsman Wants to Know" (1909), another rumination on the question "Is God the author of evil?" concludes: "If our Maker *is* all-powerful for good or evil, He is not in His right mind" (*WM* 229). Does the mere reference to "our Maker" imply an acknowledgment of God's existence? It seems doubtful: Twain is merely engaging in the rhetorical device of accepting a given position (that God is both omnipotent and benevolent) and showing that it leads to an untenable conclusion (that God is insane). It is certainly not a conclusion that any believer would want to accept.

It is easy to pluck individual utterances by Twain, written over many years and for many occasions, to convey a sense of his enduring piety; but the overwhelming majority of his public writings—and, in particular, those of his writings that he deemed too incendiary for publication in his lifetime—betray a scathing condemnation of both the metaphysical and ethical foundations of the Christian religion and the repeated failings of Christians to live up to the best features of their faith. His criticisms are harsher than those of many actual atheists who would follow in his wake, so that the question of Twain's own beliefs becomes largely moot. Emerging from Twain's tender mercies, religion has few garments left untorn.

Chapter 6

CLARENCE DARROW: RELIGION IN THE DOCK

Clarence Darrow (1857–1938) was born four years before the beginning of the Civil War and died a year before the beginning of World War II. These eighty years could well be considered the most *transformative* in the history of the United States—years that saw America expand from a fledgling and sparsely populated nation of farmers and small-businessmen to the threshold of a superpower. Darrow witnessed and, in no insignificant way, participated in the multifaceted growing pains incident to this transformation: on such issues as the relations between capital and labor, the role of women in society, the place of religion in a diverse population, and, particularly, the theoretical and practical status of crime and punishment, Darrow made signal contributions that endured far beyond the span of his own life. A lawyer first and a writer second, he nonetheless left behind a succession of treatises whose provocative content still challenges us. Darrow, a self-proclaimed rebel who sided, both intellectually and emotionally, with the minority, remains a figure to contend with.

Throughout his writings, whether on crime, religion, or morals, Darrow was convinced that our views of life are fundamentally and unalterably shaped by childhood experience. In this assertion, he may well have been considering his own upbringing, for the kernels of many facets of his thought can be found in the events of his youth and adolescence. He was born on April 18, 1857, in the village of Kinsman, in northeast Ohio, the fifth of eight children born to Amirus and Emily (Eddy) Darrow. Amirus had studied theology in his own youth, but in the process he lost his faith; that seed of religious unorthodoxy was manifestly passed on to his son Clarence in spite of his receiving a conventionally Presbyterian upbringing, with regular church attendance and Sunday school. Clarence's mother was an ardent advocate of women's rights, and he no doubt absorbed these views as well despite her early death in 1872.

Darrow's schooling was spotty: he had an undistinguished record at the local district school; in 1873 he was sent to the preparatory department of Allegheny College in Meadville, Pennsylvania, but the depression of that year dried up the family funds and forced him to leave after a year. While employed as a schoolteacher at Vernon, seven miles south of Kinsman, Darrow began studying law on the side. He entered the University of Michigan law school in 1877 but again left after a year, instead entering a law office in Youngstown and studying for the bar exam. After a few months, he took the bar exam—and passed. Darrow was, in a sense, fortunate that the standards for entering the legal profession were at this time quite low: almost any bright and motivated young man could become a lawyer with minimal study. He married a young woman from Kinsman, Jessie Ohl, on April 15, 1880.

Finding no work in his tiny hometown, Darrow set up a law office in nearby Andover. But law as such appears to have interested him less than politics, and he began both a career in public speaking and an affiliation with the local Democratic Party. His only son, Paul, was born on December 10, 1883. The election of 1884, which saw Grover Cleveland—the first Democrat to be elected president since before the Civil War—take possession of the White House, raised Darrow's fortunes, and he moved to the larger city of Ashtabula, on Lake Erie, where he was elected city solicitor in 1885.

But by this time, Darrow had developed still greater political ambitions. He felt he needed to test his skills on a national level, and the place to go was Chicago, an immensely vital city that many contemporaries predicted would become the prototypical American metropolis and eventually eclipse New York as the nation's cultural center. Darrow's move there in 1887 proved permanent and transformed him both as a man and as a lawyer.

Coming under the influence of John Peter Altgeld, whose successful campaign for governor in 1892 he managed, Darrow plunged into the convoluted thickets of the Democratic Party machine. He was first made special assessment attorney to the city of Chicago, then its chief corporation counsel. Through Altgeld, he secured a job in the legal department of the Chicago & Northwestern Railway, an immensely powerful company that largely controlled freight and trolley traffic in and around Chicago.

Darrow's decision not to follow Altgeld to Springfield, while it lessened his direct influence on state government, proved to be a blessing in disguise: Altgeld's political career was destroyed in 1893 when he issued pardons for the Haymarket anarchists, who in 1887 had been convicted (on flimsy evidence) of setting off a bomb that killed several spectators and policemen. By this time, Darrow had thrust himself deeply into the central economic conflict of the time—the struggle between capital and labor. Many fledgling labor unions, in the face of vicious and illegal reprisals by capitalists, felt they had no choice but to resort to violence themselves. Darrow took their side in several notable legal cases. The first was the trial of socialist and labor leader Eugene V. Debs, growing out of the American Railway Union's strike against the Pullman company in 1893. Darrow, in taking up the case, resigned his position with the Chicago & Northwestern Railway as an obvious conflict of interest. Debs had been accused of conspiracy in violating an injunction against the strikers issued (without precedent) by the federal government, and Darrow was withering in his arguments against the legality of the proceedings. The case against Debs was quickly dropped so as to avoid the embarrassment of having George M. Pullman, president of the Pullman company, face Darrow's tongue lashing in cross-examination, but Darrow was disappointed that the injunction itself was upheld by the Supreme Court despite his eloquent argument against it. It was one of several occasions when Darrow faced the nation's highest court.

The Debs case visibly augmented Darrow's standing as a radical firebrand and ardent friend of labor. Several sensational cases in the coming years—his successful defense of Thomas I. Kidd of the Woodworkers' Union in 1898 in a strike in Oshkosh, Wisconsin; his involvement in the anthracite arbitration case of 1902 between the United Mine Workers and coal-mine owners in Pennsylvania; and, most spectacularly, his successful defense of "Big Bill" Haywood of the Western Federation of Miners in a murder trial in Idaho in 1907—cemented that reputation. The stress of all this work proved too much for his marriage, however, and Darrow and Jessie divorced in 1897. Darrow also lost the chance at national office in 1896 when he failed to campaign vigorously as a US representative for a supposedly "safe" Democratic district in Chicago and lost narrowly to a Republican. In 1902 he was elected to the Illinois House of Representatives, the only elected office he ever held. To many people's surprise, he made a second venture into matrimony in 1903, marrying Ruby Hamerstrom, a journalist he had met four years before. They remained married for the duration of Darrow's life.

It was also in 1903 that Darrow set up a private law practice in Chicago with lawyer-poet Edgar Lee Masters and Francis Wilson. The eight-year partnership was under continual stress, with Darrow and Masters both feeling that the other was not pulling his weight. Darrow, indeed, was unwittingly setting himself up for a fall by his vigorous defense of labor cases. He was persuaded to take on the case of James B. and John J. McNamara, two brothers who were accused of murder in the bombing of the *Los Angeles Times* building on October 1, 1910. The case against the McNamaras—one of whom was a union official then engaged in fierce disputes with *Times* owner Harrison Gray Otis—was virtually airtight, and Darrow reluctantly concluded that the only way for his clients to escape the death penalty was for them to plead guilty. The result was an uproar in the labor community, which had in defiance of all the evidence believed that the McNamaras were innocent and also believed that Darrow was a miracle worker who could have gotten them off. Worse was to follow: the prosecution, perhaps because it was angered by being robbed of the death penalty, indicted Darrow himself of jury bribery. The two cases that followed took up the bulk of the years 1912 and 1913; although the first trial ended in an acquittal and the second in a hung jury, Darrow's standing as a lawyer and was seriously compromised. Darrow himself fell into a deep depression, believing that, at the age of fifty-five, his career was over and his usefulness at an end. He could scarcely have realized that his greatest triumphs were still to come.

For the next decade, Darrow attempted to pick up the pieces of his life and career. To raise money, he began lecturing more and more widely, engaging in a series of public debates on issues ranging from religion to prohibition. Forming a new law firm, he sought to handle more criminal cases, doing much work for no charge for impoverished clients whose cases he believed worthy. At a very early stage of his career, he had determined never to work for the prosecution, and all his work was as a defense attorney. He shocked his socialist colleagues by strongly advocating the Allied cause at the outbreak of World War I and urging American entry into the war from the beginning. It was, ironically, this seeming act of betrayal to his radical roots that caused Darrow's reputation to be resurrected among the public at large.

That reputation would, however, be put to a severe test by two notorious cases, occurring within a year of each other in 1924 and 1925, that permanently sealed Darrow's reputation as "America's greatest lawyer." The murder of a small boy, Robert Franks, by two wealthy youths, Nathan Leopold and Richard Loeb (the latter the son of a vice president of Sears, Roebuck & Co.), shocked the nation with its brutality and seeming lack of motivation: was it possible that two such privileged youths could kill merely for sport? As in the McNamara case, there was no likelihood that the defendants were innocent; accordingly, Darrow—by this time a relentless opponent of the death penalty—concluded that the only way for his clients to escape the hangman was a legal sleight-of-hand whereby a guilty plea was entered, thereby thrusting the case immediately into the sentencing phase. Darrow relied on the judge's leniency in sentencing, and in the event he succeeded: Judge John Caverly brought opprobrium upon himself by sentencing Leopold and Loeb to life imprisonment for murder and a concurrent sentence of ninety-nine years for kidnapping.

The circumstances surrounding Darrow's other noteworthy case of this period—the Scopes trial of 1925—were very different: from a matter of life and death to a scenario that came close to buffoonery.[1] The serious issue of the trial—the extent to which the Christian religion would be allowed to dictate the laws of a state or of the nation—was almost submerged in the atmosphere of personal rivalry between Darrow, one of the leading American agnostics of his age, and William Jennings Bryan, the long-serving Democratic statesman (whose presidential campaign in 1896 Darrow had reluctantly supported, although he did little for Bryan's campaigns of 1900 and 1908) who now came to represent the forces of small-town conservatism and religious orthodoxy. Bryan's catastrophic decision to undergo merciless cross-examination by Darrow was the fitting capstone to a trial that riveted the nation. It is frequently overlooked that the defense—Darrow, Arthur Garfield Hays, and Dudley Field

Malone, with journalist H. L. Mencken lending loud support with his pungently satirical reporting—deliberately sought a guilty verdict for the hapless teacher John Thomas Scopes, for it was only in this way that the antievolution statute passed by the Tennessee Legislature could be challenged in federal court. But the Tennessee Supreme Court, keenly aware that the state was becoming the laughingstock of the nation, quietly overturned the conviction; although the statute was not rescinded until 1967, it was essentially a dead letter and was never enforced.

It would have been difficult for any lawyer to have followed up the Leopold and Loeb and the Scopes trials with cases still more spectacular, and Darrow felt no inclination to do so. In 1925–1926 he successfully defended two African-Americans, Ossian Sweet and his brother Henry, on murder charges surrounding their moving into a largely white neighborhood in Detroit. In 1932 he took up the case of Thomas Massie, a naval officer in Hawaii who was accused of kidnapping and killing a Hawaiian man whom he suspected (erroneously, it appears) of raping his wife. At age seventy-five, Darrow's powers were finally on the wane, and even he could not secure Massie's acquittal. The leftist firebrand made his final public appearance as the chairman of the National Recovery Review Board, which was to investigate the workings of one of the pillars of the New Deal, the National Recovery Administration. Darrow's harshly critical assessments of the NRA in 1934–1936 were not well received in government circles, although they contributed to the Supreme Court's decreeing the NRA unconstitutional.

Darrow's final years were plagued by illness, and, given his views on immortality, he probably welcomed death when it came to him on March 13, 1938. Thousands payed their respects to a man who had rarely compromised his principles, however unpopular they may have been, over his half century of public life.

Darrow longed for literary success, and he was continually disappointed at his failure to attain the renown that he sought. Although, during the first two decades of the twentieth century, he could well have been considered the most popular and controversial public speaker in the United States (taking up the role that another great agnostic, Robert G. Ingersoll, had renounced upon his death in 1899), Darrow felt that his array of writings were not receiving the critical acclaim they deserved. Perhaps Darrow had an exaggerated belief in his literary powers: he may have left no single monument like his erstwhile colleague Edgar Lee Masters's *Spoon River Anthology*, but the totality of his literary work is far from insignificant. And what is more, it is motivated by a carefully conceived philosophy that, although rarely articulated in full, unites his writings on philosophy, religion, law, society, and politics.

The religious skepticism that Darrow initially derived from his father's influence was central to his outlook. It is a bit puzzling why he continually referred to himself merely as an agnostic: there seems little doubt that he was an atheist. A listener of one of Darrow's religious debates stated clearly that he "denie[d] the existence of the Deity."[2] Surely he of all people would not have worried about the general public's fear of and prejudice against the very word *atheist*. In a 1928 debate on whether there is a purpose in the universe, Darrow argues that the notion of a purpose necessarily implies a "purposer": is there such an entity? "On this question of a purposer, or a purpose, especially a purposer, I am simply an agnostic. I haven't yet had time or opportunity to explore the universe, and I don't know what I might run on to in some nook or corner. I simply say there is not a syllable of evidence in the world to sustain any such proposition, not a syllable."[3]

It is important to emphasize this point because it might otherwise seem that Darrow's screeds against religion were merely attacking the social and political failings of religion or of religious fundamentalism. Those failings are, indeed, extensive, but Darrow would not have been so vigorous in exposing them if he did not feel that the religious point of view—as regards the existence of a deity, the existence and immortality of the soul, and the place of human beings in a boundless and impersonal cosmos—were in themselves erroneous.

Many of these points are enunciated in Darrow's opening speech at the Scopes trial, held on the second day of the proceedings. Here he rightly declares that the case constitutes the "death struggle between two civilizations."[4] Some of his reasoning here is legalese—he declares that the "caption" or title of the Tennessee statute does not match the statute itself, in that the former explicitly mentions evolution while the latter speaks only of banning the teaching of "any theory that denies the conception of the divine creation of man as put in the Bible and teach in its stead that man is descended from a lower order of animal" (*W* 77), with the word *evolution* not explicitly cited—and it is a bit surprising that Darrow does not refer to what would appear to be the statute's obvious violation of the establishment clause of the First Amendment. He may have been deterred from pursuing this line of argument because it was by no means clear that either a higher Tennessee court or the Supreme Court itself would actually accept such an argument at this time. Darrow does say that the statute is "full of weird, strange, impossible and imaginary provisions" (*W* 77), the greatest of which is the appeal to the Bible itself as some kind of textbook on science. Darrow flatly declares:

> It [the Bible] is not a book of science. Never was and was never meant to be. . . . It is not a textbook or a text on chemistry. It is not big enough to be. It is not a book on geology: they knew nothing about geology. It is not a book on biology: they knew nothing about it. It is not a work on evolution; that is a mystery. It is not a work on astronomy. The man who looked out at the universe and studied the heavens had no thought but that the earth was the center of the universe. But we know better than that. (*W* 78)

Moreover, there is wide disagreement among biblical scholars and the various Christian sects as to what specifically the Bible says, so how are any teachers to know if they are violating some statement in the Bible when they teach any subject? The real reason, Darrow concludes, why his client is on trial is that "ignorance and bigotry are rampant, and it is a mighty strong combination" (*W* 79).

When the presiding judge, John T. Raulston, prohibited the testimony of scientific experts who would declare the truth or probability of evolution as a scientific principle, the defense knew that its case was hopeless. At this point, on the seventh day of the trial, Darrow concocted his scheme of placing Bryan himself on the stand. It was quite evident to both sides that this scenario was meant for public consumption, not as a phase of the trial itself—the jury, indeed, was not present during the cross-examination—and both Bryan and Darrow jumped at the opportunity. Bryan was apparently under the impression that his cleverness and knowledge of the Bible would hold him in good stead, but the upshot was a devastating blow to his standing both as a thinker and as a litigant.

What Darrow brought out through an unrelenting series of barbed questions was Bryan's utter ignorance of both the Bible itself—beyond its mere statements—and of any of the background knowledge that would be necessary to gauge the soundness of biblical teaching. Darrow brought up the numerous whoppers in the Bible—the whale swallowing Jonah, Joshua commanding the sun to stand still, Eve made from Adam's rib, the existence of Cain's wife—and teased Bryan into admitting that he had not considered the ramifications and implications of these matters. Bryan, indeed, appeared to take pride in never having examined any other religion: "The Christian religion has satisfied me, and I have never felt it necessary to look up some competing religions" (*W* 291). At times he resorted to childish banter, as when he dismissed Darrow's query as to where Cain suddenly obtained a wife, since no such person was mentioned in the creation story: "I leave the agnostics to hunt for her" (*W* 302). Incredibly, Bryan was forced to admit that the "days" cited in the creation story may not refer to literal days (in spite of the repeated mentions of "morning" and "evening"), but might have covered centuries, millennia, or even millions of years. One would suppose such an admission would have been catastrophic for Bryan's adherence to fundamentalism. At times the proceedings become testy, as when Bryan accused Darrow (falsely) of referring to the residents of Tennessee as "yokels" (this was Mencken's term of preference) and of "insulting" the people of the state, whereupon Darrow shot back: "You insult every man of science and learning in the world because he does not believe in your fool religion" (*W* 288).

There was a curious sequel to this cross-examination. Because the judge ruled that it was inadmissible as evidence, the plan to have Darrow cross-examined by Bryan was dispensed with; but Darrow happily answered nine questions that Bryan put to him as to his own religious views. Among them were whether he believed in the God of the Bible ("I do not know of any description of God in the Bible, although we are informed in one part of it that He is a spirit"), whether the Bible is inspired ("I do not believe that it was written or inspired by God"), and whether the soul is immortal ("I have been searching for truth of this all my life with the same desire to find it which is incidental to every living thing. I have never found any evidence on the subject").[5]

The subject of immortality is worth pursuing here, for it is the subject of a debate that Darrow later had with Michael Angelo Musmanno, under the title *Does Man Live Again?* (1936). Here Darrow ingeniously turns the table on his opponent with a clever argument: "Now, he tells you about all the people who believe in immortality. Nobody believes it. Nobody believes it. Some people hope about it, and some talk about it" (*CA* 75). This conclusion becomes evident by witnessing the tenacity with which people, even in severe illness, cling to life: "Did you ever see a Christian who wanted to die? I never did; I never saw any such thing, or heard him say so" (*CA* 76). Darrow continues:

> Everybody wants to live. Now, don't be silly. You all know it. Your friends may be mostly on the other side. On the other side of what? I don't know. But they don't want to go and meet their friends. [Laughter.] They are going to stick on this side, and the more they pray, the stronger they stick. [Laughter.] No, no, their conduct belies their talk in every instance. A man's wife might be in heaven, or one of his friends. Does he want to go, too? Oh, no, he will stay here just as long as he can stay. He knows that life is full of pain; he has rheumatism, or gout, and, of course, his heart goes "fluey" on him, or he awakens during the night and can't go to sleep again, because there are not enough windows to raise. But still he wants to stick here instead of being happy. (*CA* 77)

The chief harm that religion causes, in Darrow's judgment, is in its restriction of civil liberties by infringements of the separation of church and state. This is the thrust of two essays—a review of Maynard Shipley's *The War on Modern Science* (1927) and "The Lord's Day Alliance" (1928)—written shortly after the Scopes trial. Incredibly, H. L. Mencken considered the latter essay so intemperate that he rejected it for the *American Mercury*, although the actions of present-day fundamentalists who continue to rail against the teaching of evolution or protest against the "desecration" of the Sabbath may suggest that Darrow was, here as elsewhere, uncannily prescient. Darrow knew that fundamentalists would press their case as far as it could be pressed, and that the only defense was an equally vigorous counterattack by scientists: "They should . . . organize to meet the campaign [of the fundamentalists]. They should do this, not only in defense of themselves, but in defense of learning; and, still more important, in defense of religious freedom. This fight must be made by the scientists and the teachers. It is, above all others, their job" (*CA* 25). Belatedly, the scientific community appears finally to be taking up Darrow's challenge.

"The Lord's Day Alliance" is a searing indictment of the Canadian-American group that was organized toward the end of the nineteenth century and campaigned vigorously to ban a variety of activities—playing golf or baseball, or even driving a car (except to drive to church)—on Sunday. Its most visible achievement was the banning of mail delivery on Sundays. Like the Anti-Saloon League, a pressure group that targeted state legislators to press for prohibition, the Lord's Day Alliance waged a relentless campaign at the state and municipal level to enact statutes against what would seem to be the most harmless activities if performed on a Sunday. But the group was determined to eliminate any competition to churchgoing—especially because, at the time, churchgoing was alarmingly declining. As a pamphlet by the alliance quoted by Darrow states, "The old days of tithes are gone! Lack of support is making the situation more and more critical and many churches have had to be abandoned. Is the church to survive? *Are we to remain a Christian nation*?" (*CA* 47–48). Darrow cannot help observing pungently:

> The Lord's Day folk say that reading the Sunday newspapers, playing golf, riding in automobiles, and witnessing baseball games and movies is "un-American." This compound word has been used to cover a multitude of sins. What it means nobody knows. It is bunkum meant to serve every cause, good and bad alike. By what license does the Lord's Day Alliance call its caricature of Sunday an "American Sabbath"? On what grounds does it urge it as against the European Sabbath? Is this nightmare which the Lord's Day Alliance is so anxious to force upon the United States a product of America? Everyone knows that Sunday, with the rest of the Christian religion, came to us from Europe. The weird ideas of the Lord's Day Alliance are European. (*CA* 56)

In conclusion, noting that "ours is a cosmopolitan country, made up of all sorts of people with various creeds" (*CA* 58), Darrow concludes: "It is time that men should determine to defend their right to attend to their own affairs and live their own lives, regardless of the bigots who in all ages have menaced the welfare of the world and the liberty of man" (*CA* 59).

There is a currently fashionable view that the "conflict" of religion and science was merely a tendentious fantasy of certain nineteenth-century secularists, but the Scopes trial—and the actions of contemporary fundamentalists in attempting to prevent or limit the teaching of evolution or in promoting creationism or its spruced-up counterpart, "intelligent design"—embarrassingly and overwhelmingly refutes this naive view. It may well have been the case that the medieval church was one of the leading advocates of scientific inquiry—how could it not have been, since it was the sole haven of learning in European society for centuries?—but the parameters of that learning were strictly circumscribed: any advance of science that threatened religious orthodoxy was mercilessly condemned. Both Darrow and Mencken were well aware that the reconcilers of science and religion, notably the Nobel Prize–winning physicist Robert A. Millikan, were in large part attempting to cling to an increasingly attenuated and dogma-free religiosity in the wake of scientific advances that systematically cast doubt upon the fundamental tenets of religion. For Darrow, such pussyfooting was impossible: religion may have its comforts for the weak and feeble-minded, but it was only an intellectual obstacle to the person of education.

Darrow's metaphysical views are again of central importance in the subject he made his own: the punishment of criminals. While initially influenced by such treatises as John Peter Altgeld's *Our Penal Machinery and Its Victims* (1887), which proposed that the sources of criminal behavior be more carefully examined, Darrow eventually founded his views on his conceptions of the metaphysical and moral status of crime. In such debates as "Can the Individual Control His Conduct?" and other writings, Darrow made clear his disbelief in free will as ordinarily conceived. But his determinism is not (as his philosophically untutored biographer Kevin Tierney appears to believe) equivalent to fatalism. Darrow merely believed that every human action, as with every other action by any entity throughout the universe, was strictly a result of cause and effect. Human beings did not stand outside the chain of causation. The effect of this theory on the treatment of crime is evident: it is not that criminals are somehow "blameless," but that an effort must be made to understand the nature and sources of their behavior. Darrow was combating the naive and vindictive view that crime must be punished severely because the criminal was somehow different from law-abiding human beings—a view not far different, as Darrow pointed out in the lecture "What to Do about Crime" (1927), from the medieval view that mental illness was caused by demonic possession.

Darrow's writings on crime and criminals may appear to suggest an excessive sympathy toward the criminal and an insufficient awareness of the plight of the victim, but Darrow felt that the treatment of crime in his day was so counterproductive that radical steps must be taken to remedy it. His first full-length treatise, *Resist Not Evil* (1902), addresses this matter forthrightly. It is a piquant irony that the agnostic Darrow unwaveringly repudiates the vengeance of the Christian or Islamic god in preference for the mercy and kindness of the god of Jesus. Is Darrow's concluding reflection, "Hatred, bitterness, violence and force can bring only bad results—they leave an evil stain on everyone they touch. No human soul can be rightly reached except through charity, humanity and love," merely the hopelessly naive pipe-dream of a sentimentalist? A careful reading of this and other of his writings on crime—particularly *Crime: Its Cause and Treatment* (1922), his most exhaustive discussion of the subject—suggests that he seeks to prevent crime at the source rather than merely treat its symptoms after it has already occurred. His emphasis is on the proper upbringing of children so that they do not enter a life of crime; once a crime has occurred, punishing the criminal vindictively accomplishes nothing except to ingrain that behavior in the criminal.

Darrow's longtime opposition to the death penalty is based on the belief that killing the perpetrator accomplishes nothing save to exacerbate vengeance. As he states bluntly in the essay "Capital Punishment" (1928), "The real reason why so many people tenaciously cling to the idea of capital punishment is because they take pleasure in inflicting pain upon those they hate" (*CA* 154). Darrow relentlessly destroys the argument that the death penalty is in any way a deterrent to crime, specifically the crime of murder. Although he did not have access to statistics suggesting either that the death penalty has been inflicted erroneously upon the innocent or that race is a critical factor in capital cases—two of the chief motivations that lead many thoughtful persons today to renounce the death penalty—Darrow knew that "only the poor are put to death" (*CA* 159). The wealthy, like Leopold and Loeb, can afford the best legal defense possible escape the noose.

In his social and political theory, the notion of freedom is central. Whether Darrow was concerned about any possible conflict between his determinism in regard to criminal (or, in fact, all human) conduct and his advocacy of civil liberties is not apparent. It was, as we have already seen, his devotion to freedom that impelled his most vigorous attacks on the encroachment of religion or religious-based statutes upon civil society. One of his earliest essays, on "Woman Suffrage" (1893), emphasizes the role of freedom in advocating the extension of voting rights to women:

> More and more as the spirit of liberty has penetrated the darkness of the world, have rulers of high degree and low, surrendered power and place and privilege at the demand of the common people of the earth, until to-day, in the constitutions of states and nations, full political privileges are guaranteed to those who once were chattel slaves. (*CA* 164)

It was to be expected that Darrow would join his colleague H. L. Mencken in relentlessly opposing Prohibition as an unconscionable intrusion upon civil liberties, and it is no accident that his fiery screed "The Ordeal of Prohibition" appeared in Mencken's *American Mercury*. He makes an analogous argument in another *American Mercury* essay, "The Eugenics Cult," in which he tackles the increasing tendency of anthropologists and geneticists to suggest improvements to society by banning a nebulously defined group of the "unfit" from procreating. Here it was not science but pseudoscience that Darrow is criticizing, and his arguments dissect the fallacies of the eugenicist creed while simultaneously protesting the curtailment of freedom that any legislation based on eugenic principles would entail. (It is unfortunate, however, that Darrow feels obliged to add a religious argument—"haven't the eugenists . . . forgotten that man, as he stands, is created in the image of God?" [*CA* 206]—in which he manifestly did not believe.)

But if Darrow was only intermittently effective as an essayist or a philosopher, he was unfailingly on the mark when dealing with one vital subject—himself. Whether Darrow wrote one autobiography or two may be a vexed and unanswerable question: his bibliographer, Willard D. Hunsberger, refers to *Farmington* (1904) as a novel, but it is manifestly an unaffected and emotionally accurate account of Darrow's childhood and upbringing, for it is set in a fictitious town in western Pennsylvania and its first-person narrator disguises himself as John Smith. *The Story of My Life* (1932) is a more straightforward autobiography, although it may perhaps have more to say on Darrow's beliefs and outlook than on either the outward facts of his crowded career or the intimate details of his private life.

But when we turn to such pieces as "Why I Have Found Life Worth Living" (1928) or "At Seventy-two" (1929), we see the real Darrow stripped of the pyrotechnics of the defense attorney or the self-conscious literariness of the essayist in search of fame. We see the quiet dignity of the man who can gain a contentment even in the gaping absence of a loving God or the hope of life after death, who is temperamentally inclined to go against the opinions of the crowd, who finds that both the pleasures and the disappointments of life are less keen in old age than in youth. As he notes in "At Seventy-two":

> I am inclined to believe that very few who reach mature years are harassed by any thoughts of future punishment. Life has taught the pilgrim the frailty of human judgment, the prevalence of error, the shortness of human foresight, the intricate and impenetrable web of fate that enmeshes all. It has made him tolerant and kindly and understanding. It has taught him not to judge or to condemn. It does not matter what the religious faith may be, he cannot imagine a God with less understanding and charity than he has himself. (*CA* 240)

The real Clarence Darrow may not have been quite like the conflicted Spencer Tracy in the film *Inherit the Wind* or the unprincipled, radical, atheist bugaboo that the friends of capitalism and labor made him out to be; he was far more interesting and engaging—as a man, as a writer, and as a thinker—than these caricatures suggest. He was a man who, while retaining his core beliefs over a lifetime, learned from his mistakes and gained an insight both into himself and into his society that only age, experience, and struggle can bring. And at the end, he could rightly say that he had made a difference, one for the better.

Chapter 7

H. L. Mencken: Cracker-Barrel Philosopher

In a career as journalist and cultural critic that spanned nearly fifty years, Henry Louis Mencken (1880–1956) waged a relentless battle against religion and its unwarranted incursions into the realms of science, politics, and society. A native and lifelong resident of Baltimore, Mencken received no formal schooling after graduating from high school; instead, he immediately entered journalism, working first as a reporter for the *Baltimore Herald* and then, beginning in 1906, for the *Baltimore Sun*, a paper he helped raise to international prominence until he was forced to retire for health reasons in 1949. In 1910 he assisted in the founding of the *Baltimore Evening Sun*, and it was for this paper that he did the bulk of his newspaper writing. Mencken also gained celebrity as editor and voluminous contributor (mostly in the form of book reviews) of *Smart Set* (1908–1923) and *American Mercury* (1924–1933).

Because Mencken was almost entirely self-taught, he occasionally gives the impression of a cracker-barrel philosopher, tossing off outrageous or controversial statements in a deliberate attempt to provoke his audience. Mencken's penchant for satire, parody, and whimsy, along with his modified use of what he called the "American language"—a language that eschewed the stodgy dignity of formal English by the incorporation of racy slang, colloquialism, and neologisms—can occasionally make him seem flippant and irreverent and can also make it difficult to ascertain with exactitude the beliefs he himself espouses. Moreover, given that much of his writing on religion (as on other subjects) occurs in the form of newspaper articles written for specific occasions, his broader views on a number of vital issues pertaining to religion can be difficult to identify. A convenient compilation, *H. L. Mencken on Religion* (2002), provides some insight, but we shall have to draw upon a still wider range of his immense output to portray the totality of his opinions on this subject. Even his later monograph, *Treatise on the Gods* (1930; revised 1946), offers only fragments of a full answer.

In a chapter of his autobiography, *Happy Days* (1940), titled "The Schooling of a Theologian," Mencken writes entertainingly of his earliest religious training. Although he admits frankly that his father, August Mencken, was an "infidel,"[1] August nonetheless enrolled Henry and his brother Charles into a Methodist Sunday school—largely (in his son's view) to have peace and quiet on Sunday afternoons for his naps. Mencken's recollections of that experience focus largely on the rousing hymns that the boys were forced to learn: his favorite, he declared, was "Are You Ready for the Judgment Day?"—"a gay and even rollicking tune with a saving hint of brimstone in the words" (*MR* 27). Biographer Fred Hobson reports that "when Mencken was a child, a family Bible rested on the center table in the parlor, although no one ever opened it."[2] Mencken in later years clearly became intimately familiar with the Bible, even though he would occasionally make curious errors, as when he frequently asserted that Jonah swallowed the whale instead of the whale swallowing Jonah.

In an essay of 1920, Mencken referred to himself as a "theological moron"—by which he meant that "I have no sense whatever of the divine presence or of a divine personality; neither ever enters into my thinking" (*MR* 32). But Mencken is extremely cagey in declaring whether he is an actual atheist. In this essay, "Confessions of a Theological Moron," he states merely that "I am anything but a militant atheist and haven't the slightest objection to church-going, so long as it is honest" (*MR* 32); does this remark hold out the possibility that Mencken is an atheist of some kind, even if not "militant"? An amusing sketch titled "Memorial Service" (*Smart Set*, March 1922) lists dozens of gods that human beings have believed in over the millennia, and Mencken adds: "The hell of dead gods is as crowded as the Presbyterian hell for babies" (*MR* 294). Presumably, the implication is that the current god of the Christians (or the Jews or the Muslims or any other sect of believers) is similarly doomed to oblivion, but Mencken is careful not to make any explicit statement to that effect.

Mencken does not appear to have discounted the possibility of some "force" or "will" in the universe, which might perhaps be equated with a god. In a section of the column "Clinical Notes" (*American Mercury*, May 1924) called "Sabbath Meditations," Mencken is forthright in rejecting atheism:

> It seems to me to be plain that atheism, properly so-called, is nonsense, and I can recall no concrete atheist who did not appear to me to be a donkey. To deny any given god is, of course, quite reasonable, but to deny *all* gods is simply folly. For if there is anything plain about the universe it is that it is governed by law, and if there is anything plain about law it is that it can never be anything but a manifestation of will. Do the stars spin a certain way, and no other? Then it is simply because some will ordains that they shall spin that way, as the will of a juggler ordains that the balls in air shall go in certain paths. If the will failed in the one case the stars would go thundering into one another, just as if it failed in the other case the balls would drop to the stage.[3]

This is not very impressive as metaphysics, and it does little save revealing Mencken's lack of understanding of physics. The poet George Sterling, in a letter, rightly criticized Mencken's "anthropomorphism in asserting that force has to be an application of will," continuing that "it's the nature of matter to act as it does, and that it cannot act otherwise."[4]

The essay "What I Believe" (1930) is similarly ambiguous. Although Mencken clearly rejects the very notion of faith ("In my own credo there are few articles of faith; in fact, I have been quite unable, in ten days and nights of prayer and self-examination, to discover a single one" [*MR* 37]), he never addresses the issue of the existence of any kind of god. He concludes the essay: "I believe that religion, generally speaking, has been a curse to mankind—that its modest and greatly overestimated services on the ethical side have been more than overborne by the damage it has done to clear and honest thinking" (*MR* 47). Even this remark does not necessarily commit Mencken to the view that religious thinking is actually erroneous, although perhaps the implication is there.

A book review of 1932 appears to specify the god Mencken could believe in: "I see no difficulty in believing in a personal God—not, of course, the brummagem police sergeant of the Christian proletariat, but a hard-working, honest and not too intelligent Overseer of our miserable rat-hole in the cosmos, beset heavily day and night by the arbitrary and ill-natured mandates of gods still higher" (*MR* 245). If this remark is to be taken at all seriously, it suggests Mencken's belief in a god (one among many) who is not omnipotent. It is possible that Mencken actually believed in such a god, although a much earlier essay—"The Anthropomorphic Delusion" (*Smart Set*, August 1919)—treats the notion with considerable humor. Relating the many imperfections of the human body and mind ("No other animal is so defectively adapted to its environment" [*MR* 56]), Mencken lampoons the idea that we are made in God's image: "If we assume that man actually does resemble God, then we are forced into the impossible theory that God is a coward, an idiot and a bounder" (*MR* 57). In the essay "Hint to Theologians" (*American Mercury*, January 1924), Mencken asserts that the notion of a multiplicity of gods is logically superior to that of a single god:

> The theory that the universe is run by a single God must be abandoned, and that in place of it we must set up the theory that it is actually run by a board of gods, all of equal puissance and authority. Once this concept is grasped all the difficulties that have vexed theologians vanish. Human experience instantly lights up the whole dark scene. We observe in everyday life what happens when authority is divided, and great decisions are reached by consultation and compromise. We know that the effects, at times, particularly when one of the consultants runs away with the others, are very good, but we also know that they are usually extremely bad. Such a mixture of good and bad is on display in the cosmos. It presents a series of brilliant successes in the midst of an infinity of bungling failures. (*MR* 66)

But the general tone of this essay suggests satire—in particular, a satire aimed at one of Mencken's perennial bêtes noires, government.

In "What I Believe," Mencken expresses doubt about another central religious issue—the immortality of the soul. He says plainly, "I believe that the evidence for immortality is no better than the evidence for witches, and deserves no more respect" (*MR* 47). In a brief contribution to Jacob Helder's *Greatest Thoughts on Immortality* (1930), Mencken easily destroys several of the standard arguments in support of immortality—for example, the argument that it is a universal human belief and therefore true ("That desire is by no means universal. I lack it, and so do many other men" [*MR* 48–49])—and concludes: "It is my hope, as it is my belief, that death is the end" (*MR* 49). The book review of 1932 is more forthright on the subject ("When it comes to the immortality of the soul, I can only say that it seems to me to be wholly incredible and preposterous" [*MR* 246]); in fact, Mencken goes further, relying on science to cast doubt on the very existence of the soul, or at least to point to some fatal paradoxes in the conception:

> Its proponents get into serious difficulties when they undertake to say when and how the soul gets into the body, and where it comes from. Must it be specially created in each instance, or is it the offspring of the two parent souls? In either case, when does it appear, at the moment of conception or somewhat later? If the former, then what happens to the soul of a zygote cast out, say, an hour after fertilization? If the death of that soul ensues, then the soul is not immortal in all cases, which means that its immortality can be certain in none; and if, on the contrary, it goes to Heaven or Hell, or some vague realm between, then we are asked to believe that the bishops and archbishops who swarm beyond the grave are forced to associate, and on terms of equality, with shapes that can neither think nor speak, and resemble tadpoles far more than they resemble Christians. (*MR* 246–47)

Given his own skepticism, Mencken was repeatedly forced to address the issue of why, after so many centuries and so many scientific advances that appeared to refute its central claims, religion continued to exercise a tenacious hold upon the majority of the human—and, specifically, the American—populace. He was, indeed, forthright in maintaining that science had in fact overthrown many if not all of the central tenets of the Christian religion. Asserting, in the essay "The Ascent of Man" (*Smart Set*, May 1923), that religion "belongs exclusively to a very early stage of human development" (*MR* 61), Mencken saw it as a sign of human progress that religion was gradually shed with the advance of intellect and civilization.

Inspired by his reading of Andrew D. White's *History of the Warfare of Science with Theology in Christendom* (1896), which he once pronounced a "noble" work (*MR* 46), Mencken felt that there was a war to the death between religion and science, and that science must prevail if society was to become fit to live in. "There is . . . no possibility of reconciling science and religion—that is, religion of the sort preached to the peasantry by [William Jennings] Bryan" (*MR* 225), he wrote in 1925, shortly after the conclusion of the Scopes trial. This comment suggests that Mencken's target is merely the fundamentalists, who believe in the literal truth of every word of the Bible, even though it is full of internal contradictions as well as statements that are plainly false in light of current scientific knowledge; but it must be noted that Mencken believed that *all* Christians, whatever their denomination and however they try to brush certain embarrassing features of the Bible under the rug, are obliged to be at one with the fundamentalists on this point. Agreeing with the theologian J. Gresham Machen—who, in *Christianity and Liberalism* (1923) and other works, refuted the claims of the Modernists, who attempted to discard miracles and other supernatural elements from the Bible—Mencken derided the notion that one could pick and choose what one wished to believe in the Bible:

> Is Christianity actually a revealed religion? If not, then it is nothing; if so, then we must accept the Bible as an inspired statement of its principles. But how can we think of the Bible as inspired and at the same time as fallible? How can we imagine it as part divine and awful truth and part mere literary confectionary? And how, if we manage so to imagine it, are we to distinguish between the truth and the confectionary?[5]

In reviewing Montague Summers's *The History of Witchcraft and Demonology* (1927), Mencken noted with bemusement that Summers accepts the notorious statement in Exodus (22:18), "Thou shalt not suffer a witch to live," going on to say: "He can't imagine a Christian who refuses to believe in demoniacal possession, and no more can I" (*MR* 239). After all, the statement in Exodus comes right from the mouth of God, and there are any number of passages in which Jesus acknowledges a belief in demons (as when he expelled demons from one or two individuals and thrust them into the bodies of the Gadarene swine). If the Bible is an inspired document, these statements must be accepted; if they are not accepted, one has tacitly acknowledged that the Bible is not inspired and is therefore of no more value as a guide to belief and conduct than any other treatise, scriptural or secular.

Why, then, in light of these plain facts, do the vast majority of people continue to believe? Mencken was blunt on the issue: they are stupid. In "The Black Art" (*Baltimore Evening Sun*, March 6, 1922), he noted that the overwhelming number of Americans are superstitious in one way or another: "The truth is that freedom from such superstitions, like the capacity for truth and honor, is the exclusive possession of a very small minority of the human race—even in America, a country where education is free and universal, probably not more than one tenth of one per cent." (*MR* 59). Led by his early readings in Nietzsche—one of his earliest treatises was *The Philosophy of Friedrich Nietzsche* (1908)—Mencken believed that all the advances of civilization were the product of a select few exceptional individuals who dragged the rest of the mob along in their wake.

"Fundamentalism: Divine and Secular" (*Chicago Sunday Tribune*, September 20, 1925) opens resoundingly with the statement: "*Homo boobiens* is a fundamentalist for the precise reason that he is uneducable" (*MR* 120). Note the exact wording of the passage: Mencken is not saying that human beings are *uneducated*, but *uneducable*: in other words, no amount of education will ever be able to lift them from their slough of ignorance. Scientific advance has progressed to such a degree that only experts in the chosen field can now understand it, and the mob simply rejects what it cannot understand:

> The clodhopper's objection to the hypothesis of evolution is not primarily that it is heathenish; that, indeed, is only an afterthought. His primary objection is that it is complicated and unintelligible—in the late Martyr Bryan's phase, that it is "stuff and nonsense." In order to understand it a man must have a sound grounding in all the natural sciences; he must bring to the business an immense and intricate knowledge. And in order to get that grounding he must have a mind capable of taking it in. (*MR* 121)

The account of creation in Genesis, on the other hand, even though it is "incredible" and "counter to the known facts," is "divinely simple" (*MR* 120).

Mencken relentlessly drove home this connection between theology and ignorance. In "The Ghostly Fraternity" (*American Mercury*, June 1924), he denied that the average clergyman is even particularly religious; in fact, his chief motivation is to "shine in the world without too much effort. The young theologue, in brief, is commonly an ambitious but somewhat lazy and incompetent fellow, and he studies theology instead of medicine or law because it offers a quicker and easier route to an assured job and public respect" (*MR* 68). Mencken similarly denied that the Jesuits are a class of notably intelligent religious scholars. Reviewing E. Boyd Barrett's *The Jesuit Enigma* (1927), he refutes Barrett's notion that the Jesuits are "a sort of intellectual aristocracy within the Church," claiming instead: "It is, I believe, nothing of the sort. Founded by a soldier, it remains essentially military, not scholarly. Its aim is not to find out what is true, but to defend and propagate what Holy Church says is true. All the ideas that it is officially aware of are fixed ideas: it knows of no machinery for changing them, and wants to hear of none" (*MR* 108). As for Catholicism as a whole, "The church, as a church, like any other ecclesiastical organization, is highly unintelligent. It is forever making thumping errors, both in psychology and in politics, and despite its occasional brilliant successes among sentimental pseudo-intellectuals . . . it seems destined to go downhill hereafter."[6]

But Mencken did have to face the plain fact that some people of apparent intelligence were nonetheless believers. His review of Howard A. Kelly's *A Scientific Man and the Bible* (1926) betrays amazement that a founding member of the Johns Hopkins Medical School, and a man whom Mencken had known for many years, could nonetheless maintain a belief in the inerrancy of the Bible. He ponders the matter:

> By what route do otherwise sane men come to believe such palpable nonsense? How is it possible for a human brain to be divided into two insulated halves, one functioning normally, naturally and even brilliantly, and the other capable only of the ghastly balderdash which issues from the minds of Baptist evangelists? . . . Why should this be so? What is there in religion that completely flabbergasts the wits of those who believe in it?[7]

Mencken can provide no answer to these queries. The best he can do is to appeal, as he does frequently, to the splendid prose-poetry of the Bible. Mencken states unhesitatingly, "To this day no better poetry has ever been written. It is so powerful in its effects that even men who reject its content in toto are more or less susceptible to it."[8] Poetry, too, is a heritage of the infancy of the human race as a whole and of the youth of individual human beings; and the poetry that is imbedded in the entire Christian story—both on the level of language and on the level of the overall narrative—will ensure its survival: "Christianity will survive because it appeals to the sense of poetry—to what, in men of arrested development, which is to say, average men, passes for the instinct to seek and know beauty" (*MR* 65).

Mencken's forays into the metaphysics of religion were relatively few. As a practicing journalist, he was much more interested in the intrusion of individual religions, or individual religious figures, into realms he felt they did not belong; chief among them was politics. He was well aware that, in spite of the First Amendment, the United States, "save for a short while in its infancy, while the primal infidels survived, has always diluted democracy with theocracy."[9] And because this country is "a realm of faith," therefore "religious questions belong properly to its public life" (*MR* 255). This may be a surprising conclusion from one who felt that the Christian religion in particular was factually wrong on so many metaphysical, moral, and political issues, but Mencken knew that, given the importance of religion in the minds of so many Americans, there was no way to banish it from the public sphere.

Politically, Mencken was what he himself termed an extreme libertarian. In a book review column of 1922 he wrote:

> As for me, my literary theory, like my politics, is based chiefly upon one main idea, to wit, the idea of freedom. I am, in brief, a libertarian of the most extreme variety, and know of no human right that is one-tenth as valuable as the simple right to utter what seems (at the moment) to be the truth. Take away this right, and none other is worth a hoot; nor, indeed, can any other long exist.[10]

This stance led him to protest strenuously against any attempts by the religious to force their beliefs—and, even more significantly, their behavior—upon the rest of the populace. In his day, Mencken found two cases where this was done: the Sunday laws and Prohibition.

Despite the purported separation of church and state granted by the First Amendment, a wide array of Sunday laws were on the books in many states, and Mencken was well aware that such groups as the Lord's Day Alliance were vigilantly pushing their agenda. He noted tartly that, in Maryland in 1913, a symphony orchestra could not charge money for a concert held on Sunday:

> The Blue Laws were passed in 1723, and go back to the hell fire harangues of Cotton Mather, but every effort to mitigate and modernize them is opposed with truly savage violence. Under them, the impresario who had an orchestra play the nine symphonies of Beethoven on nine successive Sunday afternoons would be liable to a minimum fine of $25,550 and 220 days in jail.[11]

In "The Free Lance"—a column he wrote for the *Baltimore Evening Sun* six days a week for four and a half years (1911–1915)—Mencken tirelessly advocated the repeal of these archaic statutes. He ultimately prevailed, but only after many years. A much later essay, "On Sunday Laws" (*Baltimore Evening Sun*, March 21, 1932), Mencken summed up the issue. He had no objection to a "day of rest" whereby those who wished to attend church could do so without hindrance, but he maintained that the law must protect others as well:

> The man outside the church has rights as well as the man within. He, also, deserves to be protected in his lawful occasions. If what he wants to do is innocent in itself, and invades no other man's rights, and has no baleful effect upon the general welfare, and is supported by a preponderance of public opinion, then any law which prohibits it is a tyrannical and evil law, and ought to be repealed. And if the animus behind that law . . . is purely theological—if its actual purpose is not the general good, but simply the furthering of some fantastic and oppressive religious idea, cherished only by an obscure and anti-social sect—then it becomes utterly and intolerably abominable, and should be got rid of as soon as possible. (*MR* 265–66)

The most "fantastic and oppressive religious idea" that Mencken could imagine was that the consumption of alcohol should be prohibited by statute. Ever since the early 1910s, Mencken—one of this nation's great devotees of beer and other alcoholic beverages—had been ominously predicting the ultimate passage of a Prohibition amendment, and he saw it come to pass in 1919. One of his most controversial stances in the issue of religion and politics was his assertion that religions—specifically the Methodist and Baptist churches—were behind the movement to pass the amendment. The matter is too complex for detailed treatment here, but the historical evidence suggests that Mencken was pretty much on target in this claim. The central role of the Anti-Saloon League in advocating Prohibition, from as early as the 1890s, is not in doubt; nor is there any doubt of its fundamentally religious character and basis. F. Scott McBride, general superintendent of the league, stated: "The Anti-Saloon League was born of God. It has been led by Him, and will fight on while He leads" (quoted in *MR* 19–20). It was clearly the Baptist and Methodist churches as a whole, and not merely individual members of them acting independently, who formed the core of the Anti-Saloon League and engaged in political pressure upon politicians to pass the Prohibition amendment. While it is true that Prohibition was in part a reaction by Anglo-Saxon Americans against what they perceived to be the excessive imbibings of recent European immigrants, there was always a subtle anti-Catholic bias mixed with this xenophobic prejudice—a bias that emerged openly with the nomination in 1928 of the "wet" Democratic presidential candidate Al Smith, the first Catholic nominated by any major American party for the presidency.

Mencken expressed particular disdain for Bishop James Cannon, perhaps the leading Methodist clergyman of his time. He was a vigorous proponent of temperance, being the leading lobbyist for the Anti-Saloon League both before and after the passage of the Eighteenth Amendment. When Herbert Hoover was elected in 1928, Mencken asserted that, for all practical purposes, the First Amendment had been effectively abrogated:

> Whether for good or for ill, the old sharp separation of church and state has been definitely abandoned. The Eighteenth Amendment was fastened upon the Constitution, not as a political measure and by political devices, nor even as a moral measure and by moral devices, but as an almost purely theological measure and by devices borrowed from the camp-meeting. Its adoption was advocated and obtained, not by lawyers or sociologists or professors of political science, but by the embattled Christians of the more bucolic sects, functioning as such. And it is supported to-day by the same naïve sectarians, not on logical grounds, but on strictly dogmatic grounds—in other words, as an article of faith.[12]

Mencken must have known by this time that Prohibition was immensely unpopular throughout the nation—it was probably the most widely disobeyed law in American history. Four years later, things looked very different, and Mencken chuckled at Cannon's expense when both political parties inserted a "wet" plank in their platform, making it inevitable that Prohibition would eventually be repealed.

On occasion, Mencken's devotion to personal liberty led him into awkward stances. Consider his opinion in regard to Christian Science. Although he acknowledged that "the idea behind it is one of the few human ideas in which I can find no sense or logic whatever," and that "it is not merely erroneous; it is imbecile,"[13] he was nonetheless opposed to laws that prohibited the withholding of orthodox medicine from the children of Christian Scientists. In maintaining that such laws would prevent the spread of infection throughout the community, Mencken merely throws up his hands and remarks that "such risks . . . constitute, in truth, the irremovable hazards that life under civilization imposes upon all of us" (*MR* 146). As to the harm to the children themselves, Mencken first states that in fact the majority of them don't suffer very much, and those who do—and actually die in the process—merely rid the world of incompetents. This essay proceeds from one fallacy and absurdity to the next. Mencken was chiefly concerned about a slippery-slope effect: "If they [the Christian Scientists] were jailed to-morrow for believing in Christian Science, I should probably be jailed the next day for refusing to believe in something still sillier" (*MR* 150). But the law was not a law against belief; it was a law against child endangerment.

On another sociopolitical issue—divorce—Mencken was firmly on the side of secularism. In the fiery essay "What Is to Be Done about Divorce?" (*New York World Magazine*, January 26, 1930), he states bluntly: "I see no chance of dealing with the divorce question rationally until the discussion is purged of religious consideration" (*MR* 281). It is the Christian religion that has made divorce nearly impossible in many states; for the Christian view of religion is inherently unwholesome:

> A wife is primarily a sexual instrument and as such must not flinch her lowly duty. If she tries to avoid having children, then she is doomed to hell. If she finds her husband growing unpleasant and turns from him to another, then she is doomed to hell again. As for him, he is bound in the same way and under the same penalties. Both would be better off if they were chaste, but as long as that is impossible they must be unchaste only with each other, and accept with resignation all the more painful consequences, whether biological or theological. (*MR* 281)

The whole issue of marriage and divorce can be addressed only by a frank appraisal of facts, "uncontaminated by false assumptions and antediluvian traditions" (*MR* 282).

One other sociopolitical issue that Mencken occasionally broached is the role of religion among African Americans. Mencken—who, in spite of certain politically incorrect utterances in his private diary and elsewhere, was a true friend of African Americans, tirelessly supporting their efforts at social and political equality and vigorously promoting the work of black authors—was so incensed by the practice of lynching, especially in his own state, that in 1935 he testified before Congress in support of the Costigan-Wagner antilynching bill. Early in his career, he wrote an amusing and strikingly prescient essay urging African Americans to convert en masse to Islam as a way of battling the Ku Klux Klan in the South. Mencken shrewdly recognized that slaveowners had forced their slaves to convert to Christianity as a means of keeping them in a suitable attitude of humility, but Islam "teaches them to rise and resist—more, to take the offensive against their enemies."[14] It would be another forty years before Wallace Fard Mohammad and his successor, Elijah Mohammad, would establish the Nation of Islam for very much this same purpose.

Although, in "Treason in the Tabernacle" (*American Mercury*, June 1931), Mencken wrote optimistically, "One of the cheering signs of the times is the appearance of an anti-clerical movement among Americans of dark complexion" (*MR* 283), he must have known that religious belief was generally stronger among African Americans than among Caucasians in the United States. Only a few months earlier, in the essay "The Burden of Credulity" (*Opportunity*, February 1931), Mencken strongly urged people of color to abandon Christianity—at any rate, the kind of Christianity they had largely espoused—if they wished to improve their lot. Responding to the claim by a Baptist clergyman that, "among all the Negro Baptists in America, there was not one who was not a Fundamentalist," Mencken replied pungently: "It is a shameful thing to say of any people who aspire to advance in the world" (*MA* 142).

Mencken's most controversial claim, on this subject, was that the Ku Klux Klan itself was, like Prohibition, a Methodist-Baptist creation. Here he was on somewhat shakier ground. For the first decade or two of the Klan's existence after its reconstitution in 1915, its chief foes were not African Americans or Jews but Catholics, who were seen as symbols of the perceived immorality and social changes that were affecting the United States in the early decades of the twentieth century. Individual Klansmen, and even some Klan leaders, were indeed associated with the Baptist and Methodist churches, but there was no concerted support of the Klan by any church. Kenneth T. Jackson, historian of the Klan, writes:

> Although there was no formal connection between the Invisible Empire and any religious denomination, Fundamentalism was the central thread of the Klan program. Declaring that "America is Protestant and so it must remain," the KKK glorified the "old-time religion," rejected evolution and higher criticism, and admonished its members to attend church regularly. Protestant clergymen were reminded that Klansmen accepted the Bible as the literal and unalterable word of God. As proof of their devotion, masked Knights frequently appeared unannounced before quiescent congregations for the purpose of making a well-publicized donation.[15]

Jackson points to the Klan's role in supporting Prohibition and other conservative social and moral causes.

The event that gained Mencken the greatest celebrity—and, in the eyes of some, notoriety and even infamy—as a religious commentator was his participation as a reporter in the trial of John Thomas Scopes for teaching evolution in Tennessee in defiance of a recently passed statute prohibiting it. This event, which galvanized the nation because of its intertwining of religion, science, politics, and law, catapulted all parties—on the one side the hapless teacher Scopes, the lead defense attorney Clarence Darrow, and Mencken as an obviously partisan commentator; and, on the other side, the former secretary of state William Jennings Bryan, who had become a leader of the Christian fundamentalist movement—into unwonted celebrity during the two weeks of the trial in the sweltering summer of 1925 in Dayton, Tennessee. It later led Jerome Lawrence and Robert E. Lee to write the play *Inherit the Wind* (1955), made into a film in 1960 in which a character clearly based on Mencken was portrayed, rather inappositely, by Gene Kelly.

An important point about Mencken's involvement in the Scopes trial must be understood. As stated earlier, he and his allies (Darrow and his assistants Dudley Field Malone and Arthur Garfield Hays of the American Civil Liberties Union) actually hoped to lose the case to embarrass the entire state of Tennessee and to send the case on appeal to a federal court; Mencken gave the strategy away when he stated in one of his earliest reports from Dayton: "The real trial, in truth, will not begin until Scopes is convicted and ordered to the hulks. Then the prisoner will be the Legislature of Tennessee" (*MR* 175). The plan did not quite work out as they had hoped: although Scopes was in fact found guilty, the sentence was later overturned by the Tennessee Supreme Court. But the publicity surrounding the trial—chiefly fueled by Mencken's partisan "reporting"—had its chosen effect of making the entire state of Tennessee, as well as the entire Christian fundamentalist movement, a laughingstock throughout the nation and the world, with the result that fundamentalists retreated into relative obscurity until 1978, when the founding of the Moral Majority reintroduced them as a force in American society and politics.

Mencken's reporting of the Scopes trial revisits many points he had made against religion in his earlier writing. He is particularly forceful in noting that there can be no "reconciling" of science and religion when it comes to scientific discovery:

> For the two parties, it must be manifest, are at the farthermost poles of difference, and leaning out into space. If one of them is right at all, then the other is wrong altogether. There can be no honest compromise between them. Either Genesis embodies a mathematically accurate statement of what took place during the week of June 3, 4004 B. C. or Genesis is not actually the Word of God. If the former alternative be accepted, then all of modern science is nonsense; if the latter, then evangelical Christianity is nonsense. (*MR* 161–62)

Mencken's attack here, as elsewhere, is on those who sought to downplay the "warfare" between science and theology—which included, to his dismay, even such notable scientists as Robert A. Millikan (winner of the Nobel Prize for physics in 1923) and Henry Fairfield Osborn, paleontologist and longtime president of the American Museum of Natural History. Mencken would later declare that the only result of the work of these "reconcilers" is "to abandon a just cause to its enemies, cravenly and without excuse."[16]

Mencken repeats his assertions that the reason for the refusal of many individuals to accept evolution and other scientific discoveries because they are fundamentally stupid ("The great masses of men, even in this inspired republic, are precisely where the mob was at the dawn of history. They are ignorant, they are dishonest, they are cowardly, they are ignoble" [*MR* 165]), and that science has now become too complex for them to understand ("It puts an unbearable burden upon his meager capacity for taking in ideas" [*MR* 167]). Mencken also attempts to lay the groundwork for the hoped-for conviction of Scopes by declaring repeatedly that, in this community, there is not the remotest possibility that someone like Scopes could get a fair trial. Everyone is a fundamentalist, and even a "Northern Methodist would be regarded as virtually an atheist" (*MR* 178). As for Darrow:

> The whisper that he is an atheist has been stilled by the bucolic make-up and by the public report that he has the gift of prophecy and can reconcile Genesis and evolution. Even so, there is ample space about him when he navigates the streets. The other day a newspaper woman was warned by her landlady to keep out of the courtroom when he was on his legs. All the local sorcerers predict that a bolt from heaven will fetch him in the end. (*MR* 181–82)

One of Mencken's most engaging articles is a lengthy report on a Holy Roller revival meeting, held on a farmer's field. "It is not enough," Mencken notes, "to go to a revival once a year or twice a year; there must be a revival every night" (*MR* 182–83). His paper drips with sarcasm for the raving revival leaders and attendees, most of them poor, ignorant yokels for whom the event was the only kind of entertainment to enliven their dreary lives. Yet his reportorial skills are sharp and precise:

> From the squirming and jabbering mass a young woman gradually detached herself—a woman not uncomely, with a pathetic home-made cap on her head. Her head jerked back, the veins of her neck swelled, and her fists went to her throat as if she were fighting for breath. She bent backward until she was like half of a hoop. Then she suddenly snapped forward. We caught a flash of the whites of her eyes. Presently her whole body began to be convulsed—great convulsions that began at the shoulders and ended at the hips. She would leap to her feet, thrust her arms in air and then hurl herself upon the heap. Her praying flat-

> tened out into a mere delirious caterwauling, like that of a tomcat on a petting party. (*MR* 185)

The trial's outcome was, indeed, a foregone conclusion, especially when the presiding judge, John Tate Raulston, declared inadmissible the testimony of expert witnesses—chiefly an array of prominent biologists—who would acknowledge the high probability of the truth of evolution. Nevertheless, Mencken was present when Bryan, during a speech to the court, declared that man was not a mammal: "It seemed a sheer impossibility that any literate man should stand up in public and discharge any such nonsense. Yet the poor old fellow did it" (*MR* 199).

It should be noted that Mencken was in Dayton only for about ten days, arriving a few days before the trial and leaving after the trial was only half over. He therefore missed the most riveting moment of the trial, when Darrow, his other options stymied, made the bold move to put Bryan himself on the stand and cross-examine him. Bryan foolishly agreed, thinking that he could outwit the clever defense attorney, and his clumsy attempts to defend the Bible as a textbook of science were so disastrous that, in spite of the actual verdict against Scopes, Bryan's cause suffered a fatal setback. Matters were not helped by the fact that Bryan died a few days after the trial was over.

This stunning turn of events, according to Mencken, shook his supporters more than anything else in the entire case. Just a week earlier, Mencken had predicted that fundamentalism, led by Bryan, would seek new worlds to conquer: the trial "serves notice on the country that Neandertal [*sic*] man is organizing in these forlorn backwaters of the land, led by a fanatic, devoid of sense and devoid of conscience" (*MR* 203). But Bryan's death took the fundamentalists aback in more ways than one:

> The circumstances of Bryan's death, indeed, have probably done great damage to Fundamentalism, for it is nothing if it is not a superstition, and the rustic pastors will have a hard time explaining to the faithful why the agent of God was struck down in the midst of his first battle. How is it that Darrow escaped and Bryan fell? There is, no doubt, a sound theological reason, but I shouldn't like to have to expound it, even to a country Bible class. In the end, perhaps, the true believers will have to take refuge from the torment of doubt in the theory that the

> hero was murdered, say by the Jesuits. Even so, there will be the obvious and disquieting inference that, in the first battle, the devil really won. (*MR* 212–13)

Mencken wrote a total of four articles on Bryan immediately following his death: "Bryan" (*Baltimore Evening Sun*, July 27, 1925); "Round Two" (*Baltimore Evening Sun*, August 10, 1925), an editorial in *American Mercury* (October 1925), and a fusion of these three pieces, "In Memoriam: W. J. B.," published in *Prejudices: Fifth Series* (1926). To say that Mencken was a bit uncharitable to his late opponent would be an understatement: even in his own day, the ferocity of these articles was deprecated, and even so sympathetic a figure as the science writer L. Sprague de Camp, in his book *The Great Monkey Trial* (1968), wrote: "Mencken succeeded in being even more unjust to Bryan than Bryan had been to Darrow in his post-trial statement. He also succeeded in shocking Bryan's admirers as severely as if he had literally scalped Bryan's corpse and done a war dance around it, waving his bloody trophy."[17]

Even though Mencken incredibly remarks, "It is the national custom to sentimentalize the dead, as it is to sentimentalize men about to be hanged. Perhaps I fall into that weakness here" (*MR* 210), he delivers a scathing indictment of Bryan and all he stood for:

> Bryan was a vulgar and common man, a cad undiluted. He was ignorant, bigoted, self-seeking, blatant and dishonest. His career brought him into contact with the first men of his time; he preferred the company of rustic ignoramuses. It was hard to believe, watching him at Dayton, that he had traveled, that he had been received in civilized societies, that he had been a high officer of state. He seemed only a poor clod like those around him, deluded by a childish theology, full of an almost pathological hatred of all learning, all human dignity, all beauty, all fine and noble things. He was a peasant come home to the dung-pile. Imagine a gentleman, and you have imagined everything that he was not. (*MR* 211)

Outrageous as this sounds, it is in fact unfair? Some recent commentators on the Scopes trial have found more merit in Bryan's side than Mencken did. Edward J. Larson, in a book on the Scopes trial that is far more sympathetic to Bryan than other studies, maintained that Bryan was also concerned about the ramifications of Darwinism in the social and political sphere—specifically, the perversion of the theory of evolution that came to be called Social Darwinism. In a 1921 lecture, "The Menace of Darwinism," Bryan declared, "To destroy the faith of Christians and lay the foundations for the bloodiest war in history would seem enough to condemn Darwinism."[18] But Mencken, although himself somewhat inclined toward Social Darwinism (based upon his own misreading of Nietzsche's concept of the superman), never brought this facet of his thought to bear in his criticisms of Bryan, which rested entirely on Bryan's dogmatic assertion of biblical literalism.

Mencken, for his part, presciently noted that fundamentalism, in spite of the catastrophic setback it had suffered in the trial and its aftermath, was by no means finished. Even though, in the wake of the trial, Georgia shelved an antievolution statute it had been considering, Mencken was not entirely sanguine that his side would prevail. The fundamentalists were everywhere:

> They swarm in the country towns, inflamed by their pastors, and with a saint, now, to venerate. They are thick in the mean streets behind the gas-works. They are everywhere that learning is too heavy a burden for mortal minds, even the vague, pathetic learning on tap in little red schoolhouses. They march with the Klan, with the Christian Endeavor Society, with the Junior Order of United American Mechanics, with the Epworth League, with all the rococo bands that poor and unhappy folk organize to bring some light of purpose into their lives. They have had a thrill, and they are ready for more. (*MR* 222–23)

Mencken, like Darrow, urged scientists to step to the forefront of the battle and defend their discipline for the good of civilization.

Mencken was also outspoken about the need to debate religious issues in public. Religious views should not be given a free pass merely because they were religious; this failure to examine such views with critical scrutiny was merely a holdover from a prior era when opposition to religion by "heretics" or "infidels" could be punished by the civil authorities. In the essay "Aftermath" (*Baltimore Evening Sun*, September 24, 1925), Mencken spoke firmly on the matter:

> Even a superstitious man has certain inalienable rights. He has a right to harbor and indulge his imbecilities as long as he pleases, provided

> only he does not try to inflict them upon other men by force. He has a right to argue for them as eloquently as he can, in season and out of season. He has a right to teach them to his children. But certainly he has no right to be protected against the free criticism of those who do not hold them. He has no right to demand that they be treated as sacred. He has no right to preach them without challenge. . . .
>
> The meaning of religious freedom, I fear, is sometimes greatly misapprehended. It is taken to be a sort of immunity, not merely from governmental control but also from public opinion. A dunderhead gets himself a long-tailed coat, rises behind the sacred desk and emits such bilge as would gag a Hottentot. Is it to pass unchallenged? If so, then what we have is not religious freedom at all, but the most intolerable and outrageous variety of religious despotism. Any fool, once he is admitted to holy orders, becomes infallible. Any half-wit, by the simple device of ascribing his delusions to revelation, takes on an authority that is denied to all the rest of us. (*MR* 216)

Five years after the Scopes trial, Mencken published *Treatise on the Gods* (1930). Lengthy and substantial as it is, in some ways the book does not represent Mencken to best advantage. Although purporting to be a sober, scholarly examination of the anthropology of religion, the work is repeatedly marred both by reliance on poor source material, such as popular works by A. Hyatt Verrill and Lewis Spence, and by clumsy humor ("The Patagonian place of the dead was a vast series of caverns underground, and its chief delight was getting drunk").[19] Mencken somewhat routinely outlines both the essence of religion ("Its single function is to give man access to the powers which seem to control his destiny, and its single purpose is to induce those powers to be friendly to him" [*TG* 4]) and its evolution over the millennia. He devotes considerable space to Christianity, noting how the New Testament in particular is riddled with inconsistencies relating to the life and teachings of Jesus, while the Pentateuch "reeks with irreconcilable contradictions and patent imbecilities" (*TG* 193). As elsewhere, he asserts that the King James Bible "is probably the most beautiful piece of writing in all the literature of the world" (*TG* 205).

In 1946 Mencken produced a revised edition in which he extensively rewrote chapter 5 ("Its State Today"). Here he lays out his most severe condemnation of the Christian religion, not only for its opposition to scientific advance, but for many other failings:

> Since the earliest days the church as an organization has thrown itself violently against every effort to liberate the body and mind of man. It has been, at all times and everywhere, the habitual and incorrigible defender of bad governments, bad laws, bad social theories, bad institutions. It was, for centuries, an apologist for slavery, as it was apologist for the divine right of kings. . . . In the domain of pure ideas one branch of the church clings to the archaic speculations of Thomas Aquinas and the other labors under the preposterous nonsense of John Calvin. . . .
>
> The only real way to reconcile science and religion is to set up something that is not science and something that is not religion. . . . To argue that the gaps in knowledge which still confront the seeker must be filled, not by patient inquiry, but by intuition or revelation, is simply to give ignorance a gratuitous and preposterous dignity. When a man so indulges himself it is only to confess that, to that extent at least, he is not a scientist at all, but a theologian, for he attempts to reconcile science and religion by the sorry device of admitting that the latter is somehow superior to the former, and is thus entitled to all territories that remain unoccupied. (*TG* 260–61)

These were, for all practical purposes, Mencken's last words on religion, and their truth and relevance seem only to have increased in the sixty years since their writing.

Chapter 8

H. P. LOVECRAFT: THE WONDERS OF THE COSMOS

How does it happen that a man like H. P. Lovecraft (1890–1937)—almost entirely unknown in his time except as the author of seemingly lurid and flamboyant tales of "cosmic" horror, and who contributed almost nothing to the public discussion of the central questions of religion, politics, and society—has become, more than a half century after his death, a kind of patron saint of atheism? The conundrum might be explained in part by considering his remarkable posthumous reputation, a reputation that has seen not only the publication of his relatively small corpus of fiction in the most prestigious of venues (capped, in 2005, by the Library of America's edition of his *Tales*) but also the issuance of his essays, poetry, and especially his thousands of letters; these letters, clearly not designed for publication and written to friends and colleagues who were themselves little known, show him to have been one of the keenest minds of his generation, one who fashioned a comprehensive worldview that saw no place for God in the fabric of the universe and that appealed largely to science as the arbiter of truth, but nonetheless left room for the imaginative stimulus of art. Yet to explain Lovecraft's eminence, both as a writer and as a thinker, we may also have to look to the nearly mythic figure he has become as the gaunt, lantern-jawed creator of a plethora of "gods" in his stories who nonetheless heaped scorn on the central religious tenets of the existence of a deity, the immortality of the soul, and the cosmic significance of humankind.

Lovecraft's early life and upbringing laid the foundations for both his impressive intellect and his supernatural fiction. Born on August 20, 1890, in Providence, Rhode Island, to a Baptist mother (Sarah Susan Phillips Lovecraft) and an Anglican father (Winfield Scott Lovecraft),

Lovecraft early developed a keen taste for what he would call "the supremely rational 18th century"[1]—the century of David Hume, Edward Gibbon, and the *philosophes*. In his early childhood years, of course, it was not philosophy but literature—especially poetry—that fascinated him, and his enthusiasm for the elegant translations of Greek and Latin poetry by such poets as John Dryden and Alexander Pope led him to classical antiquity itself. One of his earliest surviving writings is an eighty-eight-line verse paraphrase of the *Odyssey*, dating to 1897. In the piquant essay "A Confession of Unfaith" (1922), Lovecraft admits that his absorption of classical myth and literature had much to do with his later atheism. In that same essay, however, he dates his first skeptical utterances to a Sunday school class he attended at age five. This would appear to conflict with a 1920 letter in which he dates his Sunday school clashes to a somewhat later period:

> How well I recall my tilts with Sunday-School teachers during my last period of compulsory attendance! I was 12 years old, and the despair of the institution. None of the answers of my pious preceptors would satisfy me, and my demands that they cease taking things for granted quite upset them. Close reasoning was something new in their little world of Semitic mythology. At last I saw that they were hopelessly bound to unfounded dogmata and traditions, and thenceforth ceased to treat them seriously. Sunday-School became to me simply a place wherein to have a little harmless fun spoofing the pious mossbacks. My mother observed this, and no longer sought to enforce my attendance.[2]

Perhaps there is no strict contradiction: Lovecraft's memories, in "A Confession of Unfaith," of attending the "infant class" of the Sunday school at the First Baptist Church in Providence seem authentic, but one suspects he may be exaggerating the degree to which he was able to "tilt" with his teachers at the tender age of five.

Lovecraft's imagination, meanwhile, had been stimulated by his early readings of Grimm's fairy tales (age four), the *Arabian Nights* (age five), and Coleridge's *The Rime of the Ancient Mariner*, in the edition illustrated by Gustave Doré (age six). These and other influences awakened his love of the fantastic, and he was writing short horror tales as early as six. These specimens are very crude, but they laid the groundwork for his later "cosmic" narratives. Equally important, however, was Lovecraft's precocious absorption of science—first chemistry, at age eight, and then astronomy, at age eleven. Lovecraft speaks truly in "A Confession of Unfaith" that these studies definitively transformed him from agnosticism to full-fledged atheism. The "myriad suns and worlds of infinite space" seemed to reduce all earth life to vanishing insignificance, and Lovecraft admits that he actually entered a period of cosmic pessimism: "The futility of all existence began to impress and oppress me."[3]

After 1908, the year he dropped out of high school because of unspecified nervous problems, Lovecraft abandoned the writing of fiction, thinking himself a failure in that capacity. But, after he had allowed some of his teenage stories to appear in amateur magazines, where they received an enthusiastic response from friends and colleagues, Lovecraft resumed writing fiction in 1917. He had no thought of publishing professionally—he had long before adopted the eighteenth-century stance of writing as an elegant amusement, later to be augmented by an "art for art's sake" attitude that vaunted pure "self-expression" and scorned the profit motive in writing—until the establishment of the pulp magazine *Weird Tales* in 1923. This was the first magazine devoted exclusively to supernatural or horror fiction, and several of Lovecraft's colleagues—who now numbered such fellow fantasists as Frank Belknap Long and Clark Ashton Smith—urged Lovecraft to submit his work. Lovecraft grudgingly did so and was pleased that it was readily accepted. Within a few years, he was a leading figure in the *Weird Tales* stable of writers, receiving its highest level of payment (the princely sum of one and a half cents per word) and consistent commendation in the letter column.

This entry into the world of professional publishing might have led to stable employment for Lovecraft, but he never produced—or sold—enough writing in the pulps to make a genuine living at it. His fiction writing was always subject to fleeting bouts of inspiration, and on occasion he would write only one or two stories a year—sometimes none. His lack of formal education barred him from clerical jobs that his general self-education would presumably have rendered him suitable for, and the regular occupation that he ultimately fashioned for himself—the freelance revision or ghostwriting of books, articles, poetry, and even textbooks—paid so poorly and was so haphazard that it scarcely brought in any significant income. Lovecraft was forced to live in increasing poverty, reliant upon revision work, sporadic sales of stories, and a dwindling family inheritance.

In 1924, Lovecraft made a brief and unsuccessful venture both at marriage (with the Russian Jewish immigrant Sonia Haft Greene) and at establishing himself in a professional capacity as a writer or an editor in New York, but the teeming hordes of America's chief megalopolis drove him to distraction, and he returned hastily to Providence in 1926, leaving his wife behind and effectively ending the marriage. This return to his hometown initiated a spurt of creativity such as he had never experienced before. Such landmark works as "The Call of Cthulhu" (1926), "The Colour out of Space" (1927), and *The Case of Charles Dexter Ward* (1927) were produced within a six-month period. The rest of Lovecraft's life can be recounted simply: he spent his time writing—some stories, some poems and essays, but mostly thousands and thousands of letters to hundreds of far-flung correspondents, some of the letters extending to forty, fifty, or even seventy pages—and, in the summertime, he would expend his small modicum of cash on antiquarian trips up and down the eastern seaboard, from as far north as Quebec to as far south as St. Augustine and Key West. Lovecraft became the hub of a complex network of literary ties, which included such notables among the pulp magazine world as Robert E. Howard, August Derleth, Donald Wandrei, Henry S. Whitehead, and E. Hoffmann Price. Young writers such as Robert Bloch, Henry Kuttner, C. L. Moore, and Fritz Leiber benefited immensely from the literary tutelage that Lovecraft bestowed upon them, almost exclusively through the venue of correspondence. And, of course, he continued to debate issues of religion, science, and politics in his letters, gradually shedding his political conservatism and becoming a moderate (non-Marxist) socialist who felt that Franklin D. Roosevelt's New Deal reforms were far tamer than they need have been to deal with the crisis of the Great Depression.

Lovecraft's unworldliness—his pose as a gentleman who wrote only for the amusement of himself and his friends—hindered him from attaining the celebrity that could have been his. His dealings with book publishers—including G. P. Putnam's Sons and Alfred A. Knopf—were in part undermined by Lovecraft's diffidence in marketing his work, and no book of his stories appeared in his lifetime. Only one book bearing his name—a misprinted small-press edition of his novella, *The Shadow over Innsmouth* (1936)—was published, a few months before his death on March 15, 1937. Yet the firm ties of friendship that Lovecraft had forged largely—and in some cases entirely—through correspondence proved to be his posthumous literary salvation. August Derleth and Donald Wandrei were so determined that Lovecraft's stories not lapse into the oblivion of the pulp magazines that they formed a publishing company, Arkham House, initially for the sole purpose of publishing Lovecraft's work in hardcover. In short order, of course, Arkham House published other writers of supernatural fiction, including many of Lovecraft's colleagues, and became the most prestigious small press in the field.

Wandrei, however, was particularly keen on embalming Lovecraft's letters in print, as he was convinced that Lovecraft was one of the great epistolarians in literary history. He spent decades editing what ultimately became the five-volume *Selected Letters* (1965–1976), a series of books that definitively established Lovecraft as a leading intellect and a forthright and highly articulate spokesman for atheism. A man who had never published an essay (much less a letter) in a major magazine or newspaper was suddenly inspiring legions of atheists, agnostics, and secularists a half century after his death. Today, articles on Lovecraft frequently appear in the freethought press,[4] yet the full extent and details of Lovecraft's atheist writing—embodied as it is chiefly in correspondence—have only recently been made available.

Lovecraft's devotion to the eighteenth century should not deceive us into thinking that he was much influenced by—or, to be frank, even much aware of—the arguments of the leading secular thinkers of that century. Although he charmingly affected eighteenth-century diction in his letters, there is little reason to assume that he was very familiar with the writings of (to quote more fully the letter cited briefly earlier) "La Mettrie, Diderot, Helvetius, Hume, and dozens of others . . . in the supremely rational 18th century."[5] Even Voltaire, the most forceful opponent of religious obscurantism and intolerance in the eighteenth century, was probably not one of Lovecraft's favorite reads, although no doubt he would have enjoyed Voltaire's unrestrained flair in attacking the "infamy" of the church.

Lovecraft's atheism was based, as was that of so many others in the early part of the twentieth century, upon a remarkable convergence of scientific advance in the course of the nineteenth century that systematically destroyed many previously unassailable pillars of religious thought. Both the "hard" sciences—astrophysics, chemistry, biology—and the social sciences, such as history and (especially) anthropology, each pursuing its own courses of research, presented naturalistic explanations for phenomena previously thought to be the work of a deity. Anthropological advances were, in a way, the capstone of this process, for it accounted with unfailing accuracy and plausibility for the origin of religious belief in the first place. Lovecraft is correct, in the *In Defence of Dagon* essays of 1921, in speaking of anthropology as the "most important of all materialistic arguments"[6] against religion. Such works as Edward Burnett Tylor's *Primitive Culture* (1871) and Sir James George Frazer's *The Golden Bough* (1890–1915) added an immense quantity of fieldwork to the highly theoretical accounts found in David Hume's *The Natural History of Religion* (1757) and other works. (Lovecraft himself may not have read Tylor's dense work, but he unquestionably read John Fiske's popularization of Tylor's theses, *Myths and Myth-Makers* [1872].)

Of course, Lovecraft was well versed in the hard sciences as well, and his absorption of Darwinian evolution—as well as of the work of Darwin's two most prominent disciples and advocates, Thomas Henry Huxley and Ernst Haeckel—laid strong foundations for his criticism of religion. His refutation of the immortality of the soul rested largely on Darwinian principles; for, as he cleverly notes, "One must ask . . . just how the evolving organism began to acquire 'spirit' after it crossed the boundary betwixt advanced ape and primitive human."[7] His understanding of chemistry and biology led him to speculate that life would one day be generated in the laboratory, thereby confounding the religious conception that life and consciousness could only have been bestowed by a god.

Astrophysics presented the greatest difficulties for Lovecraft, chiefly because his essentially layman's training prevented him from understanding some of the more abstruse theories propounded in the early twentieth century. He early announced himself as a "mechanistic materialist"—as one who believed the universe was a "mechanism" (i.e, governed by fixed deterministic laws) and is composed wholly of matter (i.e., that "soul" or "spirit" does not and cannot exist). In an early letter, he presents a keen understanding of the implications of determinism, distinguishing it from the fallacy of fatalism:

> Determinism—what you call Destiny—rules inexorably; though not exactly in the personal way you seem to fancy. We have no specific destiny against which we can fight—for the fighting would be as much a part of the destiny as the final end. The real fact is simply that every event in the cosmos is caused by the action of antecedent and circumjacent forces, so that whatever we do is unconsciously the inevitable product of Nature rather than of our own volition. If an act correspond with our wish, it is Nature that made the wish, and ensured its fulfilment. When we see an apparent chain of circumstances leading toward some striking denouement, we say it is "Fate." That is not true in the sense meant, for all of those circumstances might have been deceptive, so that a hidden and unexpected cause would have turned matters to an utterly opposite conclusion. The chain of appearances are [*sic*] as much a part of fate as the result, whichever the latter may be. . . . [8]

Mechanistic materialism was, of course, challenged on two fronts—by Einstein's theory of relativity (which saw matter and energy as interchangeable) and by Max Planck's quantum theory (which was thought by many to have destroyed causality in its ultimate sense). Lovecraft's initial response to Einstein was little short of traumatic. In 1923, when certain solar observations rendered the theory all but irrefutable, Lovecraft reacted as follows:

> My cynicism and scepticism are increasing, and from an entirely new cause—the Einstein theory. The latest eclipse observations seem to place this system among the facts which cannot be dismissed, and assumedly it removes the last hold which reality or the universe can have on the independent mind. All is chance, accident, and ephemeral illusion—a fly may be greater than Arcturus, and Durfee Hill may surpass Mount Everest—assuming them to be removed from the present planet and differently environed in the continuum of space-time. There are no values in all infinity—the least idea that there are is the supreme mockery of all. All the cosmos is a jest, and fit to be treated only as a jest, and one thing is as true as another. I believe everything and nothing—for all is chaos, always has been, and always will be.[9]

There is scarcely any reason to examine the multiple fallacies of this statement, especially Lovecraft's rash conclusions of moral nihilism. What is remarkable is that, only six years after writing the above, Lovecraft came to terms with relativity and came to see it, not as a threat to materialism (and, hence, to his ongoing attack on religious conceptions of "soul" or "spirit"), but as an ally. A 1929 letter warns a correspondent not to be tricked by the "Einstein-twisters"—of whom there were many both among scientists and litterateurs, who were using Einstein to bolster previously outmoded views regarding both God and the soul. Lovecraft concludes:

> Matter, we learn, is a definite phenomenon instituted by certain modifications of energy; *but does this circumstance make it less distinctive in itself, or permit us to imagine the presence of another kind of modified energy in places where no sign or result of energy can be discovered?* It is to laugh! The truth is, that the discovery of matter's identity with energy—and of its consequent lack of vital intrinsic difference from empty space—is *an absolute coup de grace to the primitive and irresponsible myth of "spirit." For matter, it appears, really is exactly what "spirit" was always supposed to be*. Thus it is proved *that wandering energy always has a detectable form*—that if it doesn't take the form of waves or electron-streams, *it becomes matter itself*; and that the absence of matter or any other detectable energy-form indicates *not the presence of spirit, but the absence of anything whatever.*[10]

Whether an astrophysicist would accept this conclusion or not, it is a clever resolution of the difficulty.

Quantum theory gave Lovecraft more trouble. He maintained in a 1930 letter: "What most physicists take the quantum theory, at present, to mean, is *not that any cosmic uncertainty exists* as to which of several courses a given reaction will take; but that in certain instances *no conceivable channel of information can ever tell human beings which course will be taken*, or by what exact course a certain observed result came about."[11] This conclusion is apparently false, for the "uncertainty" really does persist—on a subatomic level. But there is no question that macroatomic phenomena remain largely materialistic and deterministic, so that Lovecraft's materialism—the word, as he recognized, being used in a purely historical sense—remains largely intact.

Lovecraft was merciless in his skewering of muddle-headed thinkers who were using relativity, quantum theory, and other scientific advances to lobby for the resurrection of religious theories that had already been conclusively shown to be antiquated. He speaks of a

> new mysticism or neo-metaphysics bred of the advertised uncertainties of recent science—Einstein, the quantum theory, and the resolution of matter into force. Although these new turns of science don't really mean a thing in relation to the myth of cosmic consciousness and theology, a new brood of despairing and horrified moderns is seizing on the doubt of all positive knowledge which they imply; and is deducing therefrom that, *since nothing is true*, therefore *anything can be true* . . . whence one may invent or revive any sort of mythology that fancy or nostalgia or desperation may dictate, and defy anyone to prove that it isn't *emotionally* true—whatever that means. This sickly, decadent neo-mysticism—a protest not only against machine materialism but against pure science with its destruction of the mystery and dignity of human emotion and experience—will be the dominant creed of middle twentieth century aesthetes, as the [T. S.] Eliot and [Aldous] Huxley penumbra well prognosticate.[12]

It may be worth noting that Lovecraft did not appear to be much interested in, or very aware of, another important advance that severely called into question the inerrancy of the Bible—the school of biblical criticism called the "higher criticism," emerging in Germany in the late eighteenth century and popularized by many important books such as Ernest Renan's *Life of Jesus* (1863). The work of the "higher criticism" dethroned the conception of the Bible as a work dictated or inspired by God, especially when other commentators pointed out that it contained not a few traces of barbarism that could not possibly be suitable for contemporary society, such as the death penalty for witches (Exod. 22:18), homosexuals (Exod. 20:13), and sabbath breakers (Exod. 31:15); the ownership of wives by the husbands (Exod. 20:17); and so forth.

Lovecraft, as I say, did not pay much attention to this work, probably because he couldn't credit how any sane person could believe that the Bible was the product of some kind of stenographic dictation from God. His own (northern) Baptist tradition emphasized the Bible as a guide to moral conduct, and even here Lovecraft saw reason to be skeptical: "Half of what Buddha or Christus or Mahomet said is either simply idiocy or downright destructiveness, as applied to the western world of the twentieth century; whilst virtually *all* of the emotional-imaginative background of assumptions from which they spoke, is now proved to be sheer childish primitiveness."[13] Lovecraft was familiar with the Bible as a literary document, and he was highly taken with the style of the Anglo-Irish writer Lord Dunsany (1878–1957), who consciously used the King James Bible as the basis of his fantastic prose; but beyond that, Lovecraft exhibited little interest in the Bible as a religious text.

Lovecraft, in the final analysis, appealed to *probability* as the ultimate basis for his atheism; and, interestingly enough, he used probability as a means of distinguishing himself from agnosticism. In his mind, the probability of the truth of theism was so vanishingly small that he felt it irresponsible to refer to himself as a mere agnostic:

> All I say is that I think it is *damned unlikely* that anything like a central cosmic will, a spirit world, or an eternal survival of personality exist. They are the most preposterous and unjustified of all the guesses which can be made about the universe, and I am not enough of a hair-splitter to pretend that I don't regard them as arrant and negligible moonshine. In theory I am an *agnostic*, but pending the appearance of radical evidence I must be classed, practically and provisionally, as an atheist.[14]

One of the most provocative questions pertaining to Lovecraft and religion is the seeming paradox of a vigorously atheistic writer producing stories filled to the brim with "gods" and their worshippers. His so-called Cthulhu Mythos (a term invented by his disciple, August Derleth), a mythology that dominates the stories of the last decade of his life, seems to envision a universe populated by all-powerful gods who can crush the human race—or at least certain venturesome individuals—at will. How can this be squared with the materialistic atheist of his letters? The matter is considerably complex, but some hints can be provided here.

Some commentators have believed that Lovecraft's "evil" gods—Cthulhu, Yog-Sothoth, Nyarlathotep, Azathoth, Shub-Niggurath, and so forth—are themselves representative of the evils of religious belief, since they embody the viciousness that many of the actual gods invented by human beings, not excluding the Christian god, appear to display. I am not entirely convinced of this notion, largely because Lovecraft's "gods" are not "evil" in any meaningful sense. They are inimical to human beings only because they render our position on this earth highly tenuous and fragile, but they are as much "beyond good and evil" (as Lovecraft actually states in "The Call of Cthulhu") as we ourselves would be from an ant's perspective. Lovecraft's "gods" are symbols for the inscrutability of the cosmos: scientific materialist that he was, he knew that the universe held an infinite reservoir of mystery, and even scientific advance could do little to minimize it; as he wrote in a late letter, "the more we learn about the cosmos, the more bewildering does it appear."[15]

And, in the end, Lovecraft's gods aren't really gods at all. It is true that, in "The Call of Cthulhu" and "The Dunwich Horror," various cults are stated as worshipping Cthulhu and Yog-Sothoth; indeed, in the former story one worshipper gives a history of the eon-old cult:

> Then . . . those first men formed the cult around small idols which the Great Ones shewed them; idols brought in dim aeras [*sic*] from dark stars. That cult would never die till the stars came right again, and the secret priests would take great Cthulhu from His tomb to revive His subjects and resume His rule of earth. The time would be easy to know, for then mankind would have become as the Great Old Ones; free and wild and beyond good and evil, with laws and morals thrown aside and all men shouting and killing and revelling in joy. Then the liberated Old Ones would teach them new ways to shout and kill and revel and enjoy themselves, and all the earth would flame with a holocaust of ecstasy and freedom.[16]

The overriding question is: Are we to take this statement at face value? It is true that a virtual library of "forbidden" books invented by Lovecraft and his colleagues—ranging from the *Necronomicon* of the mad Arab, Abdul Alhazred, to the *Unaussprechlichen Kulten* of von Juntz—appear to speak in like terms of the old gods, but what one gradually discovers, as Lovecraft's work progresses, is that these cultists are as pathetically deluded about the nature of the "gods" they worship as most human beings are in their devotion to Yahweh or Allah. The critical passage comes in the short novel *At the Mountains of Madness* (1931), where an immense stone city evidently built by extraterrestrials, coming from the depths of space, is discovered by explorers penetrating a previously unknown corner of Antarctica:

> The things rearing and dwelling in this frightful masonry in the age of dinosaurs were not indeed dinosaurs, but far worse. Mere dinosaurs were new and almost brainless objects—but the builders of the city

> were wise and old, and had left certain traces in rocks even then laid down well-nigh a thousand million years . . . rocks laid down before the true life of earth had advanced beyond plastic groups of cells . . . rocks laid down before the true life of earth had existed at all. They were the makers and enslavers of that life, and above all doubt the originals of the fiendish elder myths which things like the Pnakotic Manuscripts and the *Necronomicon* affrightedly hint about.[17]

So now the stories about the "gods" as found in the *Necronomicon* have been reduced to "myths"! The gods are merely space aliens. This appears to have been Lovecraft's conception right from the beginning, for even in "The Call of Cthulhu," which launched the Cthulhu Mythos, Cthulhu and his "spawn" are merely extraterrestrials who come from some infinitely far galaxy to the earth, where they are unwittingly trapped in the underwater city of R'lyeh beneath the Pacific. Cthulhu and R'lyeh rise in that story, but not because the "stars are right" or because of any actions taken by his human cult, but merely by accident—an earthquake—and they sink back under the waves by a similar accident.

Lovecraft's signature element in his fiction is its "cosmic" quality—its suggestion of the infinite gulfs of space and time, and the resulting inconsequence of humanity within these gulfs. It is an element that Lovecraft may well have conveyed more powerfully and poignantly than any writer in literature, and it constitutes one of the chief justifications of the canonical status he has attained today. But it should be made clear that that cosmic vision strictly depends on Lovecraft's metaphysical—and, specifically, his atheistic—viewpoint. For in Lovecraft's universe, humanity is indeed alone in the cosmos; whereas the object of most religions is, in John Milton's words, to "justify the ways of God to men," Lovecraft's "anti-mythology," as it has been appropriately called,[18] establishes that human beings can appeal to no higher power when faced with threats to our fleeting sinecure on this earth. A moment ago, in cosmic terms, we did not exist; a moment hence, the universe shall have forgotten that we did exist.

It is, in truth, a bleak vision, but the prose-poetry with which Lovecraft invests it in his stories bestows upon it a strange and exhilarating beauty. In scarcely less powerful fashion, the liveliness, vigor, and at times satirical flair of his discussions of religion and atheism in his letters and essays exhibit a mind wrestling with the central questions of existence and hammering out a cogent, forward-looking philosophy shorn of outmoded religious belief and courageously prepared to face a universe in which humanity is indeed alone and friendless. Comforting as Lovecraft knew the myths of religion may be, he was determined to contemplate the universe with the blinkers removed from his eyes and mind.

Chapter 9

BERTRAND RUSSELL: THE SAGE OF CAMBRIDGE

Bertrand Russell (1872–1970) is a philosophical schizophrenic. By this I mean that, one the one hand, he wrote some of the most abstruse philosophical treatises—chiefly concerned with logic, the philosophy of mathematics, and the analysis of language—largely for the consumption of professional philosophers, and, on the other hand, he wrote a wide array of popular works on ethics, social and political problems, and religion intended for the general public. The attempt to educate and inform the philosophically challenged is admirable, but many of these popular works—his writings on religion not excluded—create the impression of superficiality and, worse, of talking down to his audience. Although they are what brought Russell his greatest celebrity (and notoriety) in the world at large, they are held in low esteem by philosophers, and their limitations in thought and expression are palpable. Yet they contain occasional penetrating insights that allow them to retain their value to the present day. But Russell apparently never learned the lesson that his colleague, the Spanish-American philosopher George Santayana, attempted to teach him as early as 1917: "People are not intelligent. It is very unreasonable to expect them to be so, and that is a fate my philosophy reconciled me to long ago. How else could I have lived for forty years in America?"[1]

Of Russell's extraordinarily long life there is little need to dwell, interesting and even fascinating as it is. His longevity produced some striking juxtapositions, such as the fact that, as a pacifist, he protested both World War I and the Vietnam War. His birth into one of the most storied upper-class families in England: his grandfather, John Russell, 1st Earl Russell, was prime minister on two separate occasions, while his father, John Russell, Viscount Amberley, was a liberal politician and forthright atheist (he was the author of *Analysis of Religious Belief*, 1877) who unquestionably influenced his son's antireligious inclinations. Russell studied mathematics at Trinity College, Cambridge, and was later appointed lecturer there. Although he taught there for only six years (1910–1916), whereupon he was dismissed for protesting the war, he helped make Cambridge a leading institution in science and philosophy.

Yet Russell admitted to an "intense interest in religion and philosophy" (*A* 1:49) in adolescence. He was taken on alternate Sundays to an Episcopalian and a Presbyterian church, and up to the age of fifteen he professed belief in Unitarianism. But then, as he tells it:

> At this age I began a systematic investigation of the supposed rational arguments in favour of fundamental Christian beliefs. I spent endless hours in meditation upon this subject; I could not speak to anybody about it for fear of giving pain. I suffered acutely both from the gradual loss of faith and from the need of silence. I thought that if I ceased to believe in God, freedom and immortality, I should be very unhappy. I found, however, that the reasons given in favour of these dogmas were very unconvincing. . . . About two years later, I became convinced that there is no life after death, but I still believed in God, because the "First Cause" argument appeared to be irrefutable. . . . Throughout the long period of religious doubt, I had been rendered very unhappy by the gradual loss of belief, but when the process was completed, I found to my surprise that I was quite glad to be done with the whole subject. (*A* 1:49–50)

The matter of the "First Cause" argument is worth pursuing here. Both in his autobiography and in the lengthy essay "Why I Am Not a Christian" (1927), he dispenses with this argument with dispatch. The thinking is that, if every event in the universe were traced back to its antecedent cause, we would come back to a First Cause that cannot itself be found to have an antecedent cause, and this must be God. Russell follows John Stuart Mill, who wrote in his autobiography: "My father taught me that the question 'Who made me?' cannot be answered, since it immediately suggests the further question, 'Who made God?'"[2] This is simply to deny that there is a First Cause, but it is not clear that it is the best way of demolishing the argument. As I have written elsewhere:

"There is no reason to postulate a *single* First Cause; given the multiplicity of phenomena throughout the universe, there is no logical reason for assuming that there could not be two, three, or many First Causes. Indeed, it is logically possible that every event in the universe could have its own First Cause."[3] Yet Russell in his autobiography testifies that Mill's argument led him to "become an atheist" (*A* 1:50).

The whole issue of whether Russell was, in fact, an atheist or merely an agnostic merits some discussion. In "What I Believe" (1925), he states bluntly that "God and immortality, the central dogmas of the Christian religion, find no support in science" (*Y* 50). He continues, however, "It cannot be said that either doctrine is essential to religion, since neither is found in Buddhism," and he also notes that "I do not pretend to be able to prove that there is no God" (*Y* 50). The late essay "Am I an Atheist or an Agnostic?" (1949), a lecture given to the Rationalist Press Association, would appear to settle the matter:

> As a philosopher, if I were speaking to a purely philosophic audience I should say that I ought to describe myself as an Agnostic, because I do not think that there is a conclusive argument by which one can prove that there is not a God. On the other hand, if I am to convey the right impression to the ordinary man on the street I think that I ought to say that I am an Atheist, because, when I say that I cannot prove that there is not a God, I ought to add equally that I cannot prove that there are not the Homeric gods. . . . I cannot prove that either the Christian God or the Homeric gods do not exist, but I do not think that their existence is an alternative that is sufficiently probable to be worth serious consideration.[4]

In other words, the likelihood of a god's existence (whichever god one chooses) is so microscopically small that, as a practical matter, atheism is the soundest position as a working hypothesis. As he declared in another late essay, "What Is an Agnostic?" (1953), "An agnostic may think the Christian God as improbable as the Olympians; in that case, he is, for practical purposes, at one with the atheists" (*CP* 11:550).

In "Why I Am Not a Christian" Russell easily destroys other arguments purporting to prove—or even to make vaguely plausible—the existence of God. The natural-law argument states that God has dictated the natural laws that rule the universe, but Russell counters that these "laws" are mere descriptions of "how things do in fact behave" (*Y* 8), and there is no reason to think that they require a concrete lawgiver. This argument leads inevitably to the argument from design, which, as I have already stated, held sway until Darwin: "everything in the world is made just so that we can manage to live in the world, and if the world was ever so little different, we could not manage to live in it" (*Y* 9). Russell advances the obvious counterargument: "Since the time of Darwin we understand much better why living creatures are adapted to their environment. It is not that their environment was made suitable to them but that they grew to be suitable to it, and that is the basis of adaptation. There is no evidence of design about it" (*Y* 10). Russell continues that it is incredible that people ever swallowed the argument from design: If the world is uniquely adapted to our benefit, why is it so filled with flaws and inconveniences? Is this the best that omnipotence could do? "Do you think that, if you were granted omnipotence and omniscience and millions of years in which to perfect your world, you could produce nothing better than the Ku Klux Klan or the Fascists?" (*Y* 10).

Russell also notes an argument that has been resurrected in our own time: "We are told that evolution is so extraordinary and produced such marvelous results that it cannot have been the result of accident. There must have been a purpose behind it. And there must have been a God guiding the whole plan in order to get such marvelous results" ("The Existence and Nature of God" [1939], *CP* 10:258–59). This is, of course, a variant of what is now called the intelligent design argument, and Russell links it to such theologically inclined scientific writers as H. G. Wells. Russell adds dryly, "I find myself in difficulties in dealing with those arguments because I am so little impressed by the results" (*CP* 10.259). Human beings aren't quite so marvelous as they think they are. In any case:

> It is quite clear, I think, that life could have developed simply by the steady operation of natural laws. Living matter is a chemical product. It hasn't come together very often. If it comes into being at all it is likely to multiply and increase. Once you get living matter you can quite easily see how on entirely mechanical principles it can develop into people like ourselves. Certainly the origin of living matter doesn't seem quite beyond the happenings of purely mechanical causes. (*CP* 10:259)

Russell then addresses the moral argument for God: If there were no God, the injustices we all face on earth could never be redressed in a future life. We have already seen that Russell early rejected the possibility of an afterlife. Indeed, in "Why I Am Not a Christian," he makes no particular attempt to argue against immortality; instead, he simply declares that the mere existence of injustice in the world "affords a moral argument against deity and not in favor of one" (*Y* 13). Elsewhere he does address the question of life after death, specifically in relation to the existence of the soul. As a result of his early rejection of Hegelian idealism, he dismisses the radical disjunction between soul and body: advances in both physics and psychology demonstrate that both body and soul are considerably less "real" than they were once thought to be. The soul or mind, if it is anything at all, is not a substance but the sum total of our habits and memories:

> If, therefore, we are to believe that a person survives death, we must believe that the memories and habits which constitute the person will continue to be exhibited in a new set of occurrences.
>
> No one can prove that this will not happen. But it is easy to see that it is very unlikely. Our memories and habits are bound up with the structure of the brain, in much the same way in which a river is connected with the riverbed. . . . But the brain, as a structure, is dissolved at death, and memory therefore may be expected to be also dissolved. ("Do We Survive Death?" [1936], *Y* 89)

Another moral argument is that we need a God to ensure upright behavior. This argument, still widely adopted today, is given short shrift by Russell: "The first and greatest objection to this argument is that, at its best, it cannot prove that there is a God but only that politicians and educators ought to try to make people think there is one" ("Is There a God?" [1952], *CP* 11:545). Russell points out that this political indoctrination can lead to very dangerous results:

> If a theology is thought necessary to virtue and if candid inquirers see no reason to think the theology true, the authorities will set to work to discourage candid inquiry. In former centuries they did so by burning the inquirers at the stake. In Russia they still have methods which are little better; but in Western countries the authorities have perfected

> somewhat milder forms of persuasion. Of these, schools are perhaps the most important: the young must be preserved from hearing the arguments in favor of the opinions which the authorities dislike, and those who nevertheless persist in showing an inquiring disposition will incur social displeasure and, if possible, be made to feel morally reprehensible. In this way, any system of morals which has a theological basis becomes one of the tools by which the holders of power preserve their authority and impair the intellectual vigor of the young. ("Can Religion Cure Our Troubles?" [1954], *Y* 196)

This was written a decade and a half after Russell was prevented from teaching at the City College of New York, so his words are more than usually heartfelt. In any case, he goes on to say, it is plain that morals do not actually derive from religion—they are so obviously a product of "social utility" (*Y* 194) that no divine source for them is necessary.

A variant of the moral argument is that we now need religion (specifically the Christian religion) as a bulwark against the godless systems of fascism and communism. Russell addresses this argument as propounded by Herbert Butterfield in *Christianity and History* (1950). He notes pointedly, "Nowhere in Professor Butterfield's work is there the faintest attempt to prove the truth of any Christian dogma. There is only the pragmatic argument that belief in Christian dogma is useful" (*Y* 200). Christianity has, in any event, not advocated a morality that is superior to that of other religions or political systems; indeed, it "has been distinguished from other religions by its greater readiness for persecution" (*Y* 202). Russell elsewhere notes that Nazism and Soviet communism are themselves dogmatic religions with an impressive machinery for persecution. Writing in 1935, he observed: "The persecution of intellectuals in Germany and Russia has surpassed, in severity, anything perpetrated by the Churches during the last two hundred and fifty years."[5] This is Russell's riposte to the argument, still widely heard today, that many of the evils of the twentieth century can be attributed to "atheistic" political systems: these systems were themselves of a religious mind-set, and it is that mind-set of inflexible dogmatism that must be combated—chiefly by the freest possible inquiry into all intellectual, social, and political issues, regardless of their results or implications.

Russell has a great deal to say about what might be called the psychological argument in support of the existence of God—that a belief in God is helpful to one's psychological well-being, since in the absence of such a belief, people might be thrown into irremediable despair. Russell, in spite of the difficulties he admitted in shedding his religious belief in youth, has little patience for this line of reasoning: "So far as this is true, it is a coward's argument. Nobody but a coward would consciously choose to live in a fool's paradise" (*CP* 11:546). He goes on to say that the argument is probably false on its face, since the happiness of most people depends on many factors, religious belief rarely being one of the most significant. Indeed, it is quite apparent that those who have no religious belief are not markedly more unhappy than those who do.

Russell's most compressed discussion of religion occurs in the treatise *Religion and Science* (1935), but this work is marred by what I have earlier stated is Russell's regrettable tendency to talk down to his audience. In any case, large parts of the monograph appear heavily dependent on earlier works on the subject, specifically Andrew D. White's *History of the Warfare of Science with Theology in Christendom* (1896), which is frequently cited in Russell's notes. He also found much fodder in an even older work, W. E. H. Lecky's landmark study, *History of the Rise and Influence of the Spirit of Rationalism in Europe* (1865), a still valuable work that dissects the gradually decreasing influence of religion in European law and government.

Russell does speak at the very outset that there has been a "prolonged conflict" (*R* 7) between religion and science—in contrast to certain recent critics who have sophistically maintained that the conflict has been exaggerated or distorted, an assertion that virtually every day's newspaper is sufficient to refute—but makes a mild concession to religion in noting: "In so far as religion consists in a way of feeling, rather than in a set of beliefs, science cannot touch it" (*R* 17). It is not entirely clear on what basis Russell comes to this conclusion, for surely that "way of feeling" is, however tenuously and remotely, based on dogmas and doctrines whose truth-value can be tested—and, by Russell's own evidence, are usually found wanting. Probably Russell is acknowledging the social good that religions have sporadically accomplished, as when he notes the "desire to diminish the sufferings of mankind, and the hope that the future will realize the best possibilities of our species" (*R* 17), an outlook that Russell explicitly declares is shared by both the religious and the nonreligious.

Russell's actual history of the conflict of religion and science over the centuries in the West is unremarkable and touches on the usual topics: the revolutionary work of Copernicus, which pried humanity loose from the center of the universe and, by implication, from any central concern of a deity; the familiar story of Galileo and the Inquisition's condemnation of the heliocentric theory, a position not reversed by the Catholic church until the nineteenth century; and the theory of evolution ("Darwinism was as severe a blow to theology as Copernicanism" [*R* 75]). Lecky is cited in regard to the witchcraft persecutions of the later Middle Ages and Renaissance, and there is a lengthy discussion of the challenges that medicine had to overcome in regard to the treatment of the insane, who religious authorities believed were possessed by the devil.

Where Russell's treatise gains its value as an original contribution to scholarship is in its latter portions, where he addresses certain issues being discussed by scientists, philosophers, and theologians of his own day. Russell begins by wondering if the conflict of religion and science is at an end—a point raised by a book, *Science and Religion: A Symposium* (1931), consisting of twelve talks broadcast by the BBC in 1930. Since "outspoken opponents of religion were, of course [!], not included" (*R* 173), the discussions may not be entirely representative of the full spectrum of opinion on the subject; and it does appear that even the scientists chosen for participation were of a somewhat mystical or theological inclination, such as J. Arthur Thomson and J. B. S. Haldane. Thomson had declared: "Science as science never asks the question *Why?* That is to say, it never inquires into the meaning, or significance, or purpose of this manifold Being, Becoming, and Having Been. . . . Thus science does not pretend to be a bedrock of truth" (*R* 175). This is a highly dubious formulation, but it leads Russell to ask: "Ought we to admit that there is available, in support of religion, a source of knowledge which lies outside science and may properly be described as 'revelation'?" (*R* 177).

Russell uses this query to launch into a discussion of mysticism. He does so probably because—although he has not explicitly stated it—the "revelations" founded in the various scriptures of the world have already been shown to be either demonstrably false or extremely unlikely, so that the only kind of "revelation" that might conceivably afford some alternate avenue to truth is that of individual mystics. Russell largely repeats the arguments he had made in his earlier treatise, *Mysticism and Logic*

(1918), pointing to the long history of mystical thought or philosophy, reaching at least as far back as the pre-Socratic thinker Parmenides and continuing on through Plato, Hegel (whose thought, let us recall, Russell himself had adopted in his earliest philosophical thinking), F. H. Bradley, and others—perhaps even including (although he is not cited by name) Alfred North Whitehead, Russell's early collaborator on the landmark treatise *Principia Mathematica* (1903).

Russell is surprisingly charitable toward mysticism, declaring that the general uniformity of many mystics' conceptions of the universe—namely, the belief that the universe is a unity and that individuality is unreal, that evil is illusory, and that time is unreal—is a point in its favor; he continues that many mystics' specific visions or conclusions are manifestly influenced by their prior religious upbringing. But in the end, Russell is aware that "mysticism expresses an emotion, not a fact; it does not assert anything, and therefore can be neither confirmed nor contradicted by science" (*R* 187). He concludes that there is no reason to believe that the mystics' conclusions are true: "I cannot admit any method of arriving at truth except that of science, but in the realm of the emotions I do not deny the value of the experiences which have given rise to religion" (*R* 189).

Where science *can* enter into the discussion is in the notion that there is some kind of cosmic purpose to the universe—a notion to which even certain "modern men of science" (*R* 190) cling. He goes back to J. Arthur Thomson's declaration that science cannot answer the *why* of phenomena. If this is so, what is the upshot? "Religion, he [Thomson] thought, can answer it. Why were stars formed? Why did the sun give birth to planets? Why did the earth cool, and at last give rise to life? Because, in the end, something admirable was going to result—I am not quite sure what, but I believe it was scientific theologians and religiously-minded scientists" (*R* 190).

This is a rare moment of mild sarcasm in Russell's treatise, but his humor is justified. The three different types of cosmic purpose that Russell identifies are the theistic, the pantheistic, and the "emergent." The theistic version is easily dismissed, because it leads to difficulties that even the religious are uncomfortable with. If an omnipotent and omniscient God designed the world to lead inextricably to the glories of the human race, why did he not go at once to humanity, rather than dithering for hundreds of millions of years with dinosaurs and other extinct species? Moreover, if the result of this cosmic purpose is necessarily morally good, why is there so much evil in the world? "What useful purpose is served by rabies and hydrophobia?" (*R* 194). Russell finds the pantheistic and emergent varieties of cosmic purpose more complex, but in the end he dismisses them also—in particular by the trump card of declaring the inevitable extinction of the human species in the coming millennia, which makes one wonder what possible basis there can be in assuming a cosmic purpose that sees humanity as its ultimate beneficiary: "The Copernican revolution will not have done its work until it has taught men more modesty than is to be found among those who think Man sufficient evidence of Cosmic Purpose" (*R* 222).

In a long chapter on religion and ethics, Russell emphatically denies that religion is necessary for moral behavior. When religionists assert that "conscience" is some kind of innate moral standard inculcated by God, Russell little difficulty in appealing to history and psychology to refute the idea: "Conscience says different things to different people; . . . [and] the study of the unconscious has given us an understanding of the mundane causes of conscientious feelings" (*R* 225). The promptings of our conscience are so obviously the product of upbringing and social conditioning that no other source need be sought for them.

Then there is the interrelation of science, ethics, and religion. The devout declare that the question of "values" is outside the domain of science. This argument continues to be aired today, even by scientists such as Stephen Jay Gould, who want to believe that science and religion cover different areas of knowledge (Gould calls them "magisteria") and that religion has a place in the world by its control of the magisterium of ethical knowledge. Russell adopts a clever ploy in refuting this conception. He begins by declaring that the devout are quite correct in one aspect of their assertion: it is true that values are outside the domain of science—but "I draw the further conclusion, which they [the devout] do not draw, that questions as to 'values' lie wholly outside the domain of knowledge" (*R* 230). To speak of "ethical knowledge" is an oxymoron, because "when we assert that this or that has 'value,' we are giving expression to our own emotions, not to a fact which would still be true if our personal feelings were different" (*R* 231).

Russell here is adopting the attitude toward moral (and metaphysical) inquiry formulated by the logical positivists, of whom he was a significant proponent, along with Rudolf Carnap and A. J. Ayer. Indeed, Ayer has succinctly outlined the essentials of the theory in *Language, Truth and Logic* (1936):

> We begin by admitting that the fundamental ethical concepts are unanalysable, inasmuch as there is no criterion by which one can test the validity of the judgements in which they occur. . . . We say that the reason why they are unanalysable is that they are mere pseudo-concepts. The presence of an ethical symbol in a proposition adds nothing to its factual content. Thus if I say to someone, "You acted wrongly in stealing that money," I am not stating anything more than if I had simply said, "You stole that money." In adding that this action is wrong I am not making any further statement about it. I am simply evincing my moral disapproval of it. It is as if I had said, "You stole that money," in a peculiar tone of horror, or written it with the addition of some special exclamation marks. The tone, or the exclamation marks, adds nothing to the literal meaning of the sentence. It merely serves to show that the expression of it is attended by certain feelings in the speaker.[6]

In other words, morals are not objective. The sentences "The sun is hot" and "Stealing is wrong" are grammatically identical, but ontologically and epistemologically they are widely different: the first makes an empirical assertion about the universe that can be verified or refuted; the other is merely the expression of an emotion—namely, the emotion of disapproval of the phenomenon called "stealing."

Russell, in *Religion and Science*, unequivocally adopts the principle of "the 'subjectivity' of values" (*R* 237), with the obvious corollary that "if two men differ about values, there is not a disagreement as to any kind of truth, but a difference in taste" (*R* 237–38). Another consequence of the principle is that "there can be no such thing as 'sin' in any absolute sense; what one man calls 'sin' another may call 'virtue,' and though they may dislike each other on account of this difference, neither can convict the other of intellectual error" (*R* 238–39). Russell could have gone on to say that even if there were complete uniformity among human beings as to morals, or to a given moral code or axiom, that itself would not constitute "knowledge" in any meaningful sense; it would only suggest a uniformity of preference. It is as if everyone happened to prefer chocolate ice cream over vanilla ice cream: this would not suggest that there is anything (factually) "wrong" about vanilla ice cream.

For all the relative politeness of Russell's general treatment of religion—a product of his evident desire not to appear a radical either in religion or politics, in spite of his advocacy of pacifism, moderate (democratic) socialism, and other doctrines that not only caused a certain controversy in their day but even led to imprisonment and dismissal from prestigious institutions of learning[7]—his disdain for the evils that religion has perpetrated, both in the intellectual and in the sociopolitical realm, was unremitting and expressed in numerous contexts. Consider the following from *Religion and Science*: "The harm that theology has done is not to *create* cruel impulses, but to give them the sanction of what professes to be a lofty ethic, and to confer an apparently sacred character upon practices which have come down from more ignorant and barbarous ages" (*R* 106).

Consider too "Why I Am Not a Christian":

> You find as you look around the world that every single bit of progress in humane feeling, every improvement of the criminal law, every step toward the diminution of war, every step toward better treatment of the colored races, or every mitigation of slavery, every moral progress that there has been in the world, has been consistently opposed by the organized churches of the world. I say quite deliberately that the Christian religion, as organized in its churches, has been and still is the principal enemy of moral progress in the world. (*Y* 20–21)

Given these sentiments, the only surprise is that Russell did not speak out more forthrightly than he did on the issue of religion. But the documents he has left behind are an eloquent enough testimonial to the principled atheism by which he led his personal and intellectual life.

Chapter 10

Madalyn Murray O'Hair: Prayer out of the Schools

Madalyn Murray O'Hair (1919–1995) has always been a bit of an embarrassment to the atheist community. Many are grateful to her for waging a years-long campaign that resulted, in 1963, in the Supreme Court's banning of officially sanctioned prayers (almost always of a Christian sort) from the public schools of the United States, but her subsequent career as an atheist spokesman—in which she boasted that she was both the "most hated woman in America" (probably true) and the leading atheist in the nation (a dubious assertion), conjoined with her brash, profanity-laden public speeches, her apparent intolerance to dissent in the organizations she founded, and the perception that she was an intellectual lightweight who did not fully understand the depth and complexity of the issues she treated—caused many to believe that she may have hurt the atheist cause more than she helped it. I think, however, that an impartial assessment will conclude that on balance her life and work were substantially more beneficial than otherwise to the cause of both religious freedom and the propagation of atheism, setting the stage for the vigorous advocacy and popularization of atheism in the work of Richard Dawkins, Sam Harris, and Christopher Hitchens.

O'Hair, born Madalyn Evalyn Mays in a suburb of Pittsburgh, led a life that was almost never devoid of interest and even turmoil. She herself describes her childhood and upbringing in idyllic terms:

> I don't believe there could have been a happier or more secure childhood than mine. My mother was beautiful. My grandmother could sew more charming flouncy dresses (with matching bloomers) for me than any little girl could dream about. My father was a knight in shiny [*sic*] armor. We lived in a house, that—incongruously in Pittsburgh, Penn-

> sylvania—was graced with catalpa punji trees. The chauffeur of our Rolls Royce was black and shiny, and he rode me on his shoulders, and seriously purchased my mud pies at my "store" for real money.[1]

This description conveys something of the economic prosperity the family enjoyed during her childhood, but much of that prosperity was lost during the stock market crash of 1929 and the subsequent national depression. Madalyn's father was a Presbyterian and her mother a Lutheran, and she herself attended a Presbyterian church and Sunday school in her youth. She claimed to have read the Bible from cover to cover in a single weekend when she was twelve or thirteen and found herself "appalled" by its contents: "I came away stunned with the hatred, the brutality, the sadomasochism, the cruelty, the killing, the ugliness."[2] This remark suggests a moral, as opposed to a metaphysical, objection to Christian doctrine—that is, a revulsion against the god who, both in the Old and the New Testaments, is depicted as vengeful, irrationally hostile, and intolerant, but it will quickly become evident that Madalyn's objections also extended to the Bible's conflicts with known laws of science.

Madalyn attended the University of Toledo and the University of Pittsburgh, but did not graduate from either institution. Instead, on October 9, 1941, at the age of twenty-two, she eloped with a steelworker, John Henry Roths. Two months later, the United States entered World War II, and Madalyn signed up for the Women's Auxiliary Army Corps (WAACs); in 1943 she was made a lieutenant, working in the cryptography division in North Africa, France, and Italy. She fell in love with another soldier, William Murray Jr., and had a child, William J. Murray III, out of wedlock in 1946. She divorced Roths but never married Murray, for the very good reason that he was a Catholic who was still married and refused to divorce his wife. Madalyn subsequently received a BA from Ashland College in Ohio and, in 1952, a JD from South Texas School of Law; she never took a bar exam, so she never practiced law.

In 1952 Madalyn's family made its fateful move to Baltimore, and in 1954 she gave birth to her second son, Jon Garth Murray—who, in fact, was not the son of William Murray Jr., but of a New York City man, Michael Fiorillo. Madalyn's luck with men was not stellar, but in 1965 she married Richard O'Hair, a man she had met in Mexico. They remained married until his death in 1978. The marriage was turbulent, and

Madalyn contemplated divorcing him, but she decided to remain with him once she learned he had been diagnosed with cancer. (From this point on, I shall refer to Madalyn as O'Hair, even though she did not adopt this name until 1965.)

O'Hair's own discussion of the events that led up to the Supreme Court case of 1963, *An Atheist Epic* (1970; revised 1989), makes for compelling reading, for all its irrelevancies, digressions, stylistic and syntactic clumsinesses (including misspelled words), and a modicum of malice toward her opponents that, in the end, might well have been justified by the torments she suffered at their hands. For reasons that will become apparent, her own account—in spite of its implausible reproduction of the exact words that she, her son, and others uttered over the course of years—appears to be substantially more reliable than a competing account by the other chief protagonist in the case, her son William (Bill) J. Murray III, who years later converted to fundamentalist Christianity and wrote his own treatise, *My Life without God* (1982).

O'Hair declares that Bill had been going to Park School, a private school (largely attended by Jewish students), but when this school decided to move from Baltimore to a distant suburb, transportation problems were created for Bill and his mother. Buses were so infrequent that Bill had to leave home at 6 AM. After several months during which Bill spent five or six hours riding buses to and from the school, O'Hair decided that she might as well enroll Bill in the nearby public school, Woodbourne Junior High School. Although O'Hair reports that she had difficulty even getting Bill enrolled in the school (the principal—whom O'Hair never names but only refers to by various opprobrious nicknames, such as "Buxom Bitch," but who was one Dorothy Duval—claimed that Bill needed a psychological exam before being allowed to sit in classes), this proved to be the least of their difficulties.

The very day that she and Bill came to the school to enroll him, they heard a prayer being spoken by the students. O'Hair reports her son's comment as follows: "He said, 'Our Lord and Saviour, Jesus Christ, Son of Mary, sired by the Holy Ghost, descendant of David, the bearer of the Holy Word, Redeemer of Life, and the Gate by which we enter Heaven and are saved, in whose Grace we walk, is praised every morning in the public schools'" (*AE* 5). This could not have been the actual prayer uttered by the students, for O'Hair continues that it was the Lord's

Prayer (*AE* 8). In any event, O'Hair declares that at this point (the year is 1960) she was already an atheist (she always capitalized the word—and never capitalized "god"—for reasons that she never seems to have clarified) and that Bill probably was one, although she deliberately refrained from indoctrinating him in either atheism or any other system of thought, leaving it up to him to decide for himself when he was ready to do so. So the issue now was: what to do about this obvious violation of Bill's constitutionally protected freedom of religion?

By this time, thirty-seven states and the District of Columbia had instituted some kind of compulsory prayers at the beginning of a school day. To be sure, they may have lasted no more than two or three minutes, but in most instances students were not allowed to forego the prayers. Maryland, founded by Roman Catholics, had had a mandatory school prayer law on its books since 1839. The first thing that O'Hair did was to ask the school administration to allow Bill to be excused from the prayers; they refused, and (by O'Hair's testimony) did so without apology: "He shall attend the services. We have made our decision now. He can refuse to say the prayer, but he will be required to move his lips as if he were saying it" (*AE* 29). O'Hair claims that, at this point, it was Bill who decided that he would "go on strike" (*AE* 31) and simply not go to school, even though this act would obviously make Bill a truant and even threaten O'Hair herself with civil and perhaps criminal penalties. Shortly thereafter, O'Hair got in touch with a reporter from the *Baltimore Sun*, who wrote up the matter in the paper; it quickly gained nationwide, and even worldwide, attention. As O'Hair pungently put it: "It was the beginning of franticville" (*AE* 46).

At the moment, however, in the opinion of the school board, Bill was merely a truant; he had not officially challenged the school's prayer policy. What O'Hair and Bill now planned to do was to have Bill show up for the morning prayer and interrupt the proceedings with the following statement: "I refuse to participate in this opening exercise of Bible reading and prayer recitation because it violates my freedom of conscience and the Constitution of the United States" (*AE* 53). But the crafty school board resorted to ingenious methods to prevent such a confrontation, specifically by locking Bill out of his homeroom class. The standoff lasted several months, during which time Bill was subjected to increasing doses of abuse, vilification, and even violence by his schoolmates, who naturally equated him with being an atheistic communist. (Matters were not helped by the fact that he had written a sober, objective account of the USSR for a class paper and was chastised by his teacher for not condemning the Soviet communist regime.) Bill in fact did manage to recite his objection to prayer, whereupon he was at once denounced as a "Commie Rat," a "Dirty Communist," an "Atheist Nazi" (?), and a "Traitor" (*AE* 96).

By November 1960, the attorney general for Maryland, C. Verdinand Sybert, ruled on the matter, stating: "Objections to exercises (of Bible reading and prayer recitation) were not a valid reason or reasons for non-compliance with the public school law"; moreover, the children of Maryland "had the right and the duty to bow their heads in humility before the Supreme Being" (quoted in *AE* 102). Bill could either stay in his class during the prayers or remain outside in the hallway (even though this was usually a form of punishment for misbehavior). Bill was similarly punished for the brutalization he had received at the hands of the students: he could eat in the cafeteria, but only by himself in a specially designated area; other restrictions were placed upon his behavior. Most incredible of all, Bill was forced to make up all the work he had missed during his "truancy"—but the amount assigned was so immense, and so advanced, that it could not possibly have been what was actually assigned to his classmates during the period in question. The whole matter was, as O'Hair bitterly notes, "almost total victory for the school board" (*AE* 102).

It was at this point, on December 8, 1960, that O'Hair, with the help of a local attorney, Leonard Kerpelman, filed suit in the Superior Court of Baltimore to prevent the school board from carrying out mandatory school prayer and Bible reading. It was this case—*Murray v. Curlett* (John N. Curlett being the president of the school board)—that ultimately went to the Supreme Court. At the very outset, however, the school board made a gaffe (as shall become evident later) in that it did not even attempt to dispute the case; instead, it filed a demurrer. As O'Hair explains:

> A demurrer is, legally, an objection to the presentation of the argument in court by the complaining party. It says that the case is insufficient to sustain an action in court of law. It refers the whole matter to the judge with a request for it to be tossed out of court as inappropriate and

> trivial. It, in essence, admits all the allegations of the party which originally complains, and it says "So what? If everything he says is true—he still hasn't got a case and we are so sure of our ground that we will go ahead *and admit that* it is all true. He still has nothing going for him." (*AE* 187)

The case was indeed thrown out in Superior Court, but O'Hair at once appealed to the Maryland Court of Appeals. She lost here also. On May 15, 1962, O'Hair appealed to the Supreme Court. About a month later, on June 25, 1962, a similar case in Pennsylvania, *Abington Township v. Schempp*, was filed at the Supreme Court. The court accepted both cases on October 8, 1962.

As for Bill, by this time, he was already out of Woodbourne Junior High—although for a time it looked as if he might not make it. The enormous amount of homework assigned to him was such that, even with O'Hair (who was not employed at this time) spending many hours helping him, it seemed likely that he might be flunked for not completing it. But a grudging truce was worked out: the school offered to graduate Bill if O'Hair dropped a suit alleging the school's complicity in the harassment that Bill had received for past year or more. Bill was, humiliatingly, placed last among those receiving a diploma, but he gained his mite of vengeance by refusing to shake the principal's hand as he received the diploma.

Meanwhile, the O'Hairs had been the victims of an incredible and appalling series of persecutions, attacks, and death threats. The windows of their house were constantly broken; O'Hair's prized flowers were brutally trampled; in one particularly vicious incident, a kitten that O'Hair had obtained as a companion for young Jon Garth (who was also subject to ostracism by his schoolmates) was killed. O'Hair, her health suffering, was forced to undergo a hysterectomy; shortly thereafter, she received an anonymous phone call reporting falsely her that her father had died. Clearly, all these actions—perpetrated by people who claimed to be Christians—were intended either to drive the family out of their house or to compel them to give up the case or even to kill them. (In one instance a bullet was fired through the living room window.)

According to O'Hair's testimony, various secular or civil liberties organizations that should have been sympathetic to their cause offered virtually no assistance in the matter. She claims that, at the outset of her case, an ACLU attorney told her: "What do you hope to gain? This is wrong. I know in my heart you are wrong. This Bible and prayer thing does not do anything to anyone. We all survive. It is nothing" (*AE* 37). Shortly thereafter, the ACLU exhibited a little more interest because of the publicity she was starting to receive, but in the end, O'Hair's indictment of the ACLU is harsh: "I wish to note here that the organization never, in any way, assisted us with the case on any level or at any time. I continued to have great hostility from it" (*AE* 233). The ACLU did lend some support to the Pennsylvania case, evidently on the assumption that the aggrieved party in that case, a Unitarian couple who had protested in a much milder fashion than O'Hair about an enforced prayer in school, presented a somewhat more appealing "victim" from a public relations standpoint than the oftentimes abrasive O'Hair. O'Hair says that other secular organizations, racked by dissension and internal feuding, also lent little assistance.

It is perhaps no surprise that the Supreme Court accepted these cases at this time. For the past fifteen years, it had been making a point of enforcing the central tenets of the establishment clause of the First Amendment: "Congress shall make no law respecting an establishment of religion." (It is followed by what is called the free exercise clause: "or prohibiting the free exercise thereof.") This clause, of course, applied only to the federal government, and it was only in 1940, in *Cantwell v. Connecticut*, that the Supreme Court explicitly declared that the states are obliged to follow Congress in enforcing both clauses of the First Amendment. In *Everson v. Board of Education* (1947), Justice Hugo Black offered a robust defense of the establishment clause:

> The "establishment of religion" clause of the First Amendment means at least this: Neither a state nor the Federal Government can set up a church. Neither can pass laws which aid one religion, aid all religions, or prefer one religion over another. Neither can force nor influence a person to go to or to remain away from church against his will or force him to profess a belief or disbelief in any religion. No person can be punished for entertaining or professing religious beliefs or disbeliefs, for church attendance, or non-attendance. (Cited in *L* 64)

For our purposes, the most critical sentence is the third, for it is eminently clear that Bill Murray was indeed being forced "to profess a belief . . . in [a] religion," specifically the religion called Christianity. In a decision, *Engal v. Vitale*, handed down the very year that the court accepted the two prayer-in-school cases, it dealt with the matter for the first time, outlawing a prayer written by the New York State Board of Regents and recited in the public schools; but this case did not deal with teacher-led student prayers, and it is clear that the court was looking for such a case to rule upon. There is, therefore, every reason to believe that, even if O'Hair (or the Schempps) had not brought a case, some other case would have been the trigger for banning prayer in public schools. But the fact remains that it was O'Hair, more than the Schempps, who aggressively forced the court into a decision.

O'Hair writes amusingly about the hapless and inexperienced Leonard Kerpelman, shaking in his boots as he faced the highest court in the land and being bailed out by a number of the justices, who came to his aid during the hearing. Meanwhile, the lawyers for the states of Maryland and Pennsylvania, realizing that they were in an untenable position, made numerous implausible and even outlandish claims. They first attempted to show that the recital of the Bible and of the Lord's Prayer was not in fact a religious ceremony, and that the proceedings were only for moral benefit. As O'Hair states, this claim was so obviously false that the justices "cut them [the state lawyers] to ribbons" (*AE* 273). Justice William O. Douglas amusingly asked, in that case, why the Koran could not be read as a morally uplifting work. The lawyers also tried to maintain that not participating in the prayers was no punishment to the students; but the state of Maryland, by its demurrer at the Superior Court, had already admitted that Bill Murray had indeed suffered ostracism and even physical injury as a result of his refusal to say the prayers.

The Supreme Court's decision, handed down on June 17, 1963, provoked a furor. In spite of the lopsided vote (8–1, with only Justice Potter Stewart dissenting), there were predictable complaints by the pious that the court had somehow "established" the "religion" of secular humanism. Their outrage was not appeased when the Supreme Court, in several decisions in 1965, banned student-led prayers that had been instituted in the wake of *Murray v. Curlett*. And, of course, there was an unappeasable thirst in both houses of Congress for a constitutional amendment allowing for prayer in public schools. In 1964, the House held eighteen days of hearings on the matter; and, in spite of wide support for one particular amendment, the Becker Amendment (which read in part: "Nothing in this Constitution shall be deemed to prohibit the offering, reading from, or listening to prayers or biblical scriptures, if participation therein is on a voluntary basis, in any governmental or public school, institution, or place" [*L* 97]), the head of the House Judiciary Committee, Emanuel Celler, lamented: "My committee, after exhaustive and comprehensive study, could not devise language for an amendment that would not do violence to the First Amendment" (*L* 97). In the Senate, the otherwise sensible Everett Dirksen of Illinois offered an amendment in 1966, but it did not receive enough votes to make it out of committee.

The state of Maryland itself had an even more extreme reaction. Even before the decision in *Murray v. Curlett* was handed down, the state, sensing that it would lose the case, proposed a bill requiring attendance at a silent meditation period each morning in school; its preamble stated, in part: "The Supreme Court . . . has drastically curtailed the right of the people in this country to hold brief religious exercises in their public schools. They [*sic*] . . . are taking away the right of a free people to give some belief and nonsectarian acknowledgment of their reliance and belief in God" (cited in *AE* 281). Although this bill passed the Maryland House by a wide margin, the Senate refused to consider it, saying that its only purpose was to "criticize the Supreme Court of the United States."

It is remarkable that the defenders of school prayer cannot see the obvious violation of constitutional principles entailed by the act. The political and religious conservative Russell Kirk, in a furious editorial, "What's Wicked about School Prayers?" (1963), fails to comprehend that the case concerns the religious freedom not only of "the tiny minority of militant atheists,"[3] but of everyone. If by chance this country happened to convert to Islam and instituted compulsory prayers to Allah, the Christians among us would be the first to howl in protest. It may well be true that the Supreme Court's handling of both the establishment clause and the free exercise clause of the First Amendment has, historically, been somewhat incoherent, but a clear strain of consistency in its many decisions rests on the critical issue of *coercion*. If, as Justice Hugo Black declared, the establishment clause means anything, it must mean that no one can be forced to express belief (or disbelief) in a religion he does not accept. And the court has shrewdly perceived that, when dealing with schoolchildren, the psychological pressures to conform are so great that enormous care must be taken that they are not put in the intolerable bind of either professing a belief hypocritically or of being ostracized for not professing it.

As for O'Hair and her family, the victory at the Supreme Court did not spell an end to their personal troubles; in many ways, it exacerbated them. Naively, O'Hair felt that the resolution of the case would engender harmony among her neighbors, but the very opposite occurred, and these "Christians" were even more furiously enraged at her. Bill, indeed, had a somewhat better time while attending high school at Baltimore Polytechnic Institute—the very school that H. L. Mencken had attended decades before—and became interested in ham radio operations, but the antenna he set up on the side of his house was repeatedly vandalized, until at last Bill and O'Hair simply gave it up. Then there was the amusing episode of the "Atheist dogs"—a pair of puppies whom O'Hair wryly named Marx and Engels, and who finally had to be given away because of neighbors' trumped-up charges that they were causing a disturbance.

In the end, after a turbulent couple of years, O'Hair and her family—now augmented by a granddaughter, Robin Murray-O'Hair, the daughter of Bill Murray—settled in Austin, Texas, where she established the American Atheist Center and began publishing the *American Atheist*, initially printed by Bill. But personal conflicts with his mother led to his leaving Austin in 1977. After a descent into alcoholism, during which he claimed that he not only saw but talked with the devil, Bill—influenced in part by the trashy novelist Taylor Caldwell's historical novel *Dear and Glorious Physician* (1959) and by a bizarre dream in which a "great winged angel" (*L* 260) stood before him—converted to fundamentalist Christianity. It is pitifully obvious that the severe trauma Bill had suffered from years of hatred, vilification, and actual violence directed toward him had exacted their toll. For the next two or three decades (he is still with us), he waged an unrelenting battle against his mother's teachings; as recently as 1995, he published a book whose title needs no explication: *Let Us Pray: A Plea for Prayer in Our Schools*.

As for O'Hair herself, she engaged in a seemingly endless array of lawsuits on church/state issues, both locally and nationally: she tackled such hot-button topics as the addition of the phrase "under God" in the Pledge of Allegiance, the motto "In God We Trust" affixed to our currency, religious displays on government property, the tax-free status of churches, and so on. She lost most of these cases. O'Hair has been accused merely of grandstanding or of seeking cheap publicity in this often quixotic litigation, but a more sympathetic interpretation may be offered: in many instances, laws and statutes of this kind do not get overturned on the first attempt, especially if they have been on the books for many years and have become enmeshed in the fabric of our society; litigation, even if it initially fails, brings attention to the constitutional and other issues surrounding these enactments so that they can be overturned later. To be sure, we are still stuck with "under God" (which a cowardly Supreme Court evaded settling in 2003 when it was challenged by the atheist Michael Newdow, since the court ruled that Newdow had no standing in the case in spite of the fact that his own daughter was forced to utter the words) and "In God We Trust" are still with us; but the right case—and the right collocation of Supreme Court justices—may ultimately engender a victory for atheists.

As it is, O'Hair was most successful in removing requirements—still on the books in many states in her day—that elected officials acknowledge the existence of a Supreme Being in their oath of office. Texas had the following paradoxical clause in its state constitution: "No religious test shall ever be required as a qualification to any office, or public trust, in this state; nor shall anyone be excluded from holding office on account of his religious sentiments, provided he acknowledge the existence of a Supreme Being." This was overturned in 1984 in *O'Hair v. Hill*. As of now, only Arkansas and Pennsylvania have similar statutes in their constitutions.[4]

As for O'Hair's own writings, they are, to put it mildly, disappointing to anyone even superficially trained in philosophy. It is highly significant that all but one of her books and pamphlets—and they number at least twenty-three, several of which underwent substantial revision over decades—were published by the American Atheist Press, which she herself founded. A number of her books are merely transcripts of lectures she delivered or talks she gave on KTBC radio in Austin. She inexplicably took great pride in a lecture she first delivered in 1961, and which she subsequently revised in 1991. It is an embarrassing piece of work. It begins:

> My name is Madalyn Murray O'Hair.
>
> I am an Atheist.
>
> I am a bit more than that—an Atheist. I am, in fact, ***the*** Atheist. The Atheist who made Americans stop to take a little stock of their accepted values. For I am the Atheist who fought a battle right up to and through the Supreme Court of the United States in order to have Bible reading and prayer recitation, as a religious ceremony, removed from the public schools in all fifty states of our Union.[5]

The speech goes on to make simple-minded philosophical assertions about materialism (to which O'Hair, both here and in a ponderous and schoolmarmish essay appended to the lecture, "The History of Materialism," professes allegiance, not realizing that the whole idealism/materialism debate has by now become utterly passé in philosophical circles) and also presents a seriously erroneous interpretation of Kant's categorical imperative, to which she also claims to adhere. It is a feeble defense of this lecture that it was intended for general, nonphilosophical audiences.

Perhaps the most compelling statement by O'Hair on atheism was a letter to the editor that was first published in a newspaper and then inserted as part of her brief in *Murray v. Curlett*:

> Your petitioners are Atheists and they define their beliefs as follows. An Atheist loves his fellow man instead of a god. An Atheist believes that Heaven is something for which we should work now—here on earth for all men together to enjoy. An Atheist believes that he can get no help through prayer, but that he must find in himself the inner conviction and strength to meet life, to grapple with it, and enjoy it. An Atheist believes that only in a knowledge of himself and a knowledge of his fellow man can he find the understanding that will help to a life of fulfillment.
>
> He seeks to know himself and his fellow man rather than to know a god. An Atheist believes that a hospital should be built instead of a church. An Atheist believes that a deed must be done instead of a prayer said. An Atheist strives for involvement in life and not escape into death. He wants disease conquered, poverty vanished, war eliminated. He wants man to understand and love man. He wants an ethical way of life. He believes that we cannot rely on god nor channel action into prayer nor hope for an end of troubles in a hereafter. He believes that we are the keepers of our own lives and that we are our brother's keeper;

> that we are responsible persons and that the job is here and the time is now. (*AE* 126–27)

Manifestly, this declaration was made as an attempt—and, in my judgment, a largely successful one—to counteract the common complaint, still heard today, that atheism is merely a "negative" creed that is intent only on denial and rejection.

The one book that O'Hair did not self-publish is *Freedom under Siege: The Impact of Organized Religion on Your Liberty and Your Pocketbook* (1974). This work, written in a sober and thoroughly researched fashion very different from much of her other work, is a compelling argument against continuing tax exemption for churches. O'Hair marshals an impressive array of evidence that shows that churches are abusing their tax-free status to become enormously wealthy (in 1974, "the churches' total real estate wealth . . . exceeds the combined assets of the nation's ten largest industrial corporations," and "the visible assets of the churches—land and buildings—are double the combined assets of the nation's five largest industrial corporations")[6] and thereby raising taxes for everyone else, resulting in a tacit tax support for churches expressly forbidden by the Constitution. But, like other of O'Hair's crusades, this one appears now a hopeless cause.

O'Hair's tragic demise—she, Jon Garth Murray, and Robin Murray-O'Hair were kidnapped by David Waters (an employee at the American Atheist Center who had a long criminal record) with the assistance of two petty criminals, Gary Karr and Danny Fry; were forced to disgorge hundreds of thousands of dollars from their bank accounts; and were then killed and their bodies dismembered—need not be dwelt upon. It was a lamentable death of a woman who, to be sure, had her share of flaws, but who exhibited remarkable courage, resilience, and determination in the face of incredible persecution for years while pursuing her cause to free the public schools of mandatory prayer. In spite of fleeting attempts to reinstitute prayer in schools, it can be safely assumed that this battle has now been decisively won. It remains O'Hair's most notable legacy, and it is one of which any of us would be proud.

Chapter 11

Gore Vidal: Taking Aim at the Sky-God

It is curious that Gore Vidal's most forthright essay on religion, "Monotheism and Its Discontents," appeared as late as 1992, for his expression of sentiments hostile to religion in general, and the Christian religion in particular, had made him notorious almost since the beginning of his career in the late 1940s. Vidal, who until recently alternated between residences in Italy and in Los Angeles, has become not only one of America's leading novelists and essayists, but an outspoken critic on a wide variety of controversial topics, including sexual liberation, homosexuality, political chicanery, and religion. Vidal has used a multiplicity of media—novels, essays, plays, political polemics, and interviews on film, television, and radio—to broadcast his views. Since the 1960s, he has himself been a media celebrity, his aristocratic features and rapier-sharp wit being instantly recognizable. And, in contrast to all the other thinkers covered in this volume, the most penetrating and distinctive of Vidal's criticisms of religion occur not in treatises but in an array of novels extending over a forty-year span.

Born to a socially and politically well-connected family on October 3, 1925, Vidal spent his childhood and adolescence in an atmosphere of privilege, where it was expected that he would excel. His grandfather was the celebrated blind senator from Oklahoma, Thomas P. Gore, who was himself an atheist but who, for political reasons, took care to mask the fact, sporadically attending a Methodist church. Vidal, who was particularly close to his grandfather, would later speak of him and of his family:

> They saw the worst of religion in the Bible Belt. And he never let on that he was not with them. My mother would complain as a child that

> she couldn't read the funny papers on Sunday. A lot of things were forbidden on the sabbath. They were trying to conform for fear that the neighbors would find out if they didn't. A lot of snooping going on. If you were doing the forbidden things on the sabbath, you were in trouble in Oklahoma. I think there were only two or three times when I went with him to church.[1]

Since Vidal's own father, Gene Vidal (a minor figure in the Franklin D. Roosevelt administration), was also an apparent atheist, Vidal seems to have received no religious training in his youth. He attended St. Albans Academy and Phillips Exeter Academy, but then passed up the opportunity to attend college and instead entered the Army. Vidal was already at this time thinking that he might wish to enter politics, and he felt that a military career would foster his chances.

It was during his three years in the Army (1943–1946) that Vidal became a writer. His first novel, *Williwaw*, based on his Army experiences, was published in 1947, before he had turned twenty-two, and several other novels written in the following years established him as a vibrant new voice in postwar American literature. One of his novels, *The City and the Pillar* (1948), not only was a bestseller but engendered intense controversy by its frank and sensitive depiction of a homosexual relationship between two young men.

It was, however, a slightly later novel, *Messiah* (1954), that constituted Vidal's first foray into the criticism of religion. The first-person narrative of Eugene Luther (an obvious play on Vidal's own full name: Eugene Luther Gore Vidal Jr.), *Messiah* tells of the emergence in California of a charismatic preacher, John Cave. Luther makes no secret of his own skepticism, telling a friend, Iris Mortimer:

> I must warn you, Iris, that I'm not a believer. And though I'm sure that the revelations of other men must be a source of infinite satisfaction to them, individually, I shouldn't for one second be so presumptuous as to make a choice among the many thousands of recorded revelations of truth, accepting one at the expense of all the others: I might so easily choose wrong and get into eternal trouble. And you must admit that the selection is wide, and dangerous to the amateur.[2]

Cave himself began his career as nothing but an undertaker's assistant (*M* 66)—but this occupation is central to his message, which is simple and devastating: "It is good to die" (*M* 72).

Luther, shaken by his witnessing of Cave and his message, warns of its dangers: "If this thing spreads it will become organized. If it becomes organized, secondary considerations will obscure the point. The truth is no truer because only a few have experienced it" (*M* 81). But Iris counters that "a society which knows what we know, which believes in Cave and what he says, will be a pleasanter place in which to live, less anxious, more tolerant" (*M* 81).

Iris's prediction is soon put to the test. Paul Himmell, "the most successful young publicist in Hollywood" (*M* 85), is hired to make Cave and Cavesword (a term coined to denote Cave's religious message) a national phenomenon—and he does just that. Using all the slick tools of media publicity, Paul makes Cave a household name. Iris has come to believe that Cave is in fact the Antichrist—but she does not interpret this in the usual fashion: "He's come to undo all the wickedness of the Christians" (*M* 116). Cave himself, who throughout the novel is deliberately portrayed as a bland, inscrutable, and perhaps psychologically empty figure, is aware that his preaching will entail a coming battle against organized religion, but he brushes this off: "'It never occurred to me that people who like to think of themselves as Christians couldn't accept both me and Christ at the same time. I know I don't promise the kingdom of heaven but I *do* promise oblivion and the loss of self, of pain'" (*M* 116).

But the ensuing religious conflict does materialize, especially after Cave says on television that churches are unnecessary and that they derive their power from superstition. Violence breaks out, leading to the destruction of St. Peter's in Rome (*M* 172). It would seem that, in the course of time, the entire world has been converted to Cavism. Presently, we hear of people committing suicide as a result of Cave's preaching; as Paul tells Luther:

> We're doing good. The people are losing their fear of death. Last month there were twelve hundred suicides in this country directly attributable to Cavesword. And these people didn't kill themselves just because they were unhappy, they killed themselves because he had made it easy, even desirable. Now you know there's never been anybody like that before in history, anywhere. (*M* 206–207)

It therefore comes as no surprise that Cave wishes to set up euthanasia chambers at every "Center" (the equivalent of churches in the Cavite religion). When Luther, who has become increasingly disenchanted with Cave, dares Cave to commit suicide himself as an example to others, Cave maintains that he will do so ("I'm not afraid" [*M* 222]); but in fact, he is later killed by Paul, who had wished him out of the way (as Luther remarks: "Paul wants full control of the establishment" [*M* 225]). Paul himself is later forced out and kills himself. At the end of the novel, Luther realizes that it is he, and not Cave, who is the real messiah.

Messiah is an extraordinarily rich and searing religious satire. The parallels between Paul Himmell and St. Paul, the true spreader of the Christian doctrine, are patent and deliberate. Vidal is therefore likening St. Paul to a Madison Avenue con artist who spread the word for purely self-serving reasons. And in emphasizing Cave's message of death, Vidal is apparently subscribing to Nietzsche's contention that Christianity itself is a religion that looks toward death, repudiating the boons of life for the false paradise of heaven. Vidal has also written a remarkably prescient fable about the rapidity with which religious fanaticism can overtake a nation and a world that consists of largely uneducated and easily indoctrinated individuals. His prophecy would, in a sense, come true a quarter century later with the rise of the religious right.

After publishing *Messiah*, Vidal took a decade-long holiday from novel writing: he came to believe that the notoriety of *The City and the Pillar* had prejudiced publishers against him. Between 1950 and 1954 he published five pseudonymous novels (including three lively detective stories under the pen name "Edgar Box"), but thereafter he pursued a career in writing for television, film, and theater. He achieved tremendous popular and critical success with two Broadway plays, *Visit to a Small Planet* (1957) and *The Best Man* (1960) and became a frequent guest on television game shows and news broadcasts. Accordingly, when he returned to novel writing with *Julian* (1964), his own celebrity helped propel that novel to bestseller status.

The subject of *Julian*, the first of the works that would make Vidal perhaps the most distinguished American historical novelist of his time, was deliberately chosen. In presenting a sympathetic account of the Roman emperor Julian who, during his brief reign (361–63 CE), attempted to stop the spread of Christianity and reinstitute Greco-

Roman paganism, Vidal was signaling his own hostility to the dominance of Christianity in the West. In a prefatory chapter of the novel, Libanius, hearing of the Emperor Theodosius's decree demanding obedience to the Nicene Creed, hopes to fight "pernicious Christian doctrine"[3] by publishing Julian's fragmentary memoir. The bulk of the novel presents that memoir.

Julian reports that he had been raised as a Christian (Christianity had become dominant in the Roman Empire following the Emperor Constantine's conversion in 324 CE), but had become intrigued by the attacks on Christianity by such pagan thinkers as Plotinus and Porphyry. His skepticism grew under the biting criticism of his teacher Maximus, who pointed out the numerous Christian borrowings from other religions:

> The Christians wish to replace our beautiful [pagan] legends with the police record of a reforming Jewish rabbi. Out of this unlikely material they hope to make a final synthesis of all the religions ever known. They now appropriate our feast days. They transform local deities into saints. They borrow from our mystery rites, particularly those of Mithras. The priests of Mithras are called "fathers." So the Christians call *their* priests "fathers." They even imitate the tonsure, hoping to impress new converts with the familiar trappings of an older cult. Now they have started to call the Nazarene "savior" and "healer." Why? Because one of the most beloved of our gods is Asklepios, whom we call "savior" and "healer." (*J* 86)

Priscus—who, with Libanius, interrupts Julian's narrative at various points to provide his own commentary—writes engagingly of Julian's battles with the early Christian pope Gregory, remarking: "The malice of a true Christian attempting to destroy an opponent is something unique in the world. No other religion ever considered it necessary to destroy others because they did not share the same beliefs. At worst, another man's belief might inspire amusement or contempt. . . . No evil ever entered the world quite so vividly or on such a vast scale as Christianity did" (*J* 142). Julian, for his part, maintains that he is not actually attempting to suppress Christianity, but merely to restore the old gods of paganism; he remarks wryly at one point, "at the rate they [the Christians] kill one another, it would be gratuitous for me to intervene" (*J* 283).

What Julian actually did, in 362, was declare religious freedom, thereby overthrowing Christianity as the state religion. At this point, Julian subjects Christian doctrine to a searching analysis:

> They base *their* religion on the idea of a single god, as though that were a novelty: from Homer to Julian, Hellenes have been monotheist. Now this single god, according to the largest of the Galilean sects, sent his son (conceived of a virgin, like so many other Asiatic gods) to preach to the world, to suffer, to rise from the dead, to judge mankind on a day which was supposed to have dawned more than three hundred years ago. (*J* 331)

The reference is to Jesus' obviously false prediction, recorded in all three of the Synoptic Gospels, that his second coming would occur within the lifetime of those who heard his preaching. As for Jesus himself:

> We must never forget that *in his own words*, Jesus was a Jew who believed in the Law of Moses. This means he could not be the son of God (the purest sort of blasphemy), much less God himself, temporarily earth-bound. There is nothing in the book of the Jews which prepares us for a messiah's kinship with Jehovah. Only by continual reinterpretation and convenient "revelations" have the Galileans been able to change this reformer-rabbi's career into a parody of one of our own gods, creating a passion of death and rebirth quite inconceivable to one who kept the Law of Moses. (*J* 332)

As for St. Paul, he "outdid all the quacks and cheats that ever existed anywhere" (ibid.).

Julian's actions now become more unrestrained. In Greece, Julian thinks that the spirit of Alexander the Great has occupied him, and he prepares for an invasion of Persia. He orders the shrine of St. Babylas to be removed: the place is sacred to Apollo. When the temple of Apollo is burned, Julian blames the Christians. He seems to be becoming a fanatic; as Libanius remarks, "I felt Julian was overdoing it. . . . He wanted everything restored at once" (*J* 383). Julian later dies in battle, his quest to halt Christianity an obvious failure. Libanius comments:

> I see nothing good ever coming of this religious system [Christianity] no matter how much it absorbs our ancient customs and puts to use for

> its own ends Hellenic wit and logic. Yet I have no doubt now that the Christians will prevail. Julian was our last hope, and he went too soon. Something large and harmful has come into the life of this old world. One recalls, stoically, the injunction of Sophocles: "And ever shall this law hold good, nothing that is vast enters into the life of mortals without a curse." (*J* 384–85)

Priscus adds: "Julian must be obliterated or at least made monster before the Christian Empire can properly be born" (*J* 405). The use of the term *empire* is deliberate: Christianity is not merely a religion, it is a means for exercising political control over human beings.

The extraordinary historical richness of *Julian*—drawing upon Julian's actual writings as well as those of Libanius, Ammianus Marcellinus, and later historians such as Edward Gibbon, J. B. Bury, and many others—justifies its high rank among Vidal's novelistic output and among the historical novels of its era. Far from being merely a mechanical re-creation of a remote epoch, *Julian* delivers a forceful message regarding the sordid means by which Christianity became established as a world religion—by distorting Jesus' message, by blatant indoctrination, by ruthless suppression of religious rivals, and by utilizing all the powers of an immense imperial apparatus to enforce outward conformity among a populace that nonetheless remained largely pagan in its deepest emotional sympathies. Vidal provides amusement at Christianity's expense by recounting in detail the frequently absurd and remarkably vicious disputes over fine points of doctrine that engaged the attention of leading Christian thinkers of the period. As Louis Auchincloss wrote in a review, Vidal's "Christians are narrow-minded, disputatious, savage to their enemies and devoid of any style or eloquence."[4]

Four years after the publication of *Julian*, Vidal became a household name with the issuance of *Myra Breckinridge* (1968), the notorious satirical novel about a man who has a sex-change operation and becomes a woman. This delightfully scabrous work is of interest in the present context only insofar as Vidal had long been of the opinion that Christianity—and Judaism—had been the spearheads of the puritanical disdain of sexual pleasure, especially of homosexual sex. In 1981, in the controversial essay "Pink Triangle and Yellow Star" (first published as "*Some* Jews and *the* Gays" in the *Nation*, November 14, 1981), Vidal boldly claimed that some Jewish leaders have made a dangerous pact with evangelical Christians, leading some of them to become gay-baiters. He singles out the right-wing Jewish commentator Norman Podhoretz and wife Midge Decter, although he also quotes Joseph Epstein as remarking, "If I had the power to do so, I would wish homosexuality off the face of the earth."[5] Vidal concludes: "Today, American evangelical Christians are busy trying to impose on the population at large their superstitions about sex and the sexes and the creation of the world" (*US* 597).

This essay evoked some furor at the time, but it was nothing compared to what a pair of later essays would produce. In "The Day the American Empire Ran out of Gas" (*Nation*, January 11, 1986 [as "Requiem for the American Empire"]), Vidal concluded that, with the United States now a debtor nation, the American Empire was officially over. Podhoretz and Decter both wrote responses to this article, to which Vidal replied with "A Cheerful Response" (*Nation*, March 22, 1986 [as "The Empire Lovers Strike Back"]). Here he maintained that the Jewish lobby, in order to secure military and economic support for Israel, has "made common cause with every sort of reactionary and anti-Semitic group in the United States, from the corridors of the Pentagon to the TV studios of the evangelical Jesus Christers" (*US* 1020). This article provoked predictable accusations that Vidal was an anti-Semite, although some recent scholarship appears to confirm Vidal's stance. Podhoretz, in particular, wrote a lengthy article, "The Hate That Dare Not Speak Its Name" (*Commentary*, November 1986), in which he axiomatically assumed that Vidal's attack on him was anti-Semitic, not merely anti-Zionist; he expressed dismay that many intellectuals he consulted on the matter did not follow his reasoning.

These articles discuss Vidal's attitude toward religion only indirectly, but that cannot be said for *Creation* (1981), an even more exhaustive treatment of the ancient world than *Julian*. Here we find ourselves several centuries before the birth of Christ, where the Persian ambassador to Greece, Cyrus Spitama, engages in an intellectual quest throughout the civilized world in search of philosophical truth. As he puts it simply at the outset: "For me there is only one subject worth pondering—creation."[6] Because the novel is set centuries before the origin of Christianity, we find none of the occasionally strident attacks on Christian doctrine that fill *Julian*. Instead, we see Cyrus canvassing the ancient world and its leading thinkers—Zoroaster (who is his grandfather), Pythagoras, Buddha, Confucius, and others—for their opinions as to the origin of the universe and other central questions of philosophy. The novel is narrated by the young Democritus (Cyrus's nephew), later to become the founder of the implicitly atheistic philosophy of atomism.

It would be fruitless to examine in detail the progression of this immense novel or even the arguments that the philosophers whom Cyrus meets expound in response to his questioning. It becomes plain that Cyrus's (and Vidal's) sympathies lie chiefly with Buddhism and Confucianism. In meeting Buddha, Cyrus believes that his system is a "perfect atheism" (*C* 237). He is amazed by two particular aspects of Buddha's teachings:

> Until I met the Buddhists, I did not think it possible for a religion or philosophy or world view of any complexity to exist without a theory of creation, no matter how imprecise. But here was a sect or order or religion which had captured the imagination of two powerful kings and many wise men, and the order had done so without ever taking seriously the only great question: How did the cosmos begin?
>
> Worse, Buddhists regard all gods with the same sort of amiable contempt that educated Athenians do. But the Athenians are fearful of prosecution by public opinion, while the Buddhists are indifferent to the superstitions of the Brahmans. They do not even care enough about the gods to turn them into devils the way Zoroaster did. The Buddhists accept the world as it is, and try to eliminate it. (*C* 235)

As for Confucius, whom he meets on a trip to China, Cyrus also concludes flatly that "Confucius was an atheist" (*C* 401). He later elaborates the point:

> I think that for all practical purposes, the Confucians are atheists. They do not believe in an afterlife or a day of judgment. They are not interested in how this world was created or for what purpose. Instead, they act as if this life is all there is and to conduct it properly is all that matters. For them, heaven is simply a word to describe correct behavior. Because the common people have all sorts of irrational feelings about heaven—a concept as old as the race—Confucius has cleverly used the

> idea of heaven in order to give a magical authority to his pronouncements on the way that men ought to treat one another. (*C* 418–19)

It is important to Vidal's purpose that Cyrus—who at the outset is a relatively orthodox Zoroastrian—acknowledges "my deep dislike of atheism" (*C* 419), but he nevertheless says of Confucius: "I have never known a man with such a clear idea of how public and private affairs should be conducted. . . . If one is going to eliminate the creator of all things, then it is a good idea to replace the creator with a very clear idea of what constitutes goodness in the human scale" (*C* 419). Vidal is also careful to conclude the novel with Democritus's resounding utterance, "Matter is all. All is matter" (*C* 488), thereby enshrining atheistic materialism as the final conclusion of this enormous novel of ideas.

It may be worth while to treat *Kalki* (1978) here. This slim but devastatingly cynical novel in some senses reprises the themes of *Messiah*. We are introduced to James J. Kelly, an American who claims that he is the Hindu messiah, Kalki. His followers hand out paper flowers and claim that the end of the world is coming. The narrator, the aviatrix Theodora Hecht Ottinger, is persuaded by Kelly to drop thousands of the paper flowers all across the world by airplane—they turn out to be poisoned and end up killing the entire human race, with the exception of a small band of Kelly's associates. Kelly's reasons for destroying humanity—overpopulation, pollution of the earth, and so on—are very largely Vidal's own, as stated in essays of the time. In the end, Kelly's plans for beginning a new, purer human race are confounded by the fact that none of his female associates are capable of bearing children.

Kalki is not explicitly antireligious in the manner of *Messiah*, but it raises many of the same issues as that novel—notably, a neoreligious cult of death. As a satirical novel, it is difficult to surpass: the revelation, halfway through the work, that nearly the entire human race has been eliminated is one of the most powerful moments in contemporary literature. One gains the impression that Vidal took a certain misanthropic pleasure in wiping the earth clean. As he wrote in his memoir, *Palimpsest* (1995): "My imagination is often triggered by the 'what if' that leads to the end of things."[7]

Vidal's most unrestrained attack on Christianity comes in the short satirical novel *Live from Golgotha* (1992), which reprises another central theme of *Messiah*—the power of the media to control human thought. It was in this year that Vidal published his essay "Monotheism and Its Discontents" (*Nation*, July 13, 1992; *US* 1048–54). The thrust of the essay is simple: "The great unmentionable evil at the center of our culture is monotheism." By this statement Vidal explicitly indicts not only Christianity but Judaism and Islam also, all three of which he labels the "sky-god religions." Strictly speaking, Vidal does not actually embrace atheism, and his remarks could theoretically be interpreted to suggest that he could envision polytheism as a viable religion; but the atheistic implications of this essay, as of the rest of his work, are unmistakable. Vidal stresses the unwarranted intrusion of religion into the secular sphere, in defiance of the First Amendment and the known views of the Founding Fathers. He maintains that monotheism has resulted only in a culture of hatred (against African Americans, women, gays, and others), and he sees the United States as increasingly polarized between the religious and the secular; indeed, he openly advocates "an all-out war on the monotheists" in the name of sanity and civilization.

Vidal's own contribution to that war was *Live from Golgotha*. It is difficult to describe the plot of this outrageous and frequently hilarious polemic, which shuttles back and forth in time between the present (and future) and the past of two thousand years ago. It is narrated by Timothy, who was born a few years after the death of Jesus. Learning from St. Paul that a strange sort of virus is erasing all copies of the Synoptic Gospels, Timothy realizes that he must write his own gospel of what actually happened to Jesus. Meanwhile, an executive at NBC has managed to go back in time, claiming that he wishes to film the crucifixion. This self-parodic science-fictional premise allows Vidal all manner of jokes at the expense of Jesus, St. Paul, and Christianity in general. Jesus himself, we learn, was not the handsome and fresh-faced youth of countless cheap paintings; instead, "Jesus was enormously fat with this serious hormonal problem—the so-called parable about the loaves and fishes was just the fantasy of somebody who could never get enough to eat."[8] And there are passing whimsies as in the offhand remark, "like so many of life's born failures, he became a Christian" (*LG* 78).

But the novel is far more than a series of abusive insults. Vidal, a thorough student of the Bible, points out many of the more troubling features of scripture and Christian doctrine. James, the brother of Jesus, is careful to point out Jesus' Jewish origins and the essential Jewishness of his entire mission, saying that Jesus "was simply a devout Jew of the Reformed Temple Party" (*LG* 110). In Ephesus, an old woman complains bitterly to Timothy about the most notorious failing of Jesus' prophesying—his failure to return to earth within the lifetime of those who had heard his preaching:

> We have been waiting patiently—lo! these many years. . . . I and my friends who first brought me to Jesus, believed Him when He said that He—as the bona-fide Messiah—would return to us while we were still alive. Well, my friends have long since crossed the shining river and I am barely clinging to the flotsam and jetsam here by de ribberside. So could you kindly share with us His latest adjusted estimated time of arrival? (*LG* 72)

St. Paul's retort—"There was, madam, no agreed-on timetable when Our Lord left us" (*LG* 72)—is, as Vidal knows full well, an evasion, for Jesus' prophecy is unequivocal: "But I tell you of a truth, there shall be some standing here, which shall not taste of death, till they see the kingdom of God" (Luke 9:27; cf. Matt. 16:28, Mark 9:1). Vidal also emphasizes how St. Paul, for all practical purposes, took over Christianity and molded it to his desires, which were not necessarily the same as Jesus': "By now the whole thing was not only pretty much his invention but it was kept together by his energy and mastery of cross-filing. . . . James and the Jerusalem crowd were, gradually, cut out of the action. No other way of putting it. They just faded away" (*LG* 144).

But the most outrageous aspect of *Live from Golgotha* is its conclusion. Here Vidal asserts that Jesus managed to escape being crucified altogether, instead allowing Judas (also represented as grossly fat) to take his place on the cross. Jesus, in fact, has gone forward in time and become a militant Zionist ("He was and is a zealot. A fanatic. A revolutionary. A Zionist first, last and always" [*LG* 192]) who, in the year 2001, intends to set off a nuclear holocaust from Tel Aviv. A bit later, Timothy comes to an even more cataclysmic conclusion: "What was becoming clearer by the moment that day in Jerusalem was the true identity of the original Jesus—he was indeed Lucifer incarnate, who had been transformed by Saint [Paul]'s faith and genius in marketing into a three-part god, highly suitable for everyone on earth to worship" (*LG* 214). But by going back in time, Timothy manages to persuade Pontius Pilate to crucify the actual Jesus instead of Judas.

The wickedly blasphemous humor of *Live from Golgotha* inspired its predictable recoil of outrage on the part of the pious, from Pat Robertson's claim that Vidal was himself the Antichrist[9] to D. M. Thomas's owlish criticism that Vidal's satire is "excessive, a product of the author's antireligious beliefs rather than a natural consequence of his artistic creation," and that the novel "might have been richer and more thought-provoking had it been written by someone less hostile to monotheistic religion."[10] But the very purpose of Vidal's novel is to deliver an antireligious polemic, and in that capacity it succeeds brilliantly. Even the Catholic Andrew Greeley admitted, "It may well be said that Vidal's *jeu d'esprit* with blasphemy is witty, ingenious and frothy, with emphasis on the last adjective."[11]

Gore Vidal, as one of the most articulate and forceful opponents of fundamentalist Christianity and of religion in general, has written a succession of novels that underscore his central concerns—the baneful effects of religion's intrusion into the secular sphere, the power of the media to disseminate religious fundamentalism, the hatred and resentment that can so easily emerge from adherence to religious doctrine, and the way in which religion can hinder social advancement of women, gays, and other groups. Precisely because Vidal has chosen to express his views in novels rather than essays or treatises, his influence may well be more enduring than that of even the most accessible philosopher.

Chapter 12

RICHARD DAWKINS: SCIENCE VS. GOD

British evolutionary biologist and popular science writer Richard Dawkins (b. 1941) is perhaps the leading contemporary advocate for atheism in the world today. Although his blockbuster *The God Delusion* (2006) appeared two years after Sam Harris's bestseller, *The End of Faith* (2004), and may have been partially influenced by it, Dawkins's long career as an eminent scientist—he held, among many other academic posts, the Simonyi Professorship for the Public Understanding of Science at Oxford from 1995 until his retirement in 2008—has led inexorably to his reasoned belief in the primacy of science as the chief arbiter of truth and in the perniciousness of religion both as a theory of the universe and as a mode of conduct in the world. Aside from Thomas Henry Huxley, he is the one figure discussed in this book who has been a practicing scientist for decades and who has made lasting contributions to his chosen field. His work as a popularizer of science is evident from his first book, *The Selfish Gene* (1976), to his most recent, *The Greatest Show on Earth: The Evidence for Evolution* (2009). He also founded the Richard Dawkins Foundation for Reason and Science.

One of the best places to begin a discussion of Dawkins's religious views is with his seminal treatment of the theory of evolution, *The Blind Watchmaker: Why the Evidence of Evolution Reveals a Universe without Design* (1986), one of the most impressive and convincing treatises on evolution ever written, not excluding Stephen Jay Gould's immense *The Structure of Evolutionary Theory* (2002). The antireligious substratum of the work is revealed in an early passage: "Darwin made it possible to be an intellectually fulfilled atheist."[1] What this means is that, although much sound work by philosophers and scientists had been accomplished up to the middle of the nineteenth century to overthrow some of the central pillars of religion—the findings of physicists such as Copernicus, Kepler, and Newton, which implicitly overthrew the notion that the earth occupied a special place in the universe and presented a viable alternative to the biblical account of creation in Genesis; the "higher criticism" school of biblical scholarship that established the mundane, human composition of the Bible and dealt serious blows against the notion of its "divine" inspiration; the work of David Hume and others arguing against the plausibility of "miracles"—it required the theory of evolution by natural selection to tackle the final argument to which religionists clung in their attempts to maintain that a religious account of the universe (and, specifically, of the origin and development of human and animal life) was more convincing than the scientific one: the argument from design.

As enunciated most famously by the British theologian William Paley in *Natural Theology* (1802), the argument from design asserted that living creatures contained such complex features (the most popular one being the eye with its extraordinary array of components—lens, cornea, retina, and so forth) that they could not have evolved by "blind chance" but must have been designed by a Creator. Paley put forth a celebrated analogy: If you were walking across a field and came upon a watch on the ground and were asked how it got there, you would have to assume that it was artificially contrived and therefore was the work of a contriver. Dawkins tackles this analogy head-on, making it in fact one element of the title of his book: he declares flatly that Paley's analogy between manufactured objects and biological objects is false. Dawkins does not, however, state that Paley's analogy is also question begging, for we know before the fact that the watch was manufactured by a "contriver" (in this case a human being), even though this is the very point that needs to be proved. In any case, Dawkins maintains—and proves with overwhelming arguments in his book—that natural selection is the only theory that fully accounts for the appearance of design in creatures, but he specifies that natural selection has no overriding "purpose" (aside from the brute preservation and continuation of species), so that it is a "*blind* watchmaker" (*BW* 5).

Dawkins is aware that he must account for "complex design" (*BW* ix)—things like the evolution of eyes, ears, and other organs—if he is to present a convincing case for evolution by natural selection as the only plausible mechanism by which living creatures could have gained these features. He explains that evolution operates by "chance" is a misconception. Each single evolutionary mutation may in fact have emerged by chance in certain members of a given species, but the cumulative effects of a succession of mutations is not a result of chance; those mutations that are evolutionarily beneficial contribute to the survival of those that have them:

> There is a big difference, then, between cumulative selection (in which each improvement, however slight, is used as a basis for future building), and single-step selection (in which each new "try" is a fresh one). If evolutionary progress had had to rely on single-step selection, it would never have got anywhere. If, however, there was any way in which the necessary conditions for *cumulative* selection could have been set up by the blind forces of nature, strange and wonderful might be the consequences. As a matter of fact that is exactly what happened on this planet, and we ourselves are among the most recent, if not the strangest and most wonderful, of those consequences. (*BW* 49)

But how could such complex organs as eyes and ears have evolved by infinitesimal stages? Did they not have to be "created" all at once? Dawkins destroys this argument by demonstrating that there is evidence for a nearly infinite number of intermediate stages between, say, a light-sensitive patch of skin on a creature's surface and a full-fledged eye. There are, in fact, eyelike organs in existing animals down to single-celled entities.

There is much other good work in *The Blind Watchmaker*: how the complex mechanism of DNA replication could have come into existence; the ubiquity of the genetic code ("The genetic code is universal. I regard this as near-conclusive proof that all organisms are descended from a single common ancestor" [*BW* 270]); the near-unanimity among biologists about the validity of evolution by natural selection ("No serious biologist doubts the fact that evolution has happened" [*BW* 287]); a stirring rebuttal to Stephen Jay Gould's "punctuated equilibrium," the notion that certain phases of evolution might have progressed by unexpected "leaps" rather than by steady and infinitesimal gradations; the lingering appeal of Lamarckism—the belief in the inheritance of acquired characteristics—which Dawkins brands as "simply false" (*BW* 290); and so on.

Perhaps the only caveat one can express about *The Blind Watchmaker* relates to its subtitle. Dawkins does not in fact pay much attention to the notion that, even if evolution is true, it indicates a lack of design *in the universe*. A lack of design on Earth, specifically relating to living creatures, is plausible enough; but why should we necessarily extend that conception to the universe at large? In *The God Delusion*, Dawkins admits that "Darwinism may not be relevant to the inanimate world—cosmology, for example,"[2] although in that work he assumes that extraterrestrial entities, if there are any, must also have evolved in an analogous manner to earthly entities—an odd assertion for Dawkins to make, given that he himself endorses Carl Sagan's resolute agnosticism as to whether any extraterrestrial entities exist at all (see *GD* 69). But this is a small point.

Dawkins maintains that his study of evolution—and of its enemies—has led inexorably to his atheism. Although many of his earlier books do not discuss religion to any great extent—even *The Blind Watchmaker* addresses creationism only in its final few pages and has nothing at all to say about the "intelligent design" movement—Dawkins has, over the past decade or more, become progressively more concerned about the perniciousness of religion both for its harm to the human intellect and for its evils in politics and society. He wrote vigorously against creationism and religion in his collection of essays, *A Devil's Chaplain* (2003), and produced a controversial two-part documentary on religion, *The Root of All Evil?* (2006)—the title was not Dawkins's—that was shown on British television (predictably, it has not been aired in the United States, although it is available on DVD) and that was the partial basis of *The God Delusion*. That book proved to be an unexpected and immense bestseller, selling more than 1.5 million copies and being translated into more than thirty languages worldwide.

One of the most peculiar criticisms of *The God Delusion* focuses not upon its substance but its tone. The belief among his opponents appears to be that Dawkins has merely written a vicious, ad hominem screed that does nothing but vilify religion by a series of rhetorical flourishes devoid of evidence. To be blunt, I cannot see how any fair-minded reader could have arrived at this conclusion. The tone of *The God Delusion* is precisely the same as that of Dawkins's other books on science—a mixture of forceful and passionate argumentation combined with some lighter moments of harmless fun. There may be a few mildly cheap shots—such as addressing the pious as "faith-heads" (*GD* 28) or referring on occasion to "the Afghan Taliban and the American Taliban [i.e., Christian fundamentalists]" (*GD* 326)—but that seems to be about it. To be sure, Dawkins's discussion of religion and religionists is nowhere near as unrestrained as Christians' attacks on Dawkins himself (and this from a religion that prides itself on being the gospel of love), of which the following example from the ineffable Ann Coulter is among the gentlest: "I defy any of my co-religionists to tell me they do not laugh at the idea of Dawkins burning in hell" (*GD* 360n).

I think the shrieks of the pious on Dawkins's purported intemperate tone have much to do with the fact—as Dawkins himself asserts in a new preface to the paperback edition of his book—that the devout are simply unaccustomed to having the most basic premises and practices of their religion challenged in such a forthright manner. Religion has long been the unworthy beneficiary of kid-gloves treatment from its opponents—a relic from the days when religion-based government could exact the severest penalties for "blasphemy" and other criticisms of religious doctrine and dogma.

In an early chapter, Dawkins outlines his own position. Establishing a seven-stage spectrum between a "strong theist" (someone who *knows* that God exists) and a "strong atheist" (someone who *knows* that God does not exist), Dawkins positions himself one stage short of strong atheism, in which the likelihood of God's existence is defined as follows: "Very low probability, but short of zero. *De facto* atheist. 'I cannot know for certain but I think God is very improbable, and I live my life on the assumption that he is not there'" (*GD* 73). I will confess, for what it is worth, that this is my position also, so I welcome Dawkins's clarification on this point. The rest of his seven-stage schema indicates varying degrees of agnosticism on the subject, ranging from the very high probability of God's existence to exact 50–50 equivalence one way or the other, and so on.

But in this generally sound schema, I believe that Dawkins does not fairly portray the proper position of agnosticism. He appears to regard it as an equivocal fence-sitting and suggests that most agnostics are either those who regard the likelihood or unlikelihood of God's existence as of exactly equal probability or are merely hiding behind agnosticism so as not to incur what in their minds is the social and political opprobrium of outright atheism. While I do not doubt that there are such agnostics, I think Dawkins is not being fair to the one agnostic he chooses to criticize—Thomas Henry Huxley. Dawkins of course has substantial respect for Huxley ("One doesn't criticize T. H. Huxley lightly" [*GD* 72]), but he nevertheless appears to distort Huxley's position. We have seen that Huxley was not one of those who argued that God's "existence and his non-existence are equiprobable" (*GD* 74), and it is simply false to maintain that Huxley "seems to have been ignoring the shading of *probability*" (*GD* 72), which, as we have seen, enters substantially into his evaluations of the possible truth of the "miracles" and other elements in the Bible. In fact, what Huxley was arguing against was both the first and the seventh stage of Dawkins's schema—the "strong theism" and "strong atheism" that professed to *know* whether God existed or did not exist; the stage just prior to strong atheism, which is Dawkins's position, would in fact be a form of agnosticism to Huxley—as in fact it is. As Bertrand Russell remarked, some agnostics are indeed "for practical purposes one with the atheists,"[3] and Dawkins would be one of these. There is also reason to doubt Dawkins's assertion that agnosticism concerning God's existence is merely *temporary* ("It is a scientific question; one day we may know the answer, and meanwhile we can say something pretty strong about the probability" [*GD* 70]): the latter half of the statement is sound enough, but the former half would amount, surely, to proving a negative.

Dawkins then undertakes a relatively brief, even cursory, examination of various "proofs" for the existence of God. There is little that is new here—a point not meant in criticism of Dawkins, since these "proofs" (ranging from Aquinas's arguments regarding the Unmoved Mover, the argument from personal experience, Pascal's wager, and so forth) have been refuted many times before, and it seems a waste of Dawkins's talents that he must engage in such tactics one more time.

Where Dawkins's book gains its greatest value is in its formidable marshaling of scientific evidence—specifically the theory of evolution—to argue that the God hypothesis is not necessary to explain any phenomenon in the universe. At this point it may be worth going into some detail as to the nature of the conflict between science and religion, and why in my estimation there will probably always be a genuine conflict, at least for the foreseeable future. It has lately become fashionable, especially among the still-numerous legions of "reconcilers" of science and religion, to downplay this conflict and to regard it as merely an antiquated holdover from the cocksure positivism of the later nineteenth century, when the two most significant treatises on the conflict—John William Draper's *History of the Conflict between Religion and Science* (1874) and Andrew D. White's *History of the Warfare of Science and Theology in Christendom* (1896)—appeared to tremendous acclaim. But this view is a serious misconstrual of the fundamental nature of the respective enterprises of science and religion.

There are two central issues to address here. The first has to do with the nature and ramifications of scientific causation. In science, when a cause is put forth to explain a given phenomenon, it is implicitly assumed to be in itself a sufficient explanation for that phenomenon; if it weren't, it would not have been put forward. This should be self-evident, but it appears that many scientists—some of whom are not very well versed in philosophical logic—are not clearly aware of the fact. What this means is that, in the realm of causation, the conflict of science and religion becomes a zero-sum game: for every genuine scientific advance that is made, to that extent religiously based causation is nullified. Indeed, the history of the past five hundred years shows a systematic replacement of supernatural causation by natural causation.

Consider the case of comets. The orthodox scientific account of comets is that they are small celestial bodies that have been captured by the gravitational pull of the sun; their "tails" are the result of solar radiation upon the comet's nucleus. This explanation renders the religious explanation (cited in many of the world's scriptures)—that comets are sent by God as baleful warnings of catastrophe, chiefly because of the "sin" of individuals or entire groups of people—immensely unlikely. No scientist has ever sat down and made an effort to disprove this religious explanation; it is simply that the scientific explanation is now so overwhelmingly convincing that the religious account has been left to die a quiet death. Science is the gainer; religion is the loser.

Some religionists have attempted to bring God into scientific causation by the back door by maintaining that God somehow "allowed" or actually "created" comets—or the big bang or evolution by natural selection—so that, under this hypothesis, there is no real "conflict" between science and religion, and the two can live happily ever after sharing the same intellectual space. But I fear that this schema plainly runs afoul of the useful logical device called Occam's razor, which correctly maintains that causes must not be unnecessarily duplicated. If B is the cause of A, it makes no sense to assert that B *and C* can also be the cause of A. By Occam's razor, if B has been established as an adequate and sufficient explanation for A, then C must be cut away as otiose. In this case, C is the religious hypothesis (for which no proof is ever offered, or can be offered) that God "allowed" some particular cause to function.

The second point has to do with the relative domains of science and religion. Dawkins is quite right to criticize his fellow evolutionary biologist Stephen Jay Gould for coming up with the foolish notion that science and religion are different "magisteria" (whatever that may mean), in that they have different realms of expertise: science deals with fact, religion deals with values. This formulation is inherently flawed for a number of reasons: first, it arbitrarily segregates religion and science into different "magisteria" with little attempt to justify why we should accept such a dichotomy; second, it obscures the fact (of which Gould was well aware) that many metaphysical presuppositions of religion are overwhelmingly likely to be false, so that its authority as a handbook of morals or values is at the very least problematical. But the most critical objection to the formulation is a very simple one: *religion has never resisted, and by its nature can never resist, poaching into the "magisterium" of science.*

I would be happy to call a truce to the "conflict" of science and religion if religion stayed within a certain restricted bound and merely offered moral advice to its adherents, but the regrettable fact is that religion has never done that and could not do so by the very nature of its enterprise. One central goal of the great majority of the sacred scriptures of the world is to offer an account of the formation of the universe, the origin of humankind, and other central issues that thinking people must address when they face an immense and frequently incomprehensible cosmos; that these scriptures do so without, in the main, offering even the slightest evidence for their dogmatic assertions is an added handicap. Religionists now have a vested interest in denying the force of this assertion, so they label it also as antiquated and nineteenth century, but the most cursory examination of the world's scriptures will convince us that virtually every one of them presents an account of the universe, and Dawkins is entirely correct in maintaining that these attempts to explain natural phenomena are manifestly scientific propositions that can, should, and must be assessed by science. It is not that science is encroaching upon religion's domain; it is that religion is, and always has, encroached upon the domains that science, by virtue of its tremendous success in actually explaining phenomena, has now rightly claimed for its own. We have a right and a duty to assess whether the origin of humanity lay in a fiat from God, in the form of a figure named Adam and a creature pulled from his rib named Eve, or whether it lay in the gradual evolution of the primates over the course of hundreds of thousands of years. How is it possible that these two views can ever be reconciled? And how is it that our inclination toward the one or the other—our ability to gauge which is the more probable and likely explanation for the origin of the human species—cannot and should not be governed by what science has learned in the course of the past several hundred years?

At this point some of the more sophisticated religionists craft a purportedly clever riposte: admitting with lofty generosity that the Bible (or the Koran or the Bhagavad-Gita) is not a scientific text, they attempt to maintain that their conception of God is not tied to the outmoded dogmas of scripture but is of a more refined and elevated sort that is not amenable to scientific analysis. It is pitifully obvious that this strategy evolved solely as a means of evading scientific scrutiny (and, in all likelihood, refutation) of the truth-claims of religion. It has gained strength in the last century or so, and it results in formulations of which the following (from the religiously inclined mathematician Alfred North Whitehead) is representative: "God is not concrete, but He is the ground for concrete actuality." If anyone can claw a meaning—concrete or otherwise—out of that collocation of words, he is doing better than I. As Walter Lippmann, who quoted this passage, remarked: "A conception of God, which is incomprehensible to all who are not highly trained logicians, is a possible God for logicians alone. It is not presumptuous to say of Mr. Whitehead's God what he himself says of Aristotle's God: that it does 'not lead him very far toward the production of a God available for religious purposes.'"[4]

This discussion may have strayed widely from *The God Delusion*, but it is implicit in much of what Dawkins has to say. His examination of the scientific evidence against the probability of God's existence is impressive, although curiously enough he begins with the evolution of life on this planet rather than with the evolution of the cosmos as a whole. In any event, his emphasis that the theory of evolution can fully explain the origin and development of life on earth is sound. His treatment of the matter, in chapter 4 of *The God Delusion*, is in some senses not quite as satisfactory as it could be; I suspect that he was so overwhelmed with the attempt to explain in a single chapter an issue whose details he has explored in several books, including *The Blind Watchmaker*, that he was not entirely comfortable producing a pared-down version for nonscientific readers.

His discussion gains force is in its mercilessly rigorous dissection of the charade of intelligent design. The proponents of this wretched cloak for creationism have been making much noise in recent years, but thankfully they have suffered serious setbacks, both intellectually and politically, that will likely cause them to shuffle off into the dustbin of pseudointellectual history. Dawkins makes the important point that intelligent design—the notion that certain features of living creatures are so "irreducibly complex" that they can be explained only by appeal to an intelligent designer—does not explain anything: not only does it discourage scientific inquiry by declaring by fiat that some phenomenon or other is irreducibly complex and that's the end of it, but it merely incites the further inquiry: what kind of intelligent designer could have created the phenomenon in question? Dawkins quotes from an article he had previously written with the geneticist Jerry Coyne:

> Why is God considered an explanation for anything? It's not—it's a failure to explain, a shrug of the shoulders, an "I dunno" dressed up in spirituality and ritual. If someone credits something to God, generally what it means is that they haven't a clue, or they're attributing it to an unreachable, unknowable sky-fairy. Ask for an explanation of where that bloke came from, and odds are you'll get a vague, pseudo-philosophical reply about having always existed, or being outside nature. Which, of course, explains nothing. (*GD* 161)

There is, however, a further point to be made here. Dawkins, being English, may not be fully aware that many American proponents of intelligent design—in particular Michael Behe, author of *Darwin's Black Box* (1996) and other tendentious treatises—are deliberately "vague" to the point of agnosticism on the central question of who or what the intelligent designer actually is. They are forced into this position not only because it is impossible if not paradoxical to come up with any coherent definition or description of an intelligent designer, but because if they did come up with such a description that in any way smacked of being akin to a "God," their relentless attempts to force intelligent design into the curricula of American public schools would be immediately halted as a plain violation of the separation of church and state established by the First Amendment. So, although they maintain a belief in an intelligent designer, they are backed into a corner by not being able to specify in any sense what such a designer could be like. Thankfully, this charade was detected in 2005 when a judge in Pennsylvania ruled unequivocally that intelligent design was merely a cover for creationism and ruled it inadmissible in the public schools in his district.

Having established satisfactorily that the God hypothesis is exceedingly unlikely, Dawkins takes up other ancillary issues, specifically why belief in God is and has been so prevalent throughout human history right down to the present day. His answers are not entirely satisfactory. With his relentlessly Darwinian perspective, Dawkins is forced to come up with an explanation of what the "Darwinian benefit" of religion might be, and he has difficulty coming up with an answer. What he concludes is that it is an unintended by-product of something else. Without going into the details of his complex argument, we can say that for Dawkins religion is a by-product of the fact that, for human existence to flourish, children must be taught to obey their elders, who have greater experience than they and can therefore steer them away from potentially dangerous features of daily life; accordingly, children are evolutionarily inclined to accept their parents' (or other respected elders') teachings on religion as well, even though these teachings are almost certain to be false.

This answer is unsatisfactory on a number of grounds, but chiefly on the ground that it fails to account for *why parents or elders began indoctrinating their children into religious belief in the first place*. Here I think that Dawkins's disinclination to bring in the results of anthropology and psychology into his discussion is highly unfortunate, even though his concomitant plea—a highly passionate one—that children should not be brainwashed into religious belief at an early age remains sound for other reasons. Dawkins is right, as I have previously indicated, to assert that the theory of evolution was the final element that made a purely secular view of the world possible, because it resolved the issue of the argument from design, which remained as religion's last trump card in its struggle to provide a satisfactory explanation of the evolution of life, but the anthropological and psychological research of the past century or more has, as I have noted earlier, in many ways resolved the ancillary question of the origin and persistence of religious belief, by showing in meticulous detail and with overwhelming probability that primitive humanity could not have evolved without adopting some religious conception of the universe to account for otherwise inexplicable phenomena. The existence of an immortal soul separate from the body in all likelihood derived from witnessing the figures of dead people in dreams; the notion of godlike creatures—beginning with primitive animism and progressing through polytheism to full-fledged monotheism—was the only feasible hypothesis to account for the array of natural phenomena that the primitive mind, able to conceive of action and volition only in human terms, faced in its daily life. Once this religious hypothesis was established, it was indeed handed down through countless generations of childhood indoctrination, but also maintained through the psychologically consoling features it provided to minds both young and old.

Dawkins, as I say, fails to elaborate on these points or even to mention them, and I think it weakens his book. Instead, he places a misguided emphasis on what he terms *memes*—which he defines as "units of cultural inheritance" (*GD* 222). Dawkins speculates—and he emphasizes that it is no more than that—that memes might have been involved in the transmission of religious ideas down through the ages. The only problem with this conjecture is that the very idea of memes is a purely hypothetical construct devised by Dawkins and some like-minded cohorts; because the term sounds like "genes" (which do exist in the real world), the concept of memes becomes a pseudoscientific "explanation" for a phenomenon—the transmission or dissemination of cultural data—that is very likely not scientific in the sense that Dawkins apparently envisions it. The fact is that cultural transmission occurs in a radically different manner from DNA replication through genes (for example, it can occur simultaneously across a wide spectrum of contemporaneously living creatures by means of the media, rather than through biological reproduction), so the meme concept seems unwieldy and even misleading.

Moreover, several examples of religious "memes" that Dawkins mentions—such as, "There are some weird things (such as the Trinity, transubstantiation, incarnation) that we are not *meant* to understand. Don't even *try* to understand one of these, for the attempt might destroy it. Learn how to gain fulfilment in calling it a *mystery*" (*GD* 232)—are so complex that they can hardly be thought of as a "unit" in any meaningful sense. I suggest that Dawkins drop the notion of memes entirely: it is simply not a useful or convincing tool to explain what he wishes to explain.

The God Delusion gains strength in its later chapters, which treats the complex issue of religion and morality. Even here some caveats can be offered. Dawkins is keen on establishing that we can have a moral sense that does not depend on religion; if he can do this, he will knock down another of the central pillars that, in the eyes of many philosophically untrained individuals, has propped religion up for centuries even in the wake of increasingly devastating evidence of its falsity on metaphysical grounds. How can we be moral without religion? Aside from maintaining that certain moral qualities that are generally valued, such as altruism, are compatible with Darwinian evolution, Dawkins maintains that there may be some "universal moral grammar" (*GD* 255) that drives most of us to have relatively similar moral outlooks regardless of what religion we believe in, if any. The argument is based on statistical surveys showing that "most people come to the same decisions when faced with [moral] dilemmas, and their agreement over the decisions themselves is stronger than their ability to articulate the reasons" (*GD* 255). This conclusion is, frankly, unsound, and it certainly does not warrant the belief that "we have a moral sense which is built into our brains, like our sexual instinct or our fear of heights" (*GD* 255). What that apparent uniformity indicates is, at best, a cultural conditioning that leads many people in a given society to think in roughly similar ways about certain moral cruxes. But the history of human society indicates such a wide array of opinions on other issues, as well as rifts within a given society—as in our own divisions over such issues as abortion, the place of gays and lesbians in society, euthanasia and assisted suicide, and so on—that it is impossible to envision what a hard-wired "moral sense" could possibly be like.

The crux of the issue, as Dawkins realizes, is that a secular morality lacks "authority." On what grounds should we behave in one way or another? I have maintained elsewhere that there are, regrettably, no grounds at all, and that the moral subjectivism evolved by Bertrand Russell, A. J. Ayer, and others is the only system of morality that is not riddled with logical errors; this is not a flaw in secular ethics, but simply an admission that this is how things are in the world.

Dawkins keenly enunciates the argument of a theist who maintains: "If you don't believe in God, you don't believe there are any absolute standards of morality. With the best will in the world you may intend to be a good person, but how do you decide what is good and what is bad? Only religion can ultimately provide your standards of good and evil. Without religion you have to make it up as you go along" (*GD* 264). This is a highly articulate exposition of the religionist's plea, and it appears unanswerable—except for the fact that, as Dawkins proceeds to examine in a subsequent chapter, the actual morality crafted by the religions of the world, as embodied in their scriptures, is oftentimes little short of barbaric (the term he uses is "obnoxious" [*GD* 268]). He mercilessly exposes the countless instances of moral doctrines in the Bible that virtually all of us have now rejected—stoning for adultery or homosexuality or sabbath breaking, the slaughter of entire populations of defeated enemies (which Dawkins rightly terms "ethnic cleansing" [*GD* 280]), and so on. The result is plain: "My main purpose here has not been to show that we *shouldn't* get our morals from scripture (although that is my opinion). My purpose has been to demonstrate that we (and that includes most religious people) as a matter of fact *don't* get our morals from scripture" (*GD* 283). What this means is that our moral sense has evolved independently of any adherence to a religious creed, so that *everyone's* morality is one that "you have to make up as you go along."

Dawkins also addresses another fancied trump card of theists: If atheism is so good, what about such atheists as Hitler and Stalin? Aren't they worse than any religious persecutors in human history, and don't their depredations indicate that atheism is even more brutal than religion? To this Dawkins has a pungent two-part answer. First, Hitler was not an atheist. In what will no doubt startle many, Dawkins establishes that Hitler was raised as a Catholic and went to Catholic school for years; as late as 1941 he stated to one of his generals, "I shall remain a Catholic for ever" (*GD* 311). Dawkins is not engaging in Catholic bashing here, for he acknowledges that Hitler may not have been "a sincerely believing Christian" (*GD* 311), but he does go on to remark soundly that the long history of Christian anti-Semitism (Jews as God-killers and so forth) unquestionably colored Hitler's racist ideology, if indeed it was not the foundation of it: a speech of 1922 makes this point irrefutable ("How terrific was His [Jesus'] fight for the world against the Jewish poison" [*GD* 312]). As for Stalin, he was indeed an atheist, but Dawkins shrewdly observes that his savagery was not a *result* of his atheism; it was surely political in origin and development. As Dawkins remarks, "Individual atheists may do evil things but they don't do evil things in the name of atheism" (*GD* 315). He could have strengthened his case by stating that the Soviet indoctrination of its citizens into dogmatic atheism was exactly equivalent to the religious indoctrination that Dawkins rightly censures, to the point that Soviet and Chinese atheistic communism *became a religion* with all the evils that religion entails.

On occasion, however, Dawkins appears to go a bit overboard in his attempt to indict religion. The very opening of his book appears to maintain that such baleful events as 9/11, the Israeli/Palestinian wars, and the "troubles" in Northern Ireland would not have occurred without religion. No one of Dawkins's intellectual acuity could really think that these conflicts would simply have been wiped off the pages of history if religion had not existed, and in a later chapter, he writes with some irritation, "Yes yes, of course the troubles in Northern Ireland are political" (*GD* 294), a point that could be made about the other conflicts he singles out; it is at least arguable that Dawkins is correct in stating that, in each of these conflicts, religion was a central catalyst for them, for the particular viciousness in which they were manifested, and for the irreconcilability of their participants. But such casually formulated hypothetical arguments do not strengthen his case against religion.

A final chapter of *The God Delusion* treats the issue of the consolations of religion. Here again I think Dawkins's discussion could have been ampler than it was. While he is unquestionably sound in asserting that there is nothing in atheism that would lead one toward depression or undue angst, and that any number of religionists have admitted that they are themselves tormented by notions of sin, everlasting perdition, and other things of this sort, it could be maintained that Dawkins does underestimate the consoling aspects of religion. Any number of surveys have found that religious people are, on the whole, generally happier than nonreligious people. The precise ramifications of such surveys remain debatable, and some words can be said to bolster the atheist side of the matter. First, the numbers are not so lopsided as to suggest anything approaching a definitive answer to the question. Second, it could be argued that a cow, with its relatively simpler cognitive and psychological makeup, is generally happier than a human being, but that doesn't mean it is better to be a cow. Third, there is something to be said for facing the world in a bold and forthright fashion without subscribing to fantasies: for how real or secure is "happiness" based upon a delusion? Is there not always the danger that disillusion will be even more shattering if believers are faced with the sudden collapse of their comforting worldview, as customarily happens when natural or human-generated disasters lead to the predictable soul-searching over the insoluble dilemma of how and why an omniscient and omnipotent god can allow bad things to happen to good people? And, finally, the poll numbers may be a statistical anomaly, since there has been little evidence to suggest that religious people are happy *because of* their religion. Given recent research indicating that psychological well-being is intimately connected to brain chemistry, it is at least conceivable that, by a statistical accident, more religious people have good brain chemistry (which is not an indication of intelligence, since it has also been widely established that increasing intelligence positively correlates to increasing religious skepticism) than nonreligious people. I, personally, am one of the most cheerful people I know, much more so than the religious people of my acquaintance, but I very much doubt that my own atheism, or my friends' religiosity, is any direct cause of my happiness or their relative lack of it. As Bertrand Russell pointed out, intellectual beliefs of this sort have relatively little to do with our sense of satisfaction or well-being.

Dawkins himself, and *The God Delusion* in particular, has been the subject of any number of attacks and attempted rebuttals. One of the most peculiar is Alister E. McGrath and Joanna Collicutt McGrath's *The Dawkins Delusion?: Atheist Fundamentalism and the Denial of the Divine* (2007), issued, predictably, by a religious publisher rather than a mainstream press. McGrath had previously attempted a more general rebuttal to Dawkins's views in *Dawkins' God* (2005), but *The Dawkins Delusion?* takes its aim directly at *The God Delusion*.

It begins curiously. Throughout the introduction, the text makes persistent references to the first-person singular ("Although I was passionately and totally persuaded of the truth and relevance of atheism as a young man"),[5] in spite of the plain fact that the book prominently lists two authors (presumably McGrath and his wife) on the title page. In fact, the "I" appears to refer only to Alister; only at the end of the book do we learn that he wrote most of it, with Joanna writing those passages relating to Dawkins's discussion of the Bible.

But that is the least of the book's problems. As my quotation from it attests, McGrath (I shall now consider him the sole author of the arguments and opinions in the work) maintains that he was once an atheist and, during or after his obtaining the DPhil at Oxford in molecular biology, he parted ways from Dawkins and became a believing Christian. But what McGrath pointedly neglects to mention (and his omission is so glaring that it amounts to disingenuousness) is that he was raised as an Irish Protestant and attended the Methodist College Belfast, so it is at least a fair conjecture that he has, for reasons only he can answer, reverted to the faith in which he was indoctrinated: he somehow became convinced, remarkably, that "Christianity was a much more interesting and intellectually exciting worldview than atheism" (*DD* 9)! All this makes it all the more curious that McGrath, while acknowledging that "Dawkins and I have thus traveled in totally different directions," feels that the dichotomy "raises some difficult questions *for Dawkins*" (*DD* 9; my emphasis). Why only for Dawkins? Given the overwhelming negative evidence that has accrued against the existence of God, the afterlife, the divinity of Jesus, and other central tenets of Christianity, why is it not more pertinent to ask why McGrath's reconversion to orthodox Christian belief raises difficult questions for *him*?

McGrath blithely claims that he could, if he wished, undertake a point-by-point rebuttal of every single matter raised in *The God Delusion*, but that such an undertaking "would be unspeakably tedious and would simply lead to a hopelessly dull book that seemed tetchy and reactive." Instead, what McGrath proposes to do is to "challenge him [Dawkins] at representative points and let readers draw their own conclusions about the overall reliability of his evidence and judgment" (*DD* 13). This consideration for the welfare of his potential readers is touching; but if there is anything that could be defined as an intellectual cop-out, this must be it. Those "representative points" prove to be merely random and quite unsystematic attempts at hitting Dawkins where McGrath thinks he is weakest, but his own analysis is so riddled with captiousness, crude caricature, willful misrepresentation, question begging, circular reasoning, and a simple lack of cogency that McGrath ends up casting serious doubt upon his own "evidence and judgment." The overall effect of McGrath's little book—the text, minus notes and bibliography, is all of 97 pages—is distressingly similar to a little boy kicking the shins of a hulking football player and thinking that he has thereby defeated his opponent. If this is the best that Dawkins's opponents can do, then he has little to worry about.

The curious thing is that McGrath ends up conceding the validity of Dawkins's contentions at key points, only to attempt to wiggle out of them with feigned caveats. For example, he fully agrees with Dawkins that childhood indoctrination into religion is a bad thing, but then warns ominously that indoctrination into dogmatic atheism would be just as bad—a suggestion that Dawkins never makes in his book and would surely oppose. As we have seen, Madalyn Murray O'Hair, who could be considered a much more strident atheist than Dawkins, herself refrained from any such indoctrination of her own children, leaving them to settle religious questions on their own when they were old enough to do so. McGrath, as someone trained in molecular biology, also disapproves of the intelligent design movement, but then makes the remarkable claim that Dawkins (as well as cognitive scientist and philosopher Daniel C. Dennett) have harmed the battle against this bogus movement by their "hysterical and dogmatic insistence on the atheist implications of Darwinism," which "is alienating many potential supporters" (*DD* 49). The claim is too preposterous even for credence: it is exactly the forceful attacks on intelligent design by Dawkins, Dennett, and other prominent scientists that have resulted in the collapse of this intellectual charade—aided, of course, by its crushing defeat in 2005 at the hands of that valiant judge in Pennsylvania.

Finally, McGrath agrees with Dawkins in deprecating religious extremism and fundamentalism—at least of the Islamic sort, although McGrath is quite in error in thinking that Dawkins's "ire is directed primarily against Islamic fundamentalism, particularly its *jihadist* forms" (*DD* 76). In fact, Islam comes up for relatively sparse discussion in Dawkins's book, and his main target is Christian extremism and fundamentalism, a point that McGrath does everything he can to obscure. This is because McGrath is unable to come to grips with the many centuries of such extremism and fundamentalism in his own religion, which resulted in untold misery for untold millions—all those "witches" who were burned at the stake; all the "heretics" who suffered the same fate; all the Jews, Muslims, and other non-Christians who were forcibly "converted" to Christianity; and so on. Nowhere in his little book does McGrath address any of these issues—nor, a fortiori, does he address the plain fact that these tactics were not considered "extreme" or "fundamentalist" until about the last century or so, but were instead central pillars of orthodox Christian belief until atheists, agnostics, and secularists shamed the church into abandoning or minimizing them. The plain fact is that these and other practices of the church, which only now are considered reprehensible by the church itself, have clear scriptural support, and they have been discarded only by the desperate expedient of brushing those embarrassing portions of scripture under the rug.

A single example of McGrath's philosophical blunders will suffice. In disputing Dawkins's (and others') attempt to account naturalistically for the origin and persistence of religious belief in the face of its overwhelming unlikelihood, McGrath convicts Dawkins of the error of circular reasoning. He paraphrases Dawkins's argument ("No spiritual realities exist outside us. Natural explanations may be given of the origins of belief in God") and concludes: "In the end, this is a circular argument, which presupposes its conclusions. It begins from the assumption that there is no God and then proceeds to show that an explanation of God can be offered which is entirely consistent with this" (*DD* 57). But Dawkins has not *presupposed* the nonexistence of God: his discussion of the origins of belief has been strategically placed *after* his meticulous argument—one that McGrath has done nothing to damage—that the existence of God is monumentally implausible in the face of what we now know about the operation of the universe. There is therefore no a priori "assumption" of the nonexistence of God; instead, once Dawkins has established the claim that the likelihood of such an existence is vanishingly small, he is obligated to offer a naturalistic account of how that belief could have arisen and could be maintained in the teeth of such overwhelming evidence.

What is striking about McGrath's little book is that it nowhere *offers a single shred of positive evidence for the existence of God, or even any evidence that could make such a belief even remotely plausible*. This cavernous omission, which besets *Dawkins' God* as well (a windy polemic that does little more than assert that Dawkins has not *definitively disproven* the existence of God—as if atheists must now undertake the philosophical impossibility of proving a negative if their claims are to stand up to scrutiny), is perhaps the most transparent indication of McGrath's intellectual desperation. While consistently criticizing Dawkins for the harshness of his tone (a criticism that, as I have already maintained, is itself wide of the mark), McGrath adopts exactly the same hostile and negative strategy: he is far more abusive toward Dawkins than Dawkins is toward religion. And the lack of intellectual substance to support this abuse renders McGrath's little book nothing more than a querulous whine.

One other attack on Dawkins may be worth addressing, since his opponents evidently set much store by it. Terry Eagleton wrote a harsh review of *The God Delusion* in the *London Review of Books* (October 19, 2006).[6] Unfortunately, Eagleton, although a gifted literary critic and theoretician, has no special training in science and—at least on the basis of his review—precious little in philosophy, so he is unable to battle Dawkins on his own turf; instead, Eagleton, who was raised Catholic and maintains that he is both a Catholic and a Marxist socialist, if that is comprehensible, can attack Dawkins only on what he believes to be his signal failing: his refusal to give religious thinkers serious discussion. "What, one wonders, are Dawkins's views on the epistemological differences between Aquinas and Duns Scotus? Has he read Eriugena on subjectivity, Rahner on grace or Moltmann on hope?" Eagleton would be mortified to learn that, outside the Catholic penumbra, few philosophers take these thinkers very seriously anymore, and in some cases they haven't for a good many centuries. In any case, since the thinkers just cited rarely engage in any debate over the existence of God—they merely assume it as a given—they are not even relevant to Dawkins's discussion. Dawkins has, in fact, taken on some contemporary theologians who actually attempt to debate the issue, such as Richard Swinburne in *Is There a God?* (1996). (Swinburne's great contribution to theology, incidentally, is his belief that the Holocaust was a good thing because it gave Jews a chance to demonstrate courage and nobility.)

Unlike McGrath, Eagleton actually does attempt to establish that there is a God and to characterize what that God could be like. Eagleton ridicules Dawkins for his view of God—"He seems to imagine God, if not exactly with a white beard, then at least as some kind of *chap*, however supersized." I think this is a false assertion, but even if it were true, might it not be because—well, because most of the world's scriptures actually portray God in this fashion? We surely do not need to resurrect the well-known "So God created man in his own image" (Gen. 1:27) to clinch the point. For his part, Eagleton goes on to offer the following luminous account: "[God] is, rather, the condition of possibility of any entity whatsoever, including ourselves. He is the answer to why there is something rather than nothing." If this is the answer (and, of course, Eagleton does nothing but merely assert it, offering no evidence of any kind), it is a rather opaque one; and, as Dawkins himself has established in his book, it only incites another query: *Why* did God create something rather than nothing? The idea that there needs to be a "why" for the existence of the universe is more than a little curious: it is precisely analogous to the little boy persistently asking his mother "Why? Why? Why?" as she, with decreasing patience, attempts to explain some elementary fact of existence.

Eagleton presents (again without evidence) further claims about this nebulous and ill-defined god. It now seems that he created the world "not [as] a measure of how very clever he is, but to suggest that he did it out of love rather than need." How does Eagleton know this? How is it not more plausible to assume, given the untold quantities of misery on this earth, that God created the world to torture any living beings that happen to have the misfortune to dwell on it? I have no evidence for this assertion, but in that regard I have just as much evidence as Eagleton has. And the rest of Eagleton's discussion—again nothing more than a series of unsupported assertions, such as the dubious contention that Jesus "reveals the Father as friend and lover [?] rather than judge"—comes alarmingly close to conceiving of God exactly as "some kind of *chap*." Once again, if this is the best that Dawkins's opponents can do, then he has little to worry about.

Whatever the possible shortcomings of *The God Delusion*, it remains one of the soundest and most compact expositions of the "case for atheism" ever written. But it is only a start: there is so much more to be said on the matter that one should use it only as a stepping-stone to further investigation. As a stepping-stone, it is not likely to be improved upon.

Chapter 13

Sam Harris: The Passionate Freethinker

Chronologically, Sam Harris (b. 1967) was the first author of recent years to publish a best-selling book about atheism—or, strictly speaking, a book attacking religion and faith as in themselves pernicious. This circumstance is remarkable enough in itself, but it is even more remarkable that his book, *The End of Faith: Religion, Terror, and the Future of Reason* (2004), was Harris's first published book. So far as I can tell, Harris had published little or no work, even magazine or newspaper articles, prior to issuing *The End of Faith*, although he now writes frequently for the *Washington Post*, *Newsweek*, and a number of online venues. Harris followed up his first book with *Letter to a Christian Nation* (2006), a slim tract that was a product of the many letters he received in response to his first book. A third work, *The Moral Landscape* (2010), is forthcoming as of this writing.

Harris has been somewhat cagey about his own religious upbringing. It appears that he was born to a Jewish mother and a Quaker father but that he refused to participate in a bar mitzvah. Elsewhere he has stated that his household was largely secular and that God and religion were rarely discussed. Harris himself attended Stanford University, majoring in English, but dropped out. Years later he returned, gaining a BA in philosophy. In 2009 he obtained his PhD in neuroscience from UCLA.

The most significant sentence in *The End of Faith* occurs on virtually the last page of the book: "I began writing this book on September 12, 2001."[1] I imagine that Harris wishes to suggest (for he does not fully clarify the relevance or ramifications of this remark) that the terrorist attacks on the United States on September 11, 2001, gave a particular urgency to sentiments he had harbored well before these cataclysmic events, but there may also be an unwitting suggestion that some of Harris's book is the product of the overwhelming emotions engendered by those attacks, with the result that some of his conclusions have been arrived at hastily and without a proper and judicious consideration of their full scope and implications. I fear that this latter suggestion, whatever its cause, is one that I found increasingly compelling as I read his book.

What Harris wishes us to understand in no uncertain terms is that religion is increasingly leading people to kill. He is fully aware of the long and bloody history of religion, about which he has little good to say, but he is particularly exercised by the nearly incomprehensible phenomenon of suicide bombers and of those who would deliberately target civilians; he believes that there must be something about religion that is now causing people to behave in this utterly irrational manner. At a minimum, Harris is to be praised for looking unflinchingly at the terrorist attacks of 9/11 and stating clearly that religion, and not merely sociopolitical advantage, must be a root cause and perhaps the sole cause behind them. And he maintains that the threat that religion poses to civilization extends well beyond Islam: we must be willing to give an unbiased and objective look at Christianity, especially Christian fundamentalism, for the social, intellectual, and political dangers it poses.

But Harris stumbles almost out of the gate. In his fervent desire to condemn all religion, he makes careless blunders that harm the very cause—the cause of reason, science, and common sense—he claims to espouse. He asserts, for example that "the central tenet of *every* religious tradition is that all others are mere repositories of error or, at best, dangerously incomplete. Intolerance is thus intrinsic to *every* creed" (*EF* 13; my emphasis). It is exactly this kind of error that Harris's religious opponents will jump upon—as, I imagine, they have. Harris knows better than this. He himself states, elsewhere in his book, that the Jain religion of India, which honors all life as sacred, right down to insects, "would endanger no one. In fact, the uncontrollable spread of Jainism throughout the world would improve our situation immensely" (*EF* 148); he further suggests that Buddhism is a fairly innocuous and nondogmatic religion, although he remarks plausibly (but without providing much evidence) that Buddhism in its original form "is not a religion of faith, or a religion at all, in the Western sense" (*EF* 283). The list could be extended significantly. Hinduism, to be sure, has its share of dogmas derived from its sacred texts, but, as Alf Hiltebeitel states, the modern conception of the religion—"that Hinduism is essentially monotheistic, that caste is not essentially Hindu, that Hindu tolerance does not deny the truths of other religions, that Hinduism is in accord with modern science"[2]—would seem anything but intolerant. The recent rise of "Hindu fundamentalism" as embodied in the Bharatiya Janata Party is, to my mind, largely a cynical political movement designed to win elections and consolidate power. Even more significantly, Greco-Roman religion was almost entirely a matter of ritual: there was no infallible "sacred text," no set of dogmas to which a citizen had to subscribe, and no connection whatever between religion and morality: the ancients left the debating of morals to the philosophers, where it belonged. Moreover, when the Greeks and Romans conquered foreign territories, they meddled relatively little with local religious practices and even made a rather far-fetched attempt to syncretize the local gods with their own pantheon. (Rome very sporadically "persecuted" Christians because it regarded the Christians—rightly as it happened—as dangers to the political stability of the empire.)

Like Richard Dawkins, Harris makes simplistic assumptions on the exclusively religious basis of well-known conflicts throughout the world. In speaking of the troubles between India and Pakistan over the past half century, particularly the bloody partition that occurred after the independence of India in 1947, in which a million or more people were killed, Harris remarks: "The cause of this behavior was not economic, it was not racial, and it was not political. . . . The only difference between these groups consists in what they believe about God" (*EF* 27). Harris must know better than this. The welter of social, political, economic, racial, and other issues surrounding the India-Pakistan dilemma—which includes such things as prejudice by lighter-skinned people against darker-skinned people (a trait found in India itself, especially as manifested in prejudice by lighter-skinned Northerners against darker-skinned Southerners), the control of key areas of land and natural resources, and the bitter legacy of British colonialism—makes such a childishly elementary analysis risible.

When addressing what is probably one of his most passionate concerns—the religious evil embodied in the figure of Osama bin Laden—Harris may also be guilty of oversimplification. He asks, in trying to understand "*why* Muslim terrorists do what they do":

> Why would someone as conspicuously devoid of personal grievances or psychological dysfunction as Osama bin Laden—who is neither poor, uneducated, delusional, nor a prior victim of Western aggression—devote himself to cave-dwelling machinations with the intent of killing innumerable men, women, and children he has never met? The answer to this question is obvious—if only because it has been patiently articulated ad nauseam by bin Laden himself. The answer is that men like bin Laden *actually* believe what they say they believe. They believe the literal truth of the Koran. (*EF* 28–29)

Well, maybe not. Quite frankly, I have no idea what bin Laden "actually" believes—and Harris doesn't either. No one does, except bin Laden himself. Since we cannot read his mind, it is at least plausible to assume that he may in part be using the bloody religion of Islam as a convenient tool for accomplishing broader sociopolitical aims. That he has not personally been a "victim of Western aggression" means nothing: Gandhi did not experience any great degree of personal victimization at the hands of the British in India, but he nevertheless felt a burning desire to free his countrymen from the British yoke. Bin Laden could well feel that his fellow Muslims, or fellow Arabs, have been ill treated by the West (through its economic, political, moral, and even aesthetic practices, as in the dissemination of books, films, the Internet, and other cultural products), so that his sense of grievance extends not to merely a Western army or Western political figures, but to the peoples of the West at large. I do not put this claim forward in extenuation of bin Laden, but merely in an attempt to come to a clear understanding of his motivations. The fact is that we do not know with any certainty what is in bin Laden's mind, since his relatively few known utterances were meant for public consumption and cannot be attributed to him in any simple or straightforward manner. If Harris were less of a scientist and more of a literary critic, he might not have succumbed so readily to the intentional fallacy.

There is, moreover, a certain alarmist sentiment that pervades *The End of Faith* and makes it seem far from the coolly reasoned treatise Harris wants it to be. When he states, "*Millions* among us, even now, are quite willing to die for unjustified beliefs, and millions more, it seems, are willing to kill for them" (*EF* 64; my emphasis), he surely exaggerates to a significant and even unconscionable degree. I am hardly one to hold a brief on behalf of religion, but this careless utterance does not accomplish any good for the cause of atheism. In *Letter to a Christian Nation*, Harris suggests that there are now 150 million Christian fundamentalists in the United States[3]—I think that number is a bit high, perhaps vastly higher than it should be—but only one or two such individuals have gone out and shot abortion doctors or committed other capital crimes. As for Islam, Harris is refreshingly blunt: "We are at war with Islam" (*EF* 109). He continues:

> We are at war with precisely the vision of life that is prescribed to all Muslims in the Koran, and further elaborated in the literature of the hadith, which recounts the sayings and actions of the Prophet. A future in which Islam and the West do not stand on the brink of mutual annihilation is a future in which most Muslims have learned to ignore most of their canon, just as most Christians have learned to do. Such a transformation is by no means guaranteed to occur, however, given the tenets of Islam. (*EF* 109–10)

It sounds pretty grim. But are we justified in thinking that the West is threatened by *millions* of Muslims who seek to kill us? In his long chapter, "The Problem with Islam," Harris blithely dismisses any sociopolitical considerations—such things as "the painful history of the Israeli occupation of the West Bank and Gaza . . . the collusion of Western powers with corrupt dictatorships . . . [and] the endemic poverty and lack of economic opportunity that now plague the Arab world." Harris continues: "But I will argue that we can ignore all of these things—or treat them only to place them safely on the shelf—because the world is filled with poor, uneducated, and exploited peoples who do not commit acts of terrorism" (*EF* 109).

Once again, Harris has presented a superficial account of an immensely complex issue. The one thing he fails to explain, in his discussion of Muslim terrorism, is: *Why is it only now, after a millennium and a half, that (a very few) Muslims have resorted to suicide attacks and other acts of terrorism*? Nowhere does Harris portray the slow, inexorable decline of what was once a flourishing Muslim world empire—the control of Spain by the Moors from 711 until they were thrown out of the region of Granada in 1492; the rise of the Ottoman Empire from its emergence in 1299 to its apogee in 1566, when it controlled significant parts of Europe; to its final defeat by the West shortly after World War I—something that no doubt colors much of the deep-seated Muslim resentment of Western economic and political power. And if Harris wishes us to take at face value the utterances of Osama bin Laden, then surely he is obliged to take seriously Osama's repeated claims that the Israeli occupation of Palestine is a central issue in his campaign. Harris even claims that Muslims were united in supporting Saddam Hussein when the United States invaded Iraq in 2003, even though Harris knows that Saddam was a *secular* Arab whom the devout Muslim should have despised: if millions of Muslims nonetheless rooted for him, how can this support have been anything but geopolitical or anticolonialist in origin?

In my judgment, the Arab world is indeed sensing that it has been left behind by history, and some fanatics are using this humiliating fact to gain what vengeance they can against a West that is now immensely more powerful than anything they can imagine. In this fight, acts of terrorism—perhaps the only actions that the powerless can take against the powerful—have now become the chosen weapon. I again assert all this not in defense of terrorism; I am merely suggesting that the motivations of terrorists are somewhat more complex than simply a literalist adherence to a sacred text.

An historical parallel might be worth considering. In the later nineteenth century, much of Europe and America were petrified by the thought of the dangers posed by anarchists—those who were inspired by the Russian thinker Mikhail Bakunin and others who explicitly advocated the violent overthrow of governments. For a time, these dangers seemed chillingly real: an American anarchist of Polish ancestry, Leon Czolgosz, assassinated President William McKinley in 1901. But the anarchists' greatest achievement—if it can be called that—occurred in what is now a virtually forgotten incident: On September 16, 1920, a time-bomb exploded at the corner of Broad and Wall Streets in lower Manhattan, killing 30 and injuring 400. The bomb had been left on a one-horse truck situated directly in front of the US Assay Office and across the street from the J. P. Morgan Building. Ultimately, 39 people would die of their injuries in what might be the deadliest terrorist attack on American soil prior to the Oklahoma City bombing of 1995. This incident bears remarkable similarities to the 9/11 attacks on the World Trade Center: in both cases, the heart of America's financial district was the target, in a deliberate attempt to disrupt markets and cause economic havoc to the nation.

Yet this incident is largely forgotten (the perpetrators were never found, even after a several-year manhunt) because the anarchist movement faded quickly away after this date, partially as a result of the US government's crackdown on communists and other perceived "subversives" and partially as a result of the intellectual poverty of the anarchist movement itself. Today, no one is afraid of anarchists. I believe it is at least arguable that Islamic terrorism might go the same way: without unduly simplifying the matter myself, I think that a number of factors—the spread of new technologies that are relieving the insularity of Arab peoples, the ultimate demise of oil as a valuable commodity, and, yes, the likelihood that there will be a kind of Arab "enlightenment" that causes many Muslims to doubt the efficacy of their religion—may allow the specter of Muslim terrorism to fade in the coming decades. It is at least as plausible a scenario as Sam Harris's own perfervid worries about an imminent collapse of world civilization.

Harris does seem to present a compelling case that the Koran is in itself a bloody text—that it frequently, even unremittingly, advocates violence toward "infidels" and "unbelievers." But what Harris seems to overlook, in the several pages of quotations to this effect that he presents, is that, with only one or two exceptions, every quotation seems straightforwardly to assert that *God* (not human beings) will punish infidels either in this life or (more frequently) in the afterlife. There is rarely any explicit command, or even a suggestion, that faithful Muslims take direct action to extirpate infidels. One exception—"Slay them wherever you find them. Drive them out of the places from which they drove you. Idolatry is worse than carnage" (2:190f.)—is indeed pretty clear on the matter, although even here it becomes doubtful whether Muslims are obligated to attack "infidels" in territory that Muslims never controlled, such as the United States. Once again, I am in no way defending the numerous vicious passages in the Koran (although in this regard they can be matched by various texts in the Bible: "Break their teeth, O God, in their mouth: break out the great teeth of the young lions, O Lord" [Psalm 58:6]); I am merely suggesting that Harris's indictment of the Koran is a bit overdone.

In several ways, Harris's work in neurobiology may actually have impeded—or, at least, muddied—his understanding of religion and the way it operates in the real world. He seems wedded to a view that one's beliefs lead immediately and irrevocably to action, when in fact the relations between belief and action are infinitely complex and unpredictable. Possibly Harris's quick dismissal of free will—he dispenses of it in a long footnote (*EF* 262–64), paying short shrift both to philosophers (such as A. J. Ayer) and scientists (such as the atheist Daniel C. Dennett) who have explored the matter in far more detail and profundity than he has and who have concluded that there may be no contradiction between a "soft" determinism and free will—has something to do with the matter. But the issue comes forth in certain alarmist assumptions Harris makes, especially in regard to Islam. He presents the results of surveys that have found wide theoretical support in Muslim countries for the moral justice of suicide bombing in defense of Islam: 73 percent of people in Lebanon, for example, support such action. Harris is perhaps right to be appalled by these statistics, but he doesn't draw a fairly obvious conclusion from them: *only a tiny fraction of such people actually become suicide bombers.* Lebanon has the highest ratio of people who support suicide bombers among the countries polled (although such nations as Saudi Arabia, Yemen, Egypt, Iran, Iraq, and others were not polled). But, although the modern phenomenon of suicide bombing could be said to have emerged in Lebanon in the early 1980s during its civil war, today we do not hear of many suicide bombings in Lebanon. Perhaps this is because there are no foreign troops in Lebanon at the moment; but we do not hear that any suicide bombers elsewhere in the world, either successful or foiled, were of Lebanese origin.

What Harris seems to overlook in this entire discussion is that religion is only one motivating force among many that govern people's behavior. Especially in the West, even in the United States, it appears that religion may not be the chief factor—or, indeed, a factor at all—in the overwhelming bulk of daily actions that human beings undertake. There may be millions of Christian fundamentalists in this country, but their behavior seems largely indistinguishable from that of other people except in a limited range of circumstances. As an unbeliever, I am continually surprised that *any* person claiming to be devout can watch *any* television show on network or cable TV, since the vast majority of such shows appear to be chock full of sex, violence (although, by a bizarre historical accident, Americans appear to have blandly inured themselves to witnessing high levels of grisly violence), and other objectionable behavior. I myself have developed a reprehensible taste for the sitcom *Two and a Half Men*, in which the lead character (played by Charlie Sheen) is a sex-obsessed but financially successful man with an expensive beachside house in Malibu who engages in repeated sexual escapades with married women (hence making them adulteresses) or in "fornication" (the very word has become comical) with a host of hot-bodied single women whom he has no intention of marrying, let alone in begetting offspring with. Yet Sheen's character is portrayed as successful, happy, and carefree—much more so than his hapless brother, who is divorced, penniless, and neurotic and has trouble getting laid. And this show, which seemingly violates religious taboos and moral dicta, is one of the most popular on television, and I know of no concerted attempt to protest its raunchiness or to launch boycotts against it or anything of the sort. Is it possible that religious people, like everyone else, are able to compartmentalize their belief systems—that they can put aside their religious and moral dogmas and enjoy a crude laugh once in a while? Is it even possible that some of these same people can gain a certain modicum of aesthetic pleasure out of the clever dialogue and situations exhibited on the show?

This general problem also afflicts Harris's analysis of the origin and maintenance of "faith" itself. In the chapter "The Nature of Belief," he presents a somewhat pedantic account of how people actually behave in ordinary circumstances, stating that most people require a certain "coherence" in their beliefs about the functioning of the normal features of their lives to get through the day. But when he then comes to the study of religion, he is unable to provide a clear account of why religious people continue to believe in their dogmas even when these dogmas do not "cohere" with the nature of the world around them. He apparently has no option but to conclude that such people are, essentially, insane:

> It takes a certain kind of person to believe what no one else believes. To be ruled by ideas for which you have no evidence (and which therefore cannot be justified in conversation with other human beings) is generally a sign that something is seriously wrong with your mind. Clearly,

> there is sanity in numbers. And yet, it is merely an accident of history that it is considered normal in our society to believe that the Creator of the universe can hear your thoughts, while it is demonstrative of mental illness to believe that he is communicating with you by having the rain tap in Morse code on your bedroom window. (*EF* 72)

This is a highly unsatisfactory account. In my more cynical moments, I would be the first to believe that religious people are crazy, but there is obviously much more to it than that. I have already examined, in my chapter on Richard Dawkins, the anthropological and psychological origins of religious belief. I can now go on to say that religious belief perseveres, even in the face of massive evidence to the contrary, because *explicit* disproof of its central contentions is either difficult or impossible. It is not possible to prove that there is *not* a god; it is certainly not possible to prove that there is no afterlife (and, incredibly, Harris seems to think that there is some "credible evidence" for the notion of reincarnation [*EF* 232]); and so forth. This lack of falsifiability (exhibited also in the realm of politics) is a central reason for the continuance of belief in an age in which science has presented enormous amounts of negative evidence to the contrary. Of course, the general public's ignorance (lack of information) and stupidity (lack of reasoning power) have much to do with the matter.

Harris's treatment of morals, in the long chapter "A Science of Good and Evil," is similarly beset with difficulties. Harris, for all his secularism, fervently yearns to be a moral absolutist—or, at any rate, a moral objectivist. In *Letter to a Christian Nation*, he states his adherence to "objective moral truths" (*LC* 23), while in *The End of Faith*, he declares: "Many people appear to believe that ethical truths are culturally contingent in a way that scientific truths are not. Indeed, this loss of purchase upon ethical *truth* seems to be one of the principal shortcomings of secularism" (*EF* 170). He spends the great bulk of the chapter attempting to present evidence opposed to this view, but, as I have stated earlier, this "shortcoming" is not a shortcoming of secularism but simply an acknowledgment of the way the universe operates.

Harris, as a scientist, seems unwilling to accept that in certain realms of human life, *facts* may not come into play except indirectly; he also seems to take a perverse pride in not deriving much benefit from previous philosophical writing on the subject: "There is a wide literature on morality and ethics . . . but like most writers who have pretensions to 'first philosophy,' I have not found much use for it here" (*EF* 267). Harris need not have made such an admission, for his philosophical naïveté is evident on every page of his account. He certainly cannot have read the atheist J. L. Mackie's *Ethics: Inventing Right and Wrong* (1977), who begins his book with the blunt statement: "There are no objective values,"[4] and who goes on to prove this contention with unremitting cogency. Harris could also have derived some benefit from reading Bertrand Russell, A. J. Ayer (*Language, Truth and Logic*), and any number of other treatises that clarify the precise ontological and epistemological status of ethics.

Most of all, Harris could have profited from reading David Hume, whose central ethical contention—one cannot derive "ought" from "is"—remains the central pillar of any ethical analysis. There is no *logical* means of proceeding from a statement of facts to a recommendation of the ethical value of those facts. This is because *ethical statements are not statements of fact, but emotional responses to facts*. Harris candidly admits that the statement, "Murder is wrong," "while being uncontroversial in most circles, has never seemed anchored to the facts of the world in the way that statements about planets or molecules appear to be" (*EF* 170). He thinks he has solved this problem, but he hasn't. This is because the statement in question really breaks down, logically, to two statements: (1) "There is such a thing as murder," and (2) "I happen not to approve of it." The first statement is a statement of fact; the second is the expression of a preference. *All ethical judgments are expressions of a preference*. They may be *based* on facts (or falsehoods), but they are not *in themselves* facts (or falsehoods).

Harris thinks he has solved this dilemma (if indeed it is a dilemma): "A rational approach to ethics becomes possible once we realize that questions of right and wrong are really questions about the happiness and suffering of sentient creatures. If we are in a position to affect the happiness or suffering of others, we have ethical responsibilities toward them" (*EF* 170–71). This is no doubt noble and worthy, and could be the foundation of an eminently workable system of ethics—*but the expression of such an ethical goal is not a statement of a fact*. I am sorry to report that someone who declares that he does not believe in promoting the happiness of others, but instead believes in augmenting their suffering, is in a *logically* impervious position. Such a person is merely expressing his preference. Harris goes to the extent of wondering if there really are any persons who would deny the validity of his chosen moral system: "What about people who do not love others, who see no value in it, and yet claim to be perfectly happy? Do such people even exist? Perhaps they do" (*EF* 187). Harris must live in a very rarefied environment if he does not sense that there can be such people. But even if there are no such people—even if, *per impossibile*, everyone's moral judgments were exactly identical—one could still not state that morals were objective: this implausible uniformity would simply mean that everyone has the same preferences.

Offensive as it may be to many, it is a brutal truth that everyone's system of morals is merely a bundle of preferences that, insofar as they are preferences, are logically shielded from refutation. To say that I prefer chocolate ice cream to vanilla ice cream is the expression of a preference; I am not (factually) "wrong" for this preference, except in the trivial sense that I would be wrong if I were lying about my preference. The difference between this preference and the belief that "Murder is wrong" is only a difference of degree, not of kind. Just as I can have no *factual* dispute with a person who prefers vanilla ice cream to chocolate ice cream, so I can have no factual dispute with someone who thinks "Murder is right"—because, for example, he believes in the extirpation of the human race as the highest moral good. Such a view is not by any means irrational, even though it has obviously been espoused by relatively few—Schopenhauer, for instance, or Tolstoi (who in fact based his belief on his understanding of Christianity). There is, indeed, an entire school of philosophy based on the theory that human consciousness is productive of such agonizing pain for the great majority of human beings that universal suicide is the only remedy.[5] But one would not even need a reason (plausible or otherwise) to justify the view that "Murder is right"; the expression of the preference would be sufficient in itself.

Harris gets himself into further trouble by heaping abuse on the much-maligned notion of moral relativism. His presentation of this idea is beset with two difficulties: first, it is a caricature of the view that the saner moral relativists have presented, and it ignores the critical fact that *moral relativism is not itself an ethical system, but an analysis of ethical systems*. Moral relativism customarily asserts that any individual's moral system is largely determined by his upbringing, education, socioeconomic status, national origin, place in human history, and any number of other factors—a view so self-evidently obvious that it is difficult to see how anyone could dispute it. Harris's own chosen ethical system—that we should maximize the happiness and minimize the suffering of "sentient creatures"—is itself a time-bound conception, since it now includes (and I am glad it does) many animals, an ethical development of extreme recency. Of course, moral objectivists like Harris find this whole notion deeply offensive and—in an ironic meeting of the minds with his religious opponents, such as the hapless Dinesh D'Souza—believe that an embrace of moral relativism is logically incoherent, or that it makes it impossible to take a firm moral stance on any issue. But this is a fatal misunderstanding of the situation.

It is entirely possible to have a firm, even a passionate, moral stance while accepting to the full the notions of moral subjectivism (all moral systems are a set of preferences) and moral relativism. D'Souza, in *What's So Great about Christianity*, maintains absurdly that I would have no reason to object if D'Souza punched me in the face, because I would simply have to maintain that he and I share different moral standards based on our education, upbringing, etc. But my objection would stem from my preference that people not be punched in the face without reason; it violates my moral code even if that code is not itself a *fact* but a preference. I happen to like my preferences and, in certain circumstances, will go pretty far in defending them. The idea that moral subjectivists or relativists could not, for example, summon up the gumption to battle against other "evils" practiced in the world is a myth. If the United States passed a law ordering the immediate execution of atheists (or Jewish Americans, or gays and lesbians, or fundamentalist Christians), I would be the first to take whatever action I could to prevent such a law from being enacted, because it is my preference that whole classes of people not be killed en masse without due process of law; this is not the kind of society I would care to live in. So the idea that moral subjectivism or relativism somehow inhibits our moral outrage or the actions that we might take based upon that outrage is simply false.

Harris is far too quick to dismiss both the cultural origins of certain moral practices and the very wide differences in moral systems and practices over the millennia. It was the understanding of the extent of these differences that led philosophers to doubt the objectivity of morals in the first place. And, indeed, moral relativism can be a useful weapon against religion itself. Present-day religionists (Christians, at any rate) are themselves moral relativists when gauged by historical standards. Five hundred years ago, a great majority of Christians would have been on the lookout for witches and heretics to execute, non-Christians to convert by force, and so on. Today's Christians think and believe very differently, for historical reasons that have been well charted, so it turns out that Christianity itself is subject to moral relativism, in spite of the loud protestations of its supporters.

Moreover, moral relativism can be turned to one's own benefit: if we are forced to recognize, at least in part, the validity (on cultural grounds) of other societies' moral systems, then they are likewise obligated to recognize our own. Hence the moral soundness of several European countries' recent attempts to ban the wearing of the Islamic burqa (the veil that covers a woman from head to foot) as a clear violation of European notions of freedom, secularism, and women's social and political equality.

The plain fact is that, without an understanding of the full extent of moral subjectivism and moral relativism, it is impossible to make sense of the seemingly implacable discord between the adherents of different sides of moral issues. It becomes immediately evident that these disputes rest not upon any knowledge (or lack of knowledge) of *facts*, but merely a difference in *preference*. Consider the question of abortion, one of our most intractable moral conundrums. Harris seems to think that opposition to abortion (which he fails to recognize is not solely religious in origin) is merely "irrational" (*EF* 165) and that a broader understanding of the matter (say, the value of stem-cell research) might change many people's minds. But that likelihood is very remote. It is true enough that one cannot find any passage in the Bible that explicitly prohibits abortion (the Catholics, of course, don't need any such passage, since their infallible popes have decreed that such a prohibition cannot be questioned), but the matter really comes down to preference: one side prefers to vaunt the moral supremacy of the fetus, the other the moral supremacy of the mother. Some headway might be made by pointing out the internal incoherence of the antiabortion position. If pro-lifers maintain that the fetus is already endowed with a soul that must be respected, what happens to the soul of the mother? Under this scenario, her own humanity would appear to be denied, so that she becomes nothing more than an incubator—

a baby-making machine whose own health and wishes appear to count for nothing, and who could therefore be thought to have been rendered soulless. Whether this argument would persuade any significant number of people is an open question, but the only way we can proceed in many moral disputes is to point out possible self-contradictions in the facts that underlie a moral stance.

Yet we should be forthright in facing the fact that most moral disputes eventually reach an impasse merely because of differing preferences. Hitler's prejudice against Jews was apparently based on his belief in their biological inferiority. This belief is scientifically false, so to that extent his prejudice against Jews is based upon a falsehood. But if he had merely stated, "I happen not to like Jews," we would not have a *factual* case against him—however much we would be within our rights to be appalled at his moral stance and to do everything in our power to prevent him from acting upon it.

I do not wish to be too hard on Sam Harris. His books are written with a passion and perspicacity that are admirable and worth emulation. It is a bit odd that he does not actually articulate his own stance, nor does he present any clear-cut refutations of conventional religious beliefs. His position seems to be that the tenets of religion are not merely *unproven* but *unprovable*. There is much to be said for this view. How, at this stage in history, are we to *prove* that Jesus was product of a virgin birth? To appeal to the Bible is useless, for two reasons: (1) the reasoning would be fatally circular, because the only way the Bible's testimony on the matter could be accepted would be to assume that it was inspired by God, which is the very point at issue, and (2) as Harris keenly points out, not only do the gospels of Mark and John say nothing about the virgin birth, and not only does Paul seem to have no knowledge of it, but it appears that the whole idea of the virgin birth was the result of a mistranslation into Greek of the Hebrew passage (Isaiah 7:14) that purportedly "predicted" such a birth. In the passage in question—translated in the King James Version as "Behold a virgin shall conceive, and bear a son"—the word translated as "virgin" in reality means "young woman." The Revised English Bible (1989) is more honest on the matter: "A young woman is with child, and she will give birth to a son."

Harris's exposure of the evils of religion (the Inquisition, the Holocaust as ultimately inspired by the legacy of Christian anti-Semitism) are relatively unremarkable, although they are expressed with verve and pungency: "Anti-Semitism is as integral to church doctrine as the flying buttress is to a Gothic cathedral" (*EF* 92). But he gets into trouble again when he maintains that the United States' "war on drugs" is also motivated by religion. This simply does not seem to be the case, and Harris presents no evidence for it, writing vaguely, "When one looks at our drug laws—indeed, our vice laws altogether—the only organizing principle that appears to make sense of them is that anything which might radically eclipse prayer or procreative sexuality as a source of pleasure has been outlawed" (*EF* 160). I have never heard such an argument offered by proponents of the drug laws, and Harris presents none. His comment would apply more pertinently to the ridiculous prohibition against prostitution, but he does not discuss this issue to any significant degree.

Some of the most valuable parts of *The End of Faith* are those that treat religious "moderation." In this country, any number of major denominations have renounced literal belief in the Bible, and to that extent are able to claim that they have dispensed with some of the more offensive parts of scripture (the death penalty for adulterers, homosexuals, and sabbath violators; the belief that the world is flat and that the Sun revolves around the Earth; the condoning of slavery), but in so doing, as Harris shrewdly notes, they have implicitly rejected the "divine" inspiration of the Bible and have rendered their own position incoherent. They are, in essence, picking and choosing what parts of scripture they wish to believe in—and that decision is based on an independent factual and moral stance that has been significantly influenced by the advance of (secular) knowledge and morals over the past several centuries. Harris also maintains that the very existence of this "liberal" or "moderate" Christianity renders it difficult to criticize religion in any sense, even fundamentalist religion:

> Moderates do not want to kill anyone in the name of God, but they want us to keep using the word "God" as though we knew what we were talking about. And they do not want anything too critical said about people who really believe in the God of their fathers, because tolerance, perhaps above all else, is sacred. To speak plainly and truthfully about the state of our world—to say, for instance, that the Bible and the Koran both contain mountains of life-destroying gibberish—is anti-

> thetical to tolerance as moderates currently perceive it. But we can no longer afford the luxury of such political correctness. We must finally recognize the price we are paying to maintain the iconography of our ignorance. (*EF* 22–23)

Letter to a Christian Nation was inspired by the thousands of letters that Harris received, mostly from Christians and many rather hostile ("The truth is that many who claim to be transformed by Christ's love are deeply, even murderously, intolerant of criticism" [*LC* vii]). As such, Harris addresses his remarks directly to fundamentalist Christians, using the second person throughout. It is a hard-hitting little book (it does not seem to contain more than 20,000 words of text) that in some instances restates the points in *The End of Faith* and in other instances addresses new issues—the biblical condoning of slavery, the intellectual incoherence of intelligent design, and so on.

What Sam Harris accomplished in *The End of Faith*, in however flawed a manner, was to bring atheism—or, since he is relatively silent about his own beliefs in that book, it would be more accurate to say the blunt and forthright criticism of religion—to the forefront, tying it (albeit in a somewhat exaggerated and even hysterical way, to my mind) with the threat it may pose to world civilization. In some ways, it is surprising that it became a bestseller at all, but the fact that it did so is the clearest indication one needs that there is a widespread desire to hold religion accountable for its manifold derelictions in the intellectual, social, and political spheres. And whatever defects there may be in Harris's discussion are virtually redeemed by the eloquent epilogue to the book, which passionately states the case for shedding religious belief to the betterment of our lives:

> No myths need be embraced for us to commune with the profundity of our circumstance. No personal God need be worshipped for us to live in awe at the beauty and immensity of creation. No tribal fictions need be rehearsed for us to realize, one fine day, that we do, in fact, love our neighbors, that our happiness is inextricable from their own, and that our interdependence demands that people everywhere be given the opportunity to flourish. The days of our religious identities are clearly numbered. Whether the days of civilization itself are numbered would seem to depend, rather too much, on how soon we realize this. (*EF* 227)

Chapter 14

Christopher Hitchens: The Evils of Religion

Christopher Hitchens (b. 1949) is a figure who rarely sidesteps controversy. Born in England and now holding both British and American citizenship, he has for decades shuttled back and forth across the Atlantic when he is not traveling even more widely as a foreign correspondent. His articles appear regularly in both British and American journals, and although he is generally of leftist political leanings—he started out as a Marxist—the events of September 11, 2001, caused him to revise his stance somewhat, to such a degree that he has been called a neoconservative, a label he rejects. It is unfortunate that he coined the term *Islamofascism* to denote Muslim terrorism, for this clumsy coinage was quickly adopted by the neoconservatives he professes to disdain as an excuse for an aggressively interventionalist foreign policy, especially the invasion of Iraq in 2003, a move Hitchens continues to support.

Atheism has been a core element in Hitchens's thinking for many years. Although his grandmother was Jewish, and even though he has been married twice (once in a Greek Orthodox ceremony to a Greek Cypriot woman, and then in a Reform Jewish ceremony), he makes no secret that his atheism has been of long standing. Although his numerous books are, for the most part, collections of his periodical essays or treatises on somewhat arcane subjects (his first book, published in 1984, was a historical study of Cyprus), he has also written significant books on George Orwell, Thomas Jefferson, and Thomas Paine's *The Rights of Man*. In 1995 he augmented his notoriety by writing a short polemic against Mother Teresa, *The Missionary Position: Mother Teresa in Theory and Practice*, and a dozen years later, he was the third recent writer to attain bestseller status with *God Is Not Great: How Religion Poisons Every-*

thing (2007). He quickly followed up this work with a serviceable anthology, *The Portable Atheist* (2007). A memoir, *Hitch-22*, was published in 2010.

From a superficial glimpse, it might be easy to conclude that *The Missionary Position* is a deliberate attempt to "bring down" a holy icon by any means necessary, even if it requires a perversion of the facts or, somewhat more innocuously, a purposefully slanted interpretation of acknowledged facts. A deeper investigation, however, reveals that if any distortion has been done in regard to Mother Teresa's reputation, it has occurred on the side of those who vaunted her as a living saint. Hitchens's small book (it is just under one hundred pages of relatively large type) grew out of a documentary he made for the BBC entitled *Hell's Angel* (1994), which predictably led to "venomous and irrational attacks"[1] on Hitchens. (There is no evidence as to whether Mother Teresa herself took note either of the documentary or of the book prior to her death in 1997.) He states that, up to the time of his writing, there were at least twenty works on Mother Teresa (probably even more than that, even by 1994; there are now—according to the online catalog of the New York Public Library—close to one hundred, including other video documentaries, of which Hitchens's is not included), and that they were all favorable to her and written in an attitude of almost abashed reverence. So is there another, darker side to the picture? It did not take Hitchens much effort to find that the answer was yes.

It is one thing to discover that, throughout her career, Mother Teresa was "keeping company with several . . . frauds, crooks and exploiters" (*MT* 8); perhaps some of this can be excused by her need to drum up charitable contributions from all possible sources for her Missionaries of Charity. But there seems to be much more to it. Why was she so keen on hanging around such lowlives as the vicious dictator Jean-Claude ("Baby Doc") Duvalier of Haiti; such politicians and financiers (and convicted criminals) as Marion Barry, former mayor of Washington, DC; and Charles Keating? Is it that their devotion to religion trumped, in her mind, any other derelictions they may have committed in the secular world? If so, her system of morals deserves serious examination. The situation with Keating was particularly egregious. He had donated more than $1 million—much or all of it gained from his avowedly criminal activities in the savings and loan scandals of the 1980s—to Mother

Teresa's charity; in return, she wrote an appalling letter to the judge overseeing his criminal case, requesting mercy in his sentencing. She began the letter with a hypocritical demurrer ("We do not mix up in Business or Politics or courts"—although that is exactly what she was doing here) and pleading that Keating had always been "kind and generous to God's poor" (*MT* 67)—except, that is, to the hapless small investors he had ripped off. In reply, Paul W. Turley, the deputy district attorney for Los Angeles County, fired back a heated but studiously polite letter stating that it would have been more in tune with the canons of justice if Mother Teresa had returned the $1 million that Keating had given to her, since it was not his money to give. To this letter (which Hitchens prints in his book for the first time [*MT* 68–70]) no reply was given.

Even this behavior might be forgiven if the charity work that Mother Teresa was doing in Calcutta for decades were actually worth doing—but of even this there are strong doubts. Her devotion to the poor, the diseased, and the friendless would seem to be exemplary of the best that religion can do. Why is it, then, that, even though one of her many bank accounts (this one in Utah) contained the sum of $50 million, her various hospitals around the world were so poorly equipped? It is bad enough that these people were sick and dying; it is worse that they were "not allowed to watch TV or smoke or drink or have friends over. Even when they are dying, close friends are not allowed" (*MT* 42). This testimony comes from Elgy Gillespie, who worked for a time at Mother Teresa's San Francisco branch. It gets worse: there is substantial evidence that in many of these clinics, patients were actually denied medical assistance for curable diseases: a fifteen-year-old boy who had a "relatively simple kidney complaint" (*MT* 40) was allowed to die rather than given antibiotics or an operation. The result, as Hitchens notes, is that Mother Teresa erected "a cult based on death and suffering and subjection" (*MT* 41).

There is a singular irony in this, because Mother Teresa herself believed that she was put on this earth to fight against what she regarded as the two greatest evils in the world: abortion and contraception. Hitchens dryly remarks, after visiting one of her orphanages in Calcutta: "It is difficult to spend any time at all in Calcutta and conclude that what it most needs is a campaign against population control" (*MT* 24). But she appeared to have one more goal: to "convert" (by stealth if necessary) as many non-Catholics as possible so that hell is not filled even more than it already is with benighted heretics and unbelievers. According to the testimony of Susan Shields, who worked with Mother Teresa in various locales around the world:

> Mother taught the sisters how to secretly baptize those who were dying. Sisters were to ask each person in danger of death if he wanted a "ticket to heaven." An affirmative reply was to mean consent to baptism. The sister was then to pretend she was just cooling the person's forehead with a wet cloth, while in fact she was baptizing him, saying quietly the necessary words. Secrecy was important so that it would not come to be known that Mother Teresa's sisters were baptizing Hindus and Moslems. (*MT* 48)

To an atheist, of course, this voodoolike mummery is entirely harmless, even if comical and preposterous, but one suspects that the adherents of other faiths would not look kindly upon this surreptitious "conversion."

One of the best parts of *The Missionary Position* is its seriocomic tale of Malcolm Muggeridge, once a keen British social and cultural critic who in his old age became something of a religious fanatic. While working on his own documentary on Mother Teresa for the BBC, aired in 1969, he felt he had experienced an authentic miracle: After filming footage in a dark residence called the House of the Dying, Muggeridge was astounded to discover, when later viewing the footage, that the images were in fact clearly visible. Muggeridge himself exclaimed: "It's divine light! It's Mother Teresa. You'll find that it's divine light, old boy" (*MT* 27). (I like that "old boy" remark—so distinctively British.) Unfortunately, Muggeridge's cameraman, Ken Macmillan, calmly pointed out that the effect was the result of a new kind of film created by Kodak. But Muggeridge's "miracle" had by this time already spread and is still being talked about. To Hitchens, however, the significance of the episode is very different: "It is the first unarguable refutation of a claimed miracle to come not merely from another supposed witness to said miracle but from its actual real-time author. As such, it deserves to be more widely known than it is" (*MT* 27). But, alas, the average person is far more inclined to believe in "miracles," however fake, than in the debunking of miracles, however real.

It is a question worth discussing whether Hitchens wrote *God Is Not Great* merely to ride the wave of atheistic bestsellers triggered by Sam Harris's *The End of Faith* and Richard Dawkins's *The God Delusion*, but there is reason to doubt it. Hitchens had made his atheist views known long before the turn of the twenty-first century, especially in the volume *Letters to a Young Contrarian* (2001), and in *God Is Not Great* he testifies that "I have been writing this book all my life and intend to keep on writing it."[2] Although he cites Harris's book on several occasions, his references to Dawkins focus entirely on the latter's work as an evolutionary biologist, leading one to believe that the had not read *The God Delusion* by the time he began (or completed) his own tract. And, indeed, his book is of a substantially different character from either Harris's or Dawkins's. It is true that Hitchens has no particular expertise in science, philosophy, theology, or any of the other specialized areas of knowledge that pertain to religion; but his native intelligence, and even more his extraordinary gift for mellifluous and, on occasion, mordant prose make his book by far the most enjoyable work of these three bestselling treatises, at least from an aesthetic perspective. And Hitchens draws keenly upon his world travels as a political journalist and sometime foreign correspondent: as a result, his book is much more *worldly* than Harris's or Dawkins's, revealing at first hand how religion actually operates in the real world.

At the outset Hitchens lays down his four "irreducible objections" to religion, "that it wholly misrepresents the origins of man and the cosmos, that because of this original error it manages to combine the maximum of servility with the maximum of solipsism, that it is both the result and the cause of dangerous sexual repression, and that it is ultimately grounded on wish-thinking" (*G* 4). I am not entirely sure how well or how exhaustively Hitchens has treated all, or any, of these issues, but he provides entertaining commentaries on a wide variety of tangentially related subjects along the way.

Although Hitchens has a relatively brief chapter titled "The Metaphysical Claims of Religion Are False," he does not present the systematic rebuttal of "proofs" of God that we find in Dawkins's *The God Delusion*. Instead, he asserts plausibly that the theological work associated with such medieval thinkers as Aquinas and Moses Maimonides is a thing of the past. "Faith of that sort—the sort that can stand up at least for a while in a confrontation with reason—is now plainly impossible" (*G* 63).

This is simply because *we now know too much about the universe*. "Today the least educated of my children knows much more about the natural order than any of the founders of religion" (*G* 64). It is for this reason that all attempts, right down to the present, to "reconcile" science and religion are doomed to failure: *We do not need God to explain anything anymore*. There is quite literally no phenomenon in the universe, including its origin, where a natural, secular explanation is not, at the very least, more plausible than any of the accounts offered by any of the religions of the world; in many cases, the secular account is so overwhelmingly superior as an explanatory tool that the religious account (for example, of lightning) simply falls by the wayside as a curiosity of intellectual history.

Hitchens devotes a pungent chapter on the conflict of religion and medicine. In medicine science has made many of its most signal achievements—oness that can be seen and understood by even the most ignorant, and which have made an incalculable difference in the life and welfare of all human beings on the planet. To many of these accomplishments religion has been implacably opposed—for the very good reason that any advance in medicine negates, to that degree, a modicum of the control that religion seeks to maintain over people's lives:

> The attitude of religion to medicine, like the attitude of religion to science, is always necessarily problematic and very often necessarily hostile. A modern believer can say and even believe that his faith is quite compatible with science and medicine, but the awkward fact will always be that both things have a tendency to break religion's monopoly, and have often been fiercely resisted for that reason. What happens to the faith healer and the shaman when any poor citizen can see the full effect of drugs and surgeries, administered without ceremonies or mystifications? (*G* 46–47)

Have we forgotten that many of the women suspected of being "witches" were really shrewd manipulators of natural remedies that were in fact far more efficacious than prayers or masses could ever be? Have we forgotten that a variety of mental illnesses were depicted by churches as signs of demonic possession—a point that remains in the Catholic church's somewhat sheepish but still strongly defended doctrine about exorcism? And we certainly don't need to be reminded of how many people of the cloth have maintained that AIDS is a punishment meted out to homosexuals for their "sinful" behavior.

A lengthy chapter on "Arguments from Design" does not add much to Dawkins's resounding defense of Darwin, but one piquant anecdote is difficult to overlook. The rabid communist-hunter Whittaker Chambers recorded in his memoir *Witness* that he abandoned atheistic communism when he experienced an epiphany: he witnessed the apparent perfection of his baby daughter's ear! As Hitchens explains, "A fleshy flap of such utter beauty must be divine." He remarks:

> Well, I too have marveled at the sweet little ears of my female offspring, but never without noticing that (a) they always need a bit of a clean-out, (b) that they look mass-produced even when set against the inferior ears of other people's daughters, (c) that as people get older their ears look more and more absurd from behind, and (d) that much lower animals, such as cats and bats, have much more fascinating and lovely and more potent ears. To echo Laplace, in fact, I would say that there are many, many persuasive arguments against Stalin-worship, but that the anti-Stalin case is fully valid without Mr. Chambers's ear-flap-based assumption. (*G* 79)

Hitchens recognizes that, however much religionists seek to defend their faith through appeals to nature, they are ultimately obliged to rely on their sacred texts; and in several tart chapters dissecting, in succession, the Old Testament, the New Testament, and the Koran, he lays bare the manifest intellectual and moral deficiencies of these texts. In his discussion of the Old Testament, Hitchens introduces the provocative notion of "antitheism": "By this I mean the view that we ought to be glad that none of the religious myths has any truth to it, or in it. The Bible may, indeed does, contain a warrant for trafficking in humans, for ethnic cleansing, for slavery, for bride-price, and for indiscriminate massacre, but we are not bound by any of it because it was put together by crude, uncultured human mammals" (*G* 102). Hitchens goes on to relate the findings of recent archaeologists and other scholars who have ascertained that the figure of Moses is almost certainly a myth and that the Israelites' exodus from Egypt is similarly fictitious. These stories were probably invented centuries after their putative occurrence. He quotes the French

Dominican archaeologist Roland de Vaux, "If the historical faith of Israel is not founded in history, such faith is erroneous, and therefore, our faith is also" (*G* 103).

Hitchens's chapter on the New Testament—"The 'New' Testament Exceeds the Evil of the 'Old' One"—is oddly titled, because it is not chiefly devoted to the moral or other "evils" of the Christian scripture but rather to the plain fact that the Gospels are all manmade (not inspired by God) and contain numerous contradictions. He presents startling evidence that one of the most affecting stories in the Gospels—the celebrated tale of the woman taken in adultery, leading to Jesus' noble utterance, "He that is without sin among you, let him first cast a stone at her" (John 8:7)—is almost certainly spurious. Professor Barton Ehrman—no raving atheist, since he attended two Christian fundamentalist academies—came to the following unnerving conclusion about this passage:

> The story is not found in our oldest and best manuscripts of the Gospel of John; its writing style is very different from what we find in the rest of John (including the stories immediately before and after); and it includes a large number of words and phrases that are otherwise alien to the Gospel. The conclusion is unavoidable: this passage was not originally part of the Gospel. (*G* 122)

In dealing with the Koran, Hitchens draws both upon his study of the text and its origins and upon some striking first-hand knowledge of the actions of present-day Muslims. Whereas Christians assert merely that the Bible was "inspired" by God, Muslims maintain that Allah actually *dictated* the Koran in some fashion. Indeed, some scholars maintain that it is both impossible and impious to translate the Koran out of Arabic, since the inevitable result would be something other than the text as handed down by Allah. To this assertion, Hitchens dryly remarks that this would mean that "god is or was an Arab (an unsafe assumption)" (*G* 124). He explains the textual uncertainties in the Koran, a result of the potentially ambiguous manner in which Arabic is written. This has produced the now celebrated conjecture that those seeking "martyrdom" (by, say, committing suicide attacks) will not be rewarded in Paradise by a passel of white "virgins" but by a cluster of white raisins.

The problem with Islam, of course, is not so much the uncertainties relating to its founding (was there even a Muhammad? did such a person ever exist?) but its present-day dangers to the stability of the world. The fatwa that the Ayatollah Khomeini of Iran issued against the novelist Salman Rushdie for *The Satanic Verses*—a fatwa that extended, in theory, to Rushdie's publishers worldwide, to booksellers, and to anyone else who even indirectly disseminated the "blasphemous" text—caught the world by surprise: this death sentence upon someone merely for writing a satirical novel seemed such a recrudescence of the darkness of the Middle Ages that many Westerners had difficulty wrapping their minds around the idea. Hitchens gained an up-close look at how this whole bizarre matter played out: he took in Rushdie for a night or two in his own apartment in Washington, DC, in 1993—the fatwa was still in effect—when Rushdie was scheduled to meet with President Clinton. An "enormous and forbidding security operation was necessary" (*G* 30) to ensure Rushdie's and Hitchens's safety, and Hitchens was later debriefed by the State Department. And one of the more shameful by-products of the whole sorry episode was that Western religious figures, including the archbishop of Canterbury, the chief Sephardic rabbi of Israel, and the cardinal archbishop of New York, spoke out on the matter—in defense of the Ayatollah. When push comes to shove, religions stick together against perceived "blasphemers." One wonders if Christians were looking a bit wistfully at the continuing political power of Islam—a power that they can only dream about, now that religion has been defanged in the West and thrown out of the seats of power.

The Rushdie scenario was repeated, after a fashion, in the 2005 controversy surrounding the publication of cartoon satirizing Islam (including one portraying Muhammad's turban in the shape of a bomb) by a Danish cartoonist. Hitchens is right to express horror and dismay at what ensued: *People were killed by Muslims because of a cartoon*. If anything indicates the madness and paranoia that religion can foster, this must surely be it. It may be that only a limited number of Muslims actually committed violence, but they were supported by a vast majority of others, and few Muslims spoke out against the resulting violence. And, once again in a reprise of the Rushdie situation, Western religious figures took exactly the wrong attitude: "Islamic mobs were violating diplomatic immunity and issuing death threats against civilians, yet the response from His Holiness the Pope and the archbishop of Canterbury was to condemn—the cartoons!" (*G* 281). That the rest of the world was being bullied into abnegating its hard-won right to freedom of expression was the worst phase of the affair.

Hitchens is, indeed, strongest when dealing with the political and social ramifications of religion—points on which Dawkins and Sam Harris are not at their best. He presents one of the most penetrating discussions of the intersection of religion and slavery that I have come upon—especially in regard to the overthrow of slavery in the West. We hardly need to rehearse the numerous passages in the Old and New Testaments that present an open-faced defense of the institution of slavery (Paul's exhortation should be sufficient for our purposes: "Servants, be obedient to them that are your masters according to the flesh, with fear and trembling, in singleness of your heart, as unto Christ" [Eph. 6:5]). It is a comforting myth that Christianity led the battle against slavery in the late eighteenth and nineteenth centuries. This canard overlooks the fact (not mentioned by Hitchens) that the first nation in the West to outlaw slavery was the atheistic France of the postrevolutionary period: it banned slavery in 1793. Even if such figures as William Wilberforce and William Lloyd Garrison were led by their understanding of Christian principles to oppose slavery, it is odd that the campaign took more than a millennium and a half to get underway—a period in which the Christian church was one of the leading slaveholders in Western society.

Turning to the twentieth century and the campaign of the Reverend Martin Luther King Jr. to rectify the multitude of social and political injustices that the mere freeing of the slaves in the United States had failed to address, Hitchens makes several pertinent remarks. First, it was the Southern churches that were at the forefront of the battle *against* civil rights for African Americans and that fought tooth and nail to preserve the status quo against "communist" agitators. As for King himself,

> many of King's inner circle and entourage were secular Communists and socialists who had been manuring the ground for a civil rights movement for several decades and helping train brave volunteers like Mrs. Rosa Parks for a careful strategy of mass civil disobedience, and these "atheistic" associations were to be used against King all the time, especially from the pulpit. (*G* 179–80)

The fact is that those upholding slavery and prejudice against African Americans had considerably better support in scripture than those on the other side.

Hitchens knows that, when all the other arguments in support of religion fail (as they invariably do), the pious play their trump card: the "atheist" regimes of the twentieth century, including Hitler's Nazis and the Soviets under Stalin, have engendered far more violence than anything the church has done in the past two millennia. Hitchens takes a number of different tacks to dispose of this issue. He does not, as with Dawkins, make the case that Hitler was himself the product of Catholic upbringing and education, although he does stress that the centuries-long legacy of Christian anti-Semitism undoubtedly played a critical role in the shaping of his own views. Instead, Hitchens presents striking evidence of the degree to which the Catholic church allied itself with both Hitler and with Mussolini. Some years after he came to power in 1922, Mussolini came to an understanding with the Vatican, in the so-called Lateran Pact of 1929: "Under the terms of this deal, Catholicism became the only recognized religion in Italy, with monopoly powers over matters such as birth, marriage, death, and education, and in return urged its followers to vote for Mussolini's party" (*G* 235). As for Nazism, the record is still more distressing. The notorious Pope Pius XII, whom the current powers-that-be in the Vatican wish to elevate to sainthood, not only wrote a shamefully ingratiating letter to Hitler only a few days after his becoming pope in February 1939 ("Here at the beginning of Our Pontificate We wish to assure you that We remain devoted to the spiritual welfare of the German people entrusted to your leadership" [*G* 239]), but orchestrated the escape of many Nazi war criminals (many of whom were professing Catholics) to South America: "It was the Vatican itself, with its ability to provide passports, documents, money, and contacts, which organized the escape network and also the necessary shelter and succor at the other end" (*G* 240).

Hitchens's overriding point, in discussing the complex interplay between the church and these "atheist" regimes, is that they shared a fundamental quality: *they were both totalitarian*. "In the early history of mankind, the totalitarian principle was the regnant one. The state religion supplied a complete and 'total' answer to all questions, from one's position in the social hierarchy to the rules governing diet and sex. Slave or not, the human was property, and the clerisy was the reinforcement of absolutism" (*G* 232).

The horrors continue. The tragedy of Darfur is largely a product of religious conflict, in which Christians are centrally involved: Sudan's campaign of murder against the Muslims in Darfur was led by a dubious individual named Joseph Kony, the leader of the "Lord's Resistance Army" who was raised as a choirboy and advocated a "fanatical preachment of Christianity" (*G* 189). So too the horror of Rwanda, "the most Christian country in Africa" (*G* 190), where prominent figures in the Rwandan Catholic church led the hideous slaughter of Tutsis by the rival Hutu tribe. And to go back a little further in history, South African apartheid was largely "Calvinism in practice" (*G* 251): the Dutch-speaking Afrikaners adhered to the vicious policy of the Dutch Reformed Church that prohibited not merely the mixing of black and white, but even the coexistence of the two races on equal terms. It took the African National Party, which contained "many atheist and agnostic militants" (*G* 252), the better part of a century to overthrow this immoral regime.

Overall, the tone of Hitchens's book is somewhat sharper than Dawkins's or Harris's: the words "stupid" and "evil" are frequently found, and throughout the text Hitchens lower-cases "god"—a deliberate insult to the pious. (This would suggest that the title of his book should properly be rendered, e. e. cummings–fashion, as *god is not great*.) At the same time, the book lacks the fiery indignation of *The End of Faith*—and does so by design, for Hitchens's evident purpose is to skewer religion not only by means of logical argument but by that dry wit, satire, and ridicule which only the British seem able to manage. This, along with the witchery of his prose, is what makes *God Is Not Great* the entertaining reading experience that it is.

Richard Dawkins, Sam Harris, and Christopher Hitchens all cover substantially different territory in their three bestselling books, but as a triumvirate, they have presented some of the most compelling arguments against religion that we are likely to see. In the face of their attacks—supported by the best science and logic that human beings have been able to marshal over the past two millennia—the supporters of religion have been left with little ground to stand on.

EPILOGUE

I trust I may end on a personal note. I will frankly confess that many of the central issues pertaining to religion—the existence of God, the existence of the soul and its survival after death, the existence of heaven and hell, the dependence of morality upon religion—have ceased to interest me because they have, to my mind, been all but settled in favor of atheism. When even respected theologians as Alvin Plantinga and Richard Swinburne present such flimsy and easily refuted defenses of religious belief, one begins to sense that religion is, intellectually, out of gas.

I do not doubt that hostile critics will brand me a dogmatic atheist or an "atheist fundamentalist" (whatever that may exactly mean) or something of the sort, but such pejorative labels fail to note the fact that, after more than thirty years of investigation of these questions, I have not found a single argument offered by the religious as even remotely compelling or convincing. Every one of them has been demolished by far superior thinkers than I, and I do not pretend to hold out hope that the pious can somehow come up with better arguments than they have. I remain open to evidence, as any rational person should, but I would be a hypocrite to deny that it will require overwhelming evidence—evidence that not only makes a religious worldview plausible but, much more significantly, that somehow overturns the immense body of data that freethinkers have amassed against the intellectual plausibility of religious belief—to effect a change in my intellectual perspective.

The question becomes: What is now to be done?

Unlike Richard Dawkins and others, I am not fervently devoted to converting people to atheism. I rather doubt, in any case, whether even such works as *The God Delusion* have converted, or will convert, any significant number of the populace who are devout, or even those who are fence-sitters; such individuals tend not to read books that might threaten the stability of their belief structure, to which they have become psychologically dependent. But even these individuals, I suspect, cannot fail to notice what is happening all around them. Atheists have, as it were, come out of the closet; we are no longer afraid to speak our minds, especially given that legal and even social punishments against such declarations have been entirely eliminated or, at the very least, substantially reduced. It has been my experience that my own open declaration of atheism has not caused any notable perturbation among friends, family, or acquaintances who profess religious belief. Such individuals, no doubt, are free to think secretly that I am consigned to hell, just as I am free to feel silent contempt for their own irrationality and desperation, but in the end, it is possible to get along as well with such people as with any others.

It is certainly true that the institutional power of religion, especially in the United States, remains strong, and it is true that many politicians and commentators in the media continue to treat religion with kid gloves and seem unwilling to call it to the carpet even for its most obvious derelictions. Nevertheless, religion in the West has been sufficiently defanged that it is now merely an intermittent nuisance. Battles against its depredations—especially in its unwarranted encroachments upon intellectual matters (as in "intelligent design") or freedom of religion (which must include freedom *from* religion)—must still be fought, and we may have to be satisfied with the peculiar dichotomy of an atheistic intellectual class, a wider class of the weakly religious, and an underclass of fundamentalists.

It may be impossible—or, at any rate, unfeasible—to eliminate religion altogether, but much can be done to minimize its reach and influence. We stand today pretty much where we stood in 1935, when John Beevers wrote prophetically: "I do not believe that Christianity holds anything more of importance for the world. It is finished, played out. The only trouble lies in how to get rid of the body before it begins to smell too much."[1]

NOTES

INTRODUCTION

1. The most recent work in English appears to be Marcel Neusch's *The Sources of Modern Atheism* (1982); it is a translation of a French work published in 1977. We hardly need take note of the hostile polemical screed *The Twilight of Atheism: The Rise and Fall of Disbelief in the Modern World* (2004), by Alister E. McGrath, published at the very time when a spate of best-selling books on atheism controverted his central thesis by indicating a renewed surge of interest in the subject. James Thrower's *A Short History of Atheism* (1971) has been reprinted by Prometheus Books (2000); it is both very short and now quite outdated. The most comprehensive work may be in German: Hermann Ley's *Geschichte der Aufklärung und Atheismus* (1966–89; 5 vols. in 9).

2. W. K. C. Guthrie, *A History of Greek Philosophy* (Cambridge: Cambridge University Press, 1962–80), 2:465.

3. W. E. H. Lecky, *History of the Rise and Influence of the Spirit of Rationalism in Europe* (1865), in *Atheism: A Reader*, ed. S. T. Joshi (Amherst, NY: Prometheus Books, 2000), p. 272.

4. See Limbaugh's *Persecution: How Liberals Are Waging War on Christianity* (2003), and my discussion of it in *The Angry Right* (Amherst, NY: Prometheus Books, 2006), pp. 197–225. Ann Coulter's *Godless: The Church of Liberalism* (2006) is a similarly tendentious volume with even less intellectual heft than Limbaugh's book.

CHAPTER 1

1. "Agnosticism," in *Science and Christian Tradition* (New York: D. Appleton, 1896), p. 235. Hereafter cited in the text under the abbreviation *SC*.

2. Cited in Adrian Desmond, *Huxley: The Devil's Disciple* (London: Michael Joseph, 1994), p. 160.

3. Cited in ibid., p. 241.

4. Cited in ibid., p. 262.

5. Cited in ibid., p. 279.

6. Cited in ibid., p. 301.

7. Ibid., p. 304.

8. Cited in ibid., p. 373.

9. Cited in Houston Peterson, *Huxley: Prophet of Science* (London: Longmans, Green, 1932), p. 240.

10. Cited in Desmond, *Huxley*, p. 328.

11. William Ewart Gladstone, "Dawn of Creation and of Worship," *Nineteenth Century* 18 (November 1885): 696.

12. *Science and Hebrew Tradition* (New York: D. Appleton, 1896), p. 140. Hereafter cited in the text under the abbreviation *H.*

13. Gladstone, "Proem to Genesis: A Plea for a Fair Trial," *Nineteenth Century* 19 (January 1886): 11. Hereafter cited in the text under the abbreviation *P.*

14. "Prolegomena" to *Evolution and Ethics and Other Essays* (New York: D. Appleton & Co., 1896), p. 6. Hereafter cited in the text under the abbreviation *EE.*

15. Gladstone, *The Impregnable Rock of Holy Scripture* (1890; Philadelphia: John D. Wattles, 1891), p. 311.

16. John McRay, "Gerasenes," in *The Anchor Bible Dictionary*, ed. David Noel Freedman (New York: Doubleday, 1992), 2.991.

17. Gladstone, "Professor Huxley and the Swine-Miracle," *Nineteenth Century* 29 (January 1891): 341.

CHAPTER 2

1. Leslie Stephen, *Social Rights and Duties* (1896); quoted in Frederic William Maitland, *The Life and Letters of Leslie Stephen* (New York: G. P. Putnam's Sons, 1906), p. 133.

2. Cited in Maitland, *Life and Letters*, p. 146.

3. *Essays on Freethinking and Plainspeaking* (New York: G. P. Putnam's Sons, 1877 [1873]), pp. 8–9. Hereafter cited in the text under the abbreviation *E.*

4. "The Religious Difficulty," *Fraser's Magazine* 1 (May 1870): 626.

5. Ibid., p. 629.

6. "Mr. Bradlaugh and His Opponents," *Fortnightly Review* 34 (1880): 178.

7. Bertrand Russell, "What Is an Agnostic?" (1953), in *The Agnostic Reader*, ed. S. T. Joshi (Amherst, NY: Prometheus Books, 2007), p. 81.

8. "Thomas Henry Huxley," *Nineteenth Century* 48 (December 1900): 905.

9. "Philosophic Doubt," *Mind* 5 (April 1880): 158, 162, 166.

10. *An Agnostic's Apology and Other Essays* (London: Smith, Elder, 1893), pp. 350–51. Hereafter cited in the text under the abbreviation *A.*

11. "Pascal," *Fortnightly Review* 68 (July 1897): 16.

12. Maitland, *Life and Letters*, p. 152.

13. "Mr. Maurice's Theology," *Fortnightly Review* 21 (1874): 595–613.

14. Cited in Leslie Stephen, "Matthew Arnold and the Church of England," *Fraser's Magazine* 82 (October 1870): 415.

15. "Belief and Conduct," *Nineteenth Century* 24 (September 1888): 379. Hereafter cited in the text under the abbreviation *B*.

16. "Cardinal Newman's Scepticism," *Nineteenth Century* 29 (February 1891): 180.

17. Noel Annan, *Leslie Stephen: The Godless Victorian* (New York: Random House, 1984), p. 322.

CHAPTER 3

1. Mill, *Autobiography* (Indianapolis: Bobbs-Merrill, 1957 [1873]), pp. 42–43. Hereafter cited in the text under the abbreviation *AM*.

2. Alan P. F. Sell, *Mill on God* (Aldershot, UK: Ashgate, 2004), p. 13.

3. *Three Essays on Religion* (New York: Greenwood Press, 1969 [1874]), pp. 128–29. Hereafter cited in the text under the abbreviation *T*.

4. Sell, *Mill on God*, p. 136.

5. David Hume, *Dialogues concerning Natural Religion* (New York: Hafner, 1948 [1779]), p. 66.

6. Alan Millar, "Mill on Religion," in *The Cambridge Companion to Mill*, ed. John Skorupski (Cambridge: Cambridge University Press, 1998), p. 198.

7. *Collected Works*, ed. J. M. Robson et al. (Toronto: University of Toronto Press; London: Routledge & Kegan Paul, 1965–91), 24.812. Hereafter cited in the text under the abbreviation *CW*.

8. *On Liberty* (Harmondsworth, UK: Penguin, 1974 [1859]), p. 103.

9. "Lord Brougham's Defence of the Church Establishment" (1834); *CW* 6.229–30.

10. Elizabeth Cady Stanton, *Bible and Church Degrade Women* (1885), in *Atheism: A Reader*, ed. S. T. Joshi (Amherst, NY: Prometheus Books, 2000), pp. 315, 319.

11. *The Subjection of Women* [with *Enfranchisement of Women* by Harriet Taylor Mill] (London: Virago, 1983 [1869]), p. 85.

CHAPTER 4

1. *Ecce Homo* (trans. Walter Kaufmann and R. J. Hollingdale), in *On the Genealogy of Morals and Ecce Homo*, ed. Walter Kaufmann (New York: Vintage, 1967), p. 218. Hereafter cited in the text under the abbreviation *EH*.

2. George A. Morgan, Jr., *What Nietzsche Means* (Cambridge, MA: Harvard University Press, 1941), p. 36.

3. Walter Kaufmann, *Nietzsche: Philosopher, Psychologist, Antichrist* (Princeton, NJ: Princeton University Press, 1974), p. 316.

4. *On the Genealogy of Morals* (trans. Walter Kaufmann), in *On the Genealogy of Morals and Ecce Homo*, p. 33. Hereafter cited in the text under the abbreviation *GM*.

5. *The Anti-Christ*, in *Twilight of the Idols and The Anti-Christ*, trans. R. J. Hollingdale (Harmondsworth, UK: Penguin, 1968), pp. 115–16. Hereafter cited in the text under the abbreviation *AC*.

6. Arthur Schopenhauer, *Studies in Pessimism*, trans. Thomas Bailey Saunders (London: Swan Sonnenschein, 1890), pp. 12, 29.

7. *Thus Spake Zarathustra*, trans. R. J. Hollingdale (Harmondsworth, UK: Penguin, 1969), p. 42.

8. *Daybreak*, trans. R. J. Hollingdale (Cambridge: Cambridge University Press, 1982), p. 84.

9. *Beyond Good and Evil*, trans. Walter Kaufmann (New York: Vintage, 1966), p. 60. Hereafter cited in the text under the abbreviation *BG*.

10. *The Gay Science*, trans. Walter Kaufmann (New York: Vintage, 1974), p. 181. Hereafter cited in the text under the abbreviation *GS*.

11. *The Will to Power*, trans. Walter Kaufmann and R. J. Hollingdale (New York: Vintage, 1968), p. 113.

CHAPTER 5

1. See Harold K. Bush, Jr., *Mark Twain and the Spiritual Crisis of His Age* (Tuscaloosa: University of Alabama Press, 2007), p. 5.

2. See William E. Phipps, *Mark Twain's Religion* (Macon, GA: Mercer University Press, 2003), p. 9. Most of my information on Twain's religious upbringing is drawn from this book, which is a far more balanced treatment than Bush's study.

3. John Hays, *Mark Twain and Religion* (New York: Peter Lang, 1989), p. 106.

4. Mark Twain, *What Is Man? and Other Irreverent Essays*, ed. S. T. Joshi

(Amherst, NY: Prometheus Books, 2009), p. 143. Hereafter cited in the text under the abbreviation *WM*.

5. See Phipps, *Mark Twain's Religion*, p. 266.

6. Bush, *Mark Twain and the Spiritual Crisis*, pp. 15, 17.

7. *The Autobiography of Mark Twain* (1924), cited in Phipps, *Mark Twain's Religion*, p. 304. The statement was written in 1904.

8. Phipps, *Mark Twain's Religion*, p. 284.

9. See Bush, *Mark Twain and the Spiritual Crisis*, pp. 3–4.

10. Albert Bigelow Paine, *Mark Twain: A Biography* (New York: Harper, 1912), 1:609.

11. William Pellowe, *Mark Twain, Pilgrim from Hannibal* (New York: Hobson, 1945), p. 214.

12. *The Mysterious Stranger*, written between 1897 and 1908, was first published in a corrupted text in 1916. Twain's original version was restored by William M. Gibson in *Mark Twain's Mysterious Stranger Manuscripts* (Berkeley: University of California Press, 1969). *Letters from the Earth* (written in late 1909) was first published in 1962.

13. H. L. Mencken, "Mark Twain" (*Smart Set*, October 1919), in *H. L. Mencken on American Literature*, ed. S. T. Joshi (Athens: Ohio University Press, 2002), p. 31.

14. *The Mysterious Stranger*, in *Great Short Works of Mark Twain*, ed. Justin Kaplan (New York: Harper & Row, 1967), p. 365.

15. Ibid., p. 366.

16. *Letters from the Earth*, ed. Bernard DeVoto (New York: Crest, 1963), p. 14. Hereafter cited in the text under the abbreviation *LE*.

17. Maxwell Geismar, *Mark Twain: An American Prophet* (Boston: Houghton Mifflin, 1970), p. 354.

CHAPTER 6

1. The best account of the day-to-day events of the Scopes trial remains L. Sprague de Camp's *The Great Monkey Trial* (1968). Edward J. Larson's *Summer of the Gods: The Scopes Trial and America's Continuing Debate over Science and Religion* (1997), although it won the Pulitzer Prize, seems to me unduly sympathetic to Bryan and the fundamentalists and insufficiently aware of the threat they posed to intellectual advance. See also Ray Giner, *Six Days or Forever: Tennessee vs. John Thomas Scopes* (1958); Jerry T. Tompkins, *D-Days at Dayton: Reflections on the Scopes Trial* (1965); and Paul Keith Conklin, *When All the Gods Trembled: Dar-*

winism, Scopes, and American Intellectuals (1998). Scopes himself wrote a memoir late in life, *Center of the Storm: Memoirs of John T. Scopes* (1967).

2. Quoted in Kevin Tierney, *Darrow: A Biography* (New York: Thomas Y. Crowell, 1979), p. 396.

3. *Closing Arguments: Clarence Darrow on Religion, Law, and Society*, ed. S. T. Joshi (Athens: Ohio University Press), p. 66. Hereafter cited in the text under the abbreviation *CA*. The other major collections of Darrow's writings are *Attorney for the Damned* (1957) and *Verdicts out of Court* (1963).

4. *The World's Most Famous Court Trial: Tennessee Evolution Case* (Cincinnati: National Book Co., 1925), p. 74. This book is the only extant transcript of the actual proceedings of the Scopes trial. It will hereafter be cited in the text under the abbreviation *W*.

5. "Text of Bryan's Nine Questions on Religion and Darrow's Replies to the Commoner," *New York Times* (22 July 1925): 2.

CHAPTER 7

1. *H. L. Mencken on Religion*, ed. S. T. Joshi (Amherst, NY: Prometheus Books, 2002), p. 25. Hereafter cited in the text under the abbreviation *MR*.

2. Fred Hobson, *Mencken: A Life* (New York: Random House, 1994), p. 51.

3. "Clinical Notes," *American Mercury* 2, no. 1 (May 1924): 60–61.

4. *From Baltimore to Bohemia: The Letters of H. L. Mencken and George Sterling*, ed. S. T. Joshi (Rutherford, NJ: Fairleigh Dickinson University Press, 2001), p. 198.

5. "The Impregnable Rock," *American Mercury* (December 1931); *MR* 136.

6. "The I.Q. of Holy Church," *American Mercury* (September 1930); *MR* 109.

7. "Fides ante Intellectum," *American Mercury* (February 1926); *MR* 230.

8. "The Ascent of Man," *MR* 64.

9. "Editorial," *American Mercury* (October 1928); *MR* 253.

10. "The Monthly Feuilleton," *Smart Set* 59, no. 4 (December 1922): 140.

11. "Good Old Baltimore," *Smart Set* (May 1913), in *Mencken's America*, ed. S. T. Joshi (Athens: Ohio University Press, 2004), p. 77. Hereafter cited in the text under the abbreviation *MA*.

12. "Overture to a Melodrama," *Baltimore Evening Sun*, January 28, 1929; *MR* 258.

13. "On Christian Science," *Baltimore Evening Sun*, October 23, 1916; *MR* 146.

14. "Venture into Therapeutics," *Smart Set* (July 1923); *MR* 271.

15. Kenneth Turner Jackson, *The Ku Klux Klan in the City 1915–1930* (New York: Oxford University Press, 1967), p. 18.

16. "Counter-Offensive," *American Mercury* (May 1926); *MR* 233.

17. L. Sprague de Camp, *The Great Monkey Trial* (Garden City, NY: Doubleday, 1968), p. 441.

18. Quoted in Edward J. Larson, *Summer for the Gods: The Scopes Trial and America's Continuing Debate over Science and Religion* (New York: Basic Books, 1997), pp. 41–42.

19. *Treatise on the Gods* (New York: Alfred A. Knopf, 1946), p. 155. Hereafter cited in the text under the abbreviation *TG*.

CHAPTER 8

1. Letter to Elizabeth Toldridge, April 24, 1930, in *Selected Letters*, ed. August Derleth, Donald Wandrei, and James Turner (Sauk City, WI: Arkham House, 1965–1976), 3:146.

2. Letter to Rheinhart Kleiner, March 7, 1920, in *Selected Letters*, 1:110–11.

3. "A Confession of Unfaith," in *Collected Essays*, ed. S. T. Joshi (New York: Hippocampus Press, 2004–2006), 5:147.

4. See, for example, Robert M. Price, "H. P. Lovecraft: Prophet of Humanism," *Humanist* 61, no. 4 (July–August 2001): 26–29. See also Price's chapter on Lovecraft in *Icons of Unbelief*, ed. S. T. Joshi (Westport, CT: Greenwood Press, 2008), pp. 223–39.

5. See note 1.

6. *In Defence of Dagon*, in *Collected Essays*, 5:60.

7. Ibid., 5:64.

8. Letter to Rheinhart Kleiner, May 13, 1921; *Selected Letters*, 1:132.

9. Letter to James F. Morton, May 26, 1923; *Selected Letters*, 1:231.

10. Letter to Frank Belknap Long, February 20, 1929; *Selected Letters*, 2:266–67.

11. Letter to Frank Belknap Long, November 22, 1930; *Selected Letters*, 3:228.

12. Letter to James F. Morton, October 30, 1929; *Selected Letters*, 3:53.

13. Ibid.; *Selected Letters*, 3:47–48.

14. Letter to Robert E. Howard, August 16, 1932; *Selected Letters*, 4:57.

15. Letter to Natalie H. Wooley, November 27, 1933; *Selected Letters*, 4:324.

16. "The Call of Cthulhu" (1926), in *H. P. Lovecraft: The Fiction* (New York: Barnes & Noble, 2008), p. 367.

17. *At the Mouintains of Madness* (1931); in *H. P. Lovecraft: The Fiction*, p. 769.

18. See David E. Schultz, "From Microcosm to Macrocosm: The Growth of Lovecraft's Cosmic Vision," in *An Epicure in the Terrible: A Centennial Anthology of Essays in Honor of H. P. Lovecraft*, ed. David E. Schultz and S. T. Joshi (Rutherford, NJ: Fairleigh Dickinson University Press, 1991), p. 212.

CHAPTER 9

1. George Santayana, Letter to Bertrand Russell (c. December 1917), cited in *The Autobiography of Bertrand Russell* (Boston: Little, Brown, 1967–1969), 2:57. Hereafter cited in the text under the abbreviation *A*.

2. Cited in Russell, *Why I Am Not a Christian* (New York: Simon & Schuster, 1957), p. 6. Hereafter cited in the text under the abbreviation *Y*.

3. S. T. Joshi, *God's Defenders: What They Believe and Why They Are Wrong* (Amherst, NY: Prometheus Books, 2003), pp. 16–17.

4. *Collected Papers of Bertrand Russell* (London: George Allen & Unwin, 1983–1989; London: Routledge, 1990–), 11:91–92. Hereafter cited in the text under the abbreviation *CP*.

5. Bertrand Russell, *Religion and Science* (New York: Oxford University Press, 1935), pp. 247–48. Hereafter cited in the text under the abbreviation *R*.

6. A. J. Ayer, *Language, Truth and Logic* (1936; rev. ed. 1946; rpt. New York: Dover, 1952), p. 107.

7. There does not seem to be any purpose in discussing at length Russell's dismissal from the City College of New York in 1940–41—or, rather, the successful efforts made by certain opponents, many of whom were clergymen, to prevent him from teaching there—since the causes for the opposition to him stemmed not so much from his atheism but rather from what was perceived to be his advocacy of free love and other sexual irregularities. See Paul Edwards's long appendix to *Y* (207–59).

CHAPTER 10

1. Madalyn Murray O'Hair, *An Atheist Epic* (1970; rev. ed. Austin, TX: American Atheist Press, 1989), p. ix. Hereafter cited in the text under the abbreviation *AE*.

2. Cited in Bryan F. Le Beau, *The Atheist: Madalyn Murray O'Hair* (New

York: New York University Press, 2003), p. 21. Hereafter cited in the text under the abbreviation *L.*

3. Russell Kirk, *Confessions of a Bohemian Tory* (New York: Fleet, 1963), p. 224.

4. See Frank Zindler, "Madalyn Murray O'Hair," in *Icons of Unbelief*, ed. S. T. Joshi (Westport, CT: Greenwood Press, 2008), p. 330.

5. *Why I Am an Atheist* (1966; 2nd rev. ed. Austin, TX: American Atheist Press, 1991), p. 5.

6. *Freedom under Siege: The Impact of Organized Religion on Your Liberty and Your Pocketbook* (Los Angeles: J. P. Tarcher, 1974), p. 181.

CHAPTER 11

1. Cited in Fred Kaplan, *Gore Vidal: A Biography* (New York: Doubleday, 1999), p. 45.

2. *Messiah* (New York: E. P. Dutton, 1954), pp. 62–63. Hereafter cited in the text under the abbreviation *M.*

3. *Julian* (Boston: Little, Brown, 1964), p. 4. Hereafter cited in the text under the abbreviation *J.*

4. Louis Auchincloss, "The Best Man, Vintage 361 A.D.," *Life* 56, no. 24 (12 June 1964): 19.

5. *United States: Essays 1952–1992* (New York: Random House, 1993), p. 605. Hereafter cited in the text under the abbreviation *US.*

6. *Creation* (New York: Random House, 1981), p. 10. Hereafter cited in the text under the abbreviation *C.*

7. *Palimpsest* (New York: Random House, 1995), p. 173.

8. *Live from Golgotha* (New York: Random House, 1992), p. 29. Hereafter cited in the text under the abbreviation *LG.*

9. See Laura Cumming, "The Gospel According to Gore Vidal," *Manchester Guardian Weekly* 147, no. 17 (25 October 1992): 25.

10. D. M. Thomas, "God's Own Media Event," *New York Times Book Review* (4 October 1992): 13.

11. Andrew M. Greeley, "Is Nothing Sacred?" *Washington Post Book World* (20 September 1992): 2.

CHAPTER 12

1. *The Blind Watchmaker* (New York: W. W. Norton, 1986), p. 6. Hereafter cited in the text under the abbreviation *BW*.

2. *The God Delusion* (2006; paperback ed. Boston: Houghton Mifflin, 2008), p. 139. Hereafter cited in the text under the abbreviation *GD*.

3. Bertrand Russell, "What Is an Agnostic?" (1953), in *The Agnostic Reader*, ed. S. T. Joshi (Amherst, NY: Prometheus Books, 2007), p. 81.

4. Walter Lippmann, *A Preface to Morals* (1929), in *The Agnostic Reader*, p. 335.

5. Alister E. McGrath and Joanna Collicutt McGrath, *The Dawkins Delusion?* (Downers Grove, IL: IVP Books, 2007), p. 9. Hereafter cited in the text under the abbreviation *DD*.

6. The review can now be found at http://lrb.co.uk/v28/n20/terry-eagleton/lunging-flailing-mispunching.

CHAPTER 13

1. *The End of Faith: Religion, Terror, and the Future of Reason* (New York: W. W. Norton, 2004), p. 323. Hereafter cited in the text under the abbreviation *EF*.

2. Alf Hiltebeitel, "Hinduism," in *The Religious Traditions of Asia*, ed. Joseph M. Kitigawa (New York: Macmillan, 1989), p. 28. The articles in this book are taken from Mircea Eliade's *Encyclopedia of Religion*.

3. *Letter to a Christian Nation* (New York: Knopf, 2006), p. ix. Hereafter cited in the text under the abbreviation *LC*.

4. J. L. Mackie, *Ethics: Inventing Right and Wrong* (Harmondsworth, UK: Penguin, 1977), p. 15.

5. See Thomas Ligotti, *The Conspiracy against the Human Race* (New York: Hippocampus Press, 2010).

CHAPTER 14

1. *The Missionary Position: Mother Teresa in Theory and Practice* (London: Verso, 1995), p. xii. Hereafter cited in the text under the abbreviation *MT*.

2. *God Is Not Great: How Religion Poisons Everything* (New York: Twelve, 2007), p. 285. Hereafter cited in the text under the abbreviation *G*.

EPILOGUE

1. John Beevers, *World without Faith* (London: Hamish Amilton, 1935), p. 64

INDEX

SCHOLASTIC

Leveled Read-Aloud Plays
U.S. CIVIC HOLIDAYS

by J. M. Wolf

NEW YORK • TORONTO • LONDON • AUCKLAND • SYDNEY
MEXICO CITY • NEW DELHI • HONG KONG • BUENOS AIRES

Teaching Resources

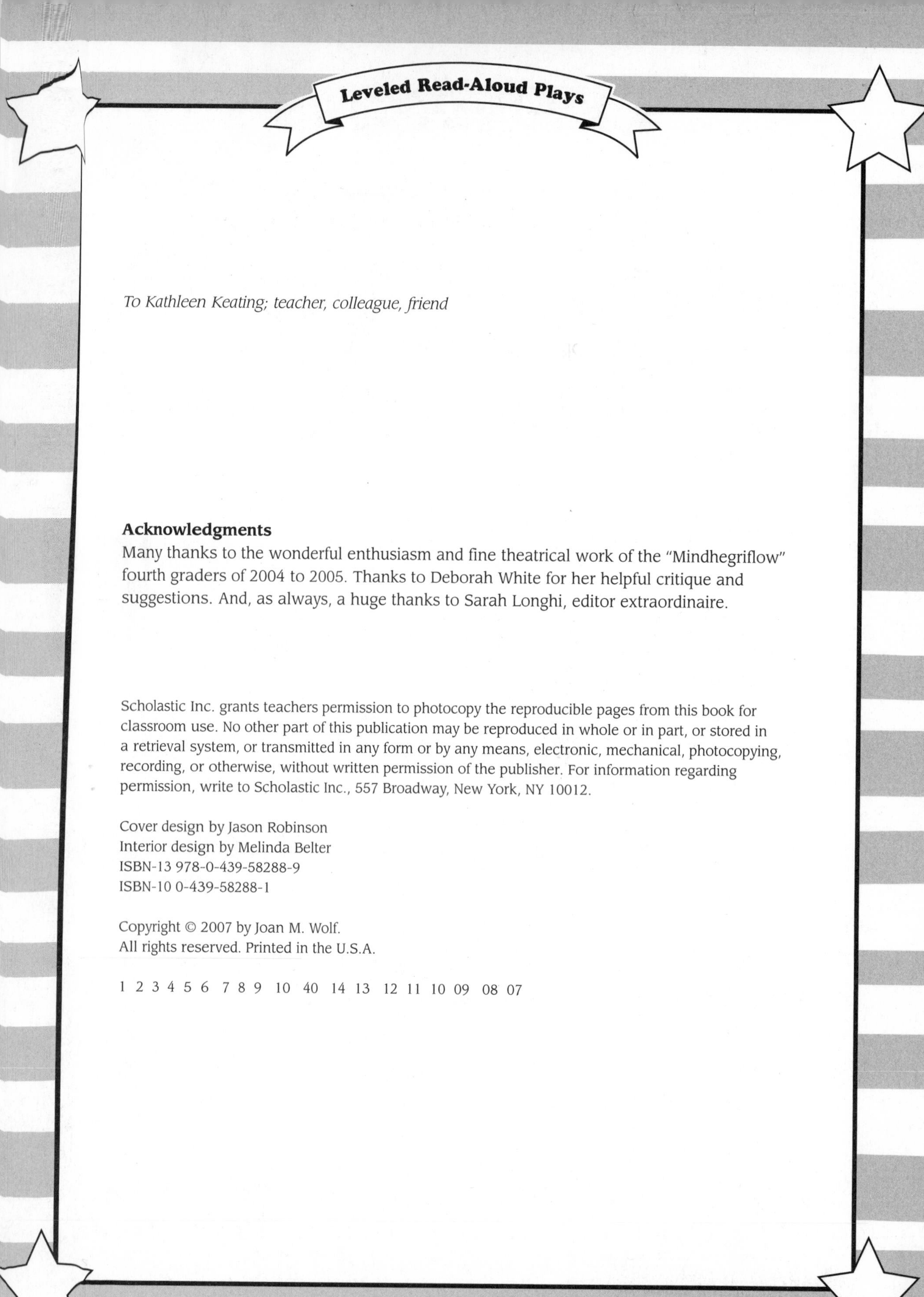

To Kathleen Keating; teacher, colleague, friend

Acknowledgments
Many thanks to the wonderful enthusiasm and fine theatrical work of the "Mindhegriflow" fourth graders of 2004 to 2005. Thanks to Deborah White for her helpful critique and suggestions. And, as always, a huge thanks to Sarah Longhi, editor extraordinaire.

Cover design by Jason Robinson
Interior design by Melinda Belter
ISBN-13 978-0-439-58288-9
ISBN-10 0-439-58288-1

1 2 3 4 5 6 7 8 9 10 40 14 13 12 11 10 09 08 07

Contents

Introduction

First, There Was History . . .

Give it a try. Ask your students how Memorial Day originated. Find out why they think Labor Day is a United States holiday. Chances are students will be able to tell you that Memorial Day has something to do with remembering soldiers or that Labor Day marks the end of summer, but they may not know that we first began to observe Memorial Day at the end of the Civil War or that Labor Day honors those who work in industry.

The plays and activities in this book are designed to help students better understand the meaning and history behind five United States civic holidays: Presidents' Day, Earth Day, Memorial Day, Independence Day, and Labor Day. The plays are designed to be both educational and fun, and intended to help kids appreciate that there is more to these holidays than simply time off from school or work.

Each play is structured for use in whatever way works best for teachers and students. You may wish to have students simply read the plays, scripts in hand, in traditional Readers Theater style. Or you may wish to produce an evening show for families, in which students memorize lines, create sets and costumes, and perform in theatrical style.

Over the past 16 years, I have regularly used drama in my classroom—from informal, small groups to read-alouds to complex, polished productions. Each time students engage in a script, bringing life to a new character or working together to rehearse their lines, I see positive changes for my students as readers and learners. Reading-based drama activities have the power to boost student self-esteem, increase oral fluency, and teach kids things they will not learn in a traditional textbook. Molly, one of my former fourth graders, said it best in a letter she wrote at the end of our year together: "I'll never forget the plays. We learned how to work as a team and learned that without one or two actors, the play wouldn't work. Best of all, we learned

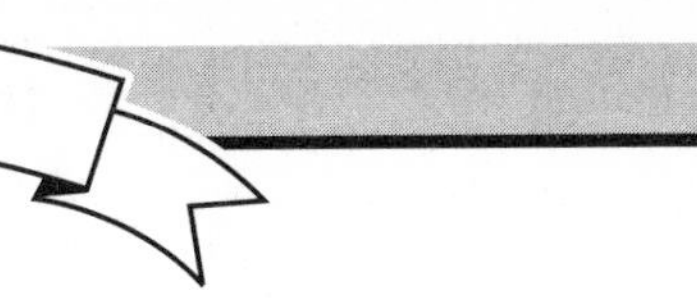

that every person on a team is important and that if we left out one character, the play wouldn't be as special. The characters are just as important as the meaning." Who can argue with this?

And Then There Was This Book . . .

Each play in this book begins with a page designed especially for teachers. Here, you will find ideas for sets and costumes, as well as a brief historical introduction about the holiday in focus. The parts in each play are leveled for grades 2 through 5 so that you can more easily assign parts based on students' reading abilities. Giving students appropriately leveled parts can help both struggling and proficient readers find success in reading and feel that they're a part of a group.

Standards-based language arts and social studies activities follow each play. These activities are designed to extend the information from the play, engage students even further in United States history, and help students research, write, and stretch their learning skills.

No matter how you choose to use the plays and activities, both you and your students will come away having learned something you may not have known before.

Happy civic holiday history!
Sincerely,
Joan M. Wolf

"Who Wants to Be President?"

A read-aloud play for
Presidents' Day,
celebrated the third Monday in February

In "Who Wants to Be President?" students learn interesting facts about past presidents through the fun and engaging format of a game show.

History

Although we usually think of Presidents' Day as the celebration of both Abraham Lincoln's and George Washington's birthdays, originally it was the celebration of Washington's birthday only. Washington's birthday was celebrated on February 22 while Lincoln's birthday was typically celebrated separately, on February 12. It wasn't until 1968 that Congress passed legislation combining both birthdays in one holiday.

Both Washington and Lincoln played pivotal roles in United States history. In 1789, Washington was unanimously selected by the electoral college to be our country's first president. Lincoln, as the 16th U.S. president, guided our country through one of the most divisive times in our history, the Civil War, and helped facilitate the abolition of slavery.

If You Stage the Play . . .

Set: For a game-show atmosphere, place several student desks next to each other for contestants. A podium can serve as the station for the game show host, and chairs can be placed apart from the contestants for the show's audience. You may wish to provide a pretend microphone for the host and a bell or buzzer for each student. Presidents may stand hidden from contestants, but in view of the audience. You may also wish to have the names of contestants printed and hanging from their desks.

Costumes: Let students brainstorm one distinctive costume item for each president, such as a top hat for Lincoln, glasses for Teddy Roosevelt, or a cane for Franklin Roosevelt. The game show host may wear a suit and have a real or pretend microphone.

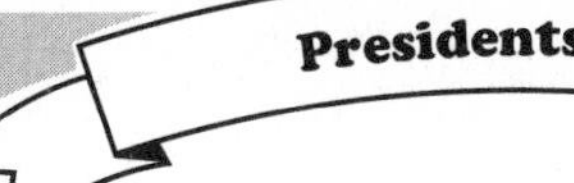

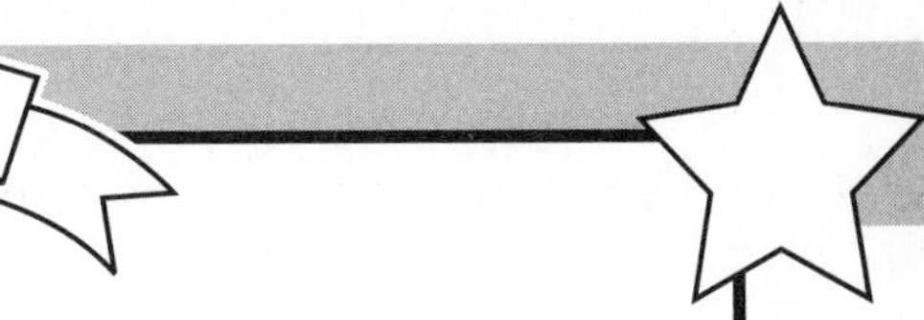

Each contestant may have an item that represents his or her distinctive personality, such as a notepad and pen for Tallia Why, a stuffed animal for Kara Lott, a small scale of justice for Justin Truth, and a megaphone for Lee Durr. They may also wear name tags.

The Cast

(in order of reading level)

Grade 2

GAME SHOW AUDIENCE (three to five people)

ROD CAST (announcer)

Grade 3

PROLOGUE ANNOUNCER (optional)

ANITA ANSWER (assistant #1)

LINN FORMATION (assistant #2)

Grade 3/Low 4

(Students may have difficulty reading the presidents' names.)

KARA LOTT (contestant #3)

TALLIA WHY (contestant #4)

LEE DURR (contestant #1)

Grade 4

MYSTERY PRESIDENT #1: TEDDY ROOSEVELT

MYSTERY PRESIDENT #2: ABRAHAM LINCOLN

JUSTIN TRUTH (contestant #2)

LUCKEE CHANSE (game show host)

Grade 5

MYSTERY PRESIDENT #3: FRANKLIN ROOSEVELT

Vocabulary

address *noun* an important speech.

candidate *noun* a person who is working to be elected.

capable *adjective* having the strength or ability to do a job.

contestant *noun* someone who takes part in a game or contest.

pardon *noun* a ruling that sets someone free.

polio *noun* an illness that strikes nerves and muscles, often causing victims to have trouble walking or moving.

quality *noun* a trait or feature of something.

swear in *verb* to give official permission for a person to take office or do a job.

Who Wants to Be President?

HONORING PRESIDENTS' DAY, CELEBRATED ON THE THIRD MONDAY IN FEBRUARY

THE CAST
(in order of appearance)

PROLOGUE ANNOUNCER (optional)
LUCKEE CHANSE (game show host)
GAME SHOW AUDIENCE (three to five people or more)
LEE DURR (contestant #1) • JUSTIN TRUTH (contestant #2)
KARA LOTT (contestant #3) • TALLIA WHY (contestant #4)
MYSTERY PRESIDENT #1: TEDDY ROOSEVELT
MYSTERY PRESIDENT #2: ABRAHAM LINCOLN
MYSTERY PRESIDENT #3: FRANKLIN ROOSEVELT
ANITA ANSWER (assistant #1) • LINN FORMATION (assistant #2)
ROD CAST (announcer)

PROLOGUE (optional): Presidents' Day is a day to think about the personal qualities and qualifications that a person needs to have to be president of our nation.

Presidents' Day was first celebrated in 1796 on February 22. This was George Washington's birthday. The United States began to celebrate Abraham Lincoln's birthday on February 12, 1866. Eventually, both birthdays were combined into one holiday and we have celebrated Presidents' Day in honor of all presidents ever since. (*exits*)

(*Game Show Audience enters and members take places.*)

Luckee Chanse: (*enters with microphone, with energy*) Hello and welcome to another exciting game of . . . (*points to Game Show Audience*)

Game Show Audience: (*happily*) Who Wants to Be President? (*cheers and applause*)

Luckee Chanse: I'm your host, Luckee Chanse, and today, four young people will compete to see if they have what it takes to be the leader of our great nation. Let's begin by meeting our players. (*Game Show Audience claps as all four contestants enter and are seated*) Contestant number one, please introduce yourself and tell us why you think you would make a great president.

Lee Durr: (*smiling and waving to the audience*) Hello, Luckee, my name is Lee Durr and I think I would make a good president because presidents have to lead and I've had a lot of experience in that area. I am a safety patrol at school and I have to lead kindergartners to their bus every day. At home, I have two little sisters who are always following me around and I have to lead my puppy on walks, too. I was born to lead!

Luckee Chanse: Thank you, Lee. Contestant number two, please tell us a little about yourself.

Justin Truth: Hi, Luckee. My name is Justin Truth and one time I found five dollars on the playground and instead of buying baseball cards, which is what I wanted to do, I gave it to my teacher so she could find out who lost it. I am very honest and presidents, as you know, must be honest people!

Luckee Chanse: Right you are, Justin. And now, contestant number three, please introduce yourself and tell us why you think you would make a great president.

Kara Lott: Sure, Luckee. My name is Kara Lott and I think I'd be a good president because I really care about people. I think presidents have to care about people and care about what happens to them. Every single weekend, when my mom goes to school, I have to take care of my little brother. I also care a lot about animals. I have five different pets at home and I take care of them every single day.

Luckee Chanse: Thank you, Kara. And last, but certainly not least, contestant number four, please introduce yourself.

Tallia Why: Thanks, Luckee. (*quickly, with energy*) Well, my name is Tallia Why and I think I would make a good president because presidents have to make a lot of speeches and I'm really good at talking and convincing people. One time, I decided that we needed to recycle at school and my teacher let me make a speech and it worked and now we are recycling. I also really like to talk on the phone a lot and I call my friends almost every night and I would talk more, except my parents told me I'm not allowed to talk on the phone so much and . . .

Luckee Chanse: (*interrupting*) Okay, Tallia. I think we understand. It looks like we've got some great players today. And now, audience, it's time to play . . . (*points to Game Show Audience*)

Game Show Audience: (*with energy*) Who Wants to Be President? (*cheers and applause*)

Luckee Chanse: (*to contestants*) Now, as you know, we have three mystery presidents who will come out one at a time and give clues about themselves. If you think you know who the mystery president is, ring your bell and make a guess. A correct answer will give you two points. Whoever gets the most points by the end of our game has the chance to become our next president for a whole day. Contestants, are you ready? (*contestants nod*) Audience? (*Game Show Audience cheers*) Okay, mystery president number one, please come on out.

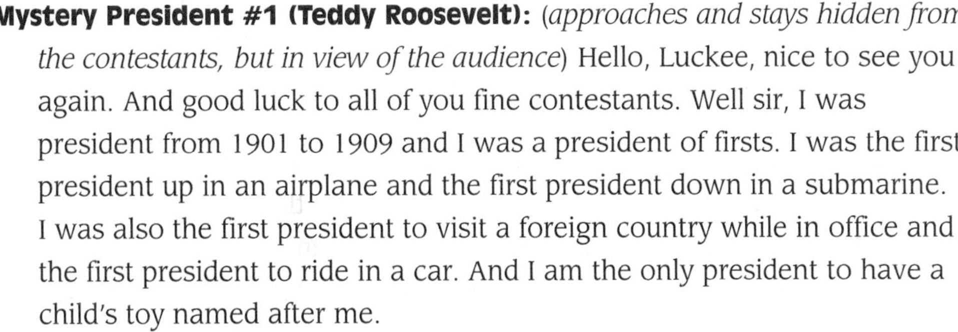

Mystery President #1 (Teddy Roosevelt): (*approaches and stays hidden from the contestants, but in view of the audience*) Hello, Luckee, nice to see you again. And good luck to all of you fine contestants. Well sir, I was president from 1901 to 1909 and I was a president of firsts. I was the first president up in an airplane and the first president down in a submarine. I was also the first president to visit a foreign country while in office and the first president to ride in a car. And I am the only president to have a child's toy named after me.

Justin Truth: (*rings bell*) William McKinley! You're William McKinley! I know that because you were a very honest president. You were the first president to have regular meetings with newspaper and radio reporters.

Teddy Roosevelt: (*chuckles*) You're close, young man, but William McKinley was the president right before me. Another clue for you is that I liked animals. Why one time, I even saved an animal from being killed while I was hunting. As a result, this child's toy was forever named after me. It was . . .

Kara Lott: (*rings bell*) Oh, oh, oh . . . It was the teddy bear. The teddy bear is named after you!

Luckee Chanse: Okay, but can you name this president, Kara?

Kara Lott: Yes, it's Teddy Roosevelt! You're Teddy Roosevelt.

Teddy Roosevelt: That's right.

Luckee Chanse: And the first two points go to Kara Lott. (*Game Show Audience cheers*)

Tallia Why: Teddy Roosevelt! Oh, I know all about you. You liked to give speeches and you were very strong. My grandmother told me that one time you were giving a speech after you had been shot in the chest and you just kept right on talking for an hour because you wanted to finish the speech before you went to the hospital and you . . . (*Teddy Roosevelt exits, waving to the audience*)

Luckee Chanse: (*interrupting*) Okay, Tallia, thank you for that information. Now, while our next president is getting ready, my assistant, Anita Answer, is going to give all of you the chance to answer some presidential trivia questions. Each question will be worth one point. Anita?

Anita Answer: (*enters*) Thank you, Luckee. (*reading from a card*) Contestants, this president was so popular that when he ran for a second term, no one else ran against him. Who was he?

Lee Durr: (*rings bell*) James Monroe! No one wanted to run against him because he was such a strong leader. He was president from 1817 to 1825.

Anita Answer: Very good. One point goes to Lee Durr (*Game Show Audience cheers*). And now, contestants, your second question (*reads from card*). During the First World War, so many men were fighting in the war that there weren't enough left in Washington D.C. to take care of the White House lawn. So this president replaced the White House gardeners with sheep. The sheep ate the grass to keep it short and this president sent the sheep's wool to the Red Cross to be made into soldier's uniforms. Of course, the sheep got a little carried away and ate more than just the grass . . .

Kara Lott: (*rings bell*) Woodrow Wilson! That was Woodrow Wilson. He was president from 1913 to 1921 and he cared so much about his sheep that he actually let one, named Old Ike, chew tobacco.

Game Show Audience: Gross! Yuck! (*assorted negative responses to "tobacco"*)

Anita Answer: Well, they didn't know how dangerous tobacco was at that time. Kara Lott got that question right and wins one point. (*Game Show Audience cheers*) And now, here's our final question before our next mystery president. (*reads card*) Who are the four presidents carved on the Mount Rushmore National Monument?

Justin Truth: (*rings bell*) I know this one. I know this one! They were all men of great character!

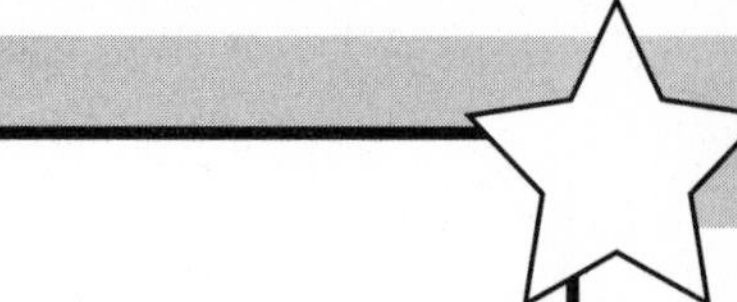

Luckee Chanse: Okay, Justin. Your answer, please.

Justin Truth: The presidents are George Washington, Thomas Jefferson, Teddy Roosevelt, and Abraham Lincoln. And Mount Rushmore is in the Black Hills of South Dakota. My family went there one summer on vacation. It's pretty cool.

Anita Answer: You are correct, Justin. (*Game Show Audience cheers*) You get one point. And now, Luckee, back to the game. *(exits)*

Luckee Chanse: Thanks, Anita. To review, Kara Lott leads the game so far with three points. Lee Durr and Justin Truth both have one point each and Tallia . . .

Tallia Why: (*interrupting*) Oh, don't worry about it, Luckee. I know I don't have any points at all, but I am having lots of fun playing the game and, you know, there are still a few rounds left and I just think . . .

Luckee Chanse: (*interrupting*) Thanks, thanks, Tallia. I'm glad you're having fun. But now we are ready for our next mystery president. Mr. President?

Mystery President #2 (Abraham Lincoln): (*approaches and stays hidden from contestants, dignified*) Good afternoon, contestants. I was the president during very troubled times for our country and even though I believed in what I did, I was not well liked at the time. Education was important to me, although I had only one year of formal schooling in my whole life. I did love books, though, and reading and learning and . . .

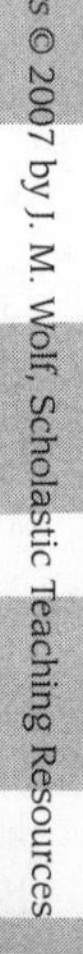

Lee Durr: (*rings bell*) I think I know who you are.

Luckee Chanse: Yes, Lee?

Lee Durr: I think you might be Millard Fillmore, our president from 1850 to 1853, the first president to have a library in the White House.

Luckee Chanse: No, I'm sorry, Lee, that is incorrect.

(*Sympathy groan from Game Show Audience.*)

Luckee Chanse: (*to Abraham Lincoln*) Mr. President, please give us another clue.

Abraham Lincoln: Well, I began a tradition that not a lot of people know about. One Christmas, my young son was very upset to learn that his pet turkey was going to be our Christmas meal. To make my son feel better, I granted his turkey an official Presidential Pardon so it would never be eaten. Since then, every president has granted one turkey a Presidential Pardon at Thanksgiving.

(*Members of Game Show Audience murmur to each other, trying to figure out who the president is. Contestants scratch their heads and look confused.*)

Luckee Chanse: Time's up, contestants. Mr. President, please give us your final clue.

Abraham Lincoln: Well, I failed at many things in my life. I lost many elections before becoming president. I lost money in business. I faced many other difficulties in my life. But one thing I did succeed in was officially freeing people from slavery in 1863.

Tallia Why: (*rings bell*) Abraham Lincoln! You're Abraham Lincoln and you gave a very famous speech, the Gettysburg Address.

Luckee Chanse: Right you are, Tallia. You have two points!

Tallia Why: (*does a victory dance while the Game Show Audience applauds*) Yea for me! Yea for me! I got two points! (*Abraham Lincoln exits and Linn Formation enters*)

Luckee Chanse: And now, my second assistant, Linn Formation, will give our contestants the chance to win additional points with more presidential trivia questions. Linn?

Linn Formation: Hello, everyone. Here's our first question, for one point. (*reads from note card*) This president brought the very first Siamese kitten to the United States to be his pet. (*all contestants look at Kara Lott*)

Kara Lott: (*holding up her hands*) What? I know it's an animal question, but I don't know this one.

Justin Truth: (*rings bell*) Oh, wait, I know! I know! It was the same president who offered legal assistance to runaway slaves. He was Rutherford B. Hayes, the president from 1877 to 1881.

Linn Formation: You are right, Justin. You now have two points. (*Game Show Audience cheers and Lee Durr gives Justin a high five*) Okay, here is question number two. (*pulls out and reads second card*) This president never ran for office. His Democratic friends nominated him, but he never made one campaign speech.

Tallia Why: (*rings bell*) Oh, that was Franklin Pierce, who was president from 1853 to 1857. Can you believe he never made even one campaign speech? I just don't know how he was able to get voters' support without making even one single speech, but then, you know, some people actually don't like to talk a lot. Can you imagine?

Luckee Chanse: Yes, I think we can imagine. (*Game Show Audience laughs*) You now have three points, Tallia. Linn, the final question please.

Linn Formation: Okay, Luckee. (*reads from card*) Who was the oldest man to be elected president of the United States?

Justin Truth: (*rings bell*) John F. Kennedy. That was John F. Kennedy.

Linn Formation: No, Justin, I'm sorry. John F. Kennedy was the *youngest* man to be elected president. He was 43.

Game Show Audience: (*in sympathy for Justin*) Ooh.

Lee Durr: (*rings bell*) Wait, wait. Ronald Reagan was the oldest man to be elected president. He was 69 years old and that just goes to show that senior citizens can be leaders, too!

Linn Formation: That is right, Lee. You have two points. (*Game Show Audience cheers and Justin gives Lee a high five*) And now it's time for our final mystery president. (*exits*)

Luckee Chanse: Okay, contestants, as we enter our final round, Justin and Lee have two points and Kara and Tallia are tied for the lead with three points each. Oh, it's close. Buckle up and get ready for our last mystery president on today's show. Mr. President?

Mystery President #3 (Franklin Roosevelt): (*enters*) Well, hello, everyone. It's nice to be here today. I had the privilege of serving this fine country as president longer than anyone else, before or after me. I was president for three terms, twelve years in all.

Luckee Chanse: Contestants? Any guesses? (*Contestants shake their heads; members of Game Show Audience mumble among themselves*)

Franklin Roosevelt: A lesser-known fact about me is that I liked pigs. I liked them so much, I even kept a collection of miniature pigs in my White House bedroom.

Kara Lott: (*rings bell*) Oh, oh—you're the sheep president. Are you Woodrow Wilson? Uh, no . . . No, wait. Maybe you're the teddy bear president. Ahhh.

Luckee Chanse: No, sorry, Kara. You're incorrect on both.

Kara Lott: (*snaps fingers*) Rats!

(*Game Show Audience gives a sympathy groan.*)

Luckee Chanse: Mr. President, I think we need another clue.

Franklin Roosevelt: Well, Luckee, not many pictures exist of me, because I didn't like being photographed. After suffering from polio as an adult, I spent a great deal of my presidency in a wheelchair and had to have help

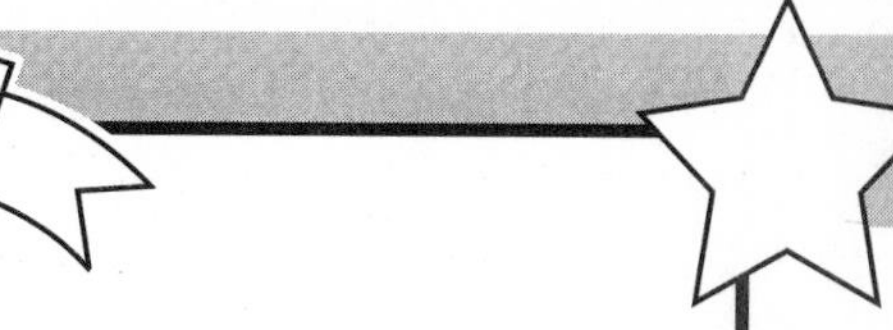

standing. In my time, people with disabilities were not always considered capable or smart. Luckily, things have changed since then.

Tallia Why: (*rings bell, excited*) Oh, oh! Franklin Roosevelt. You're Franklin Roosevelt, the president from 1933 to 1945. You started giving famous speeches on the radio called "fireside chats." And you were a great leader who helped us get through World War II! I'm a big fan of yours, sir.

Franklin Roosevelt: Well, thank you. I appreciate it!

Luckee Chanse: (*with energy*) You're absolutely right, Tallia. That correct answer brings you up to five points and makes you the winner of our game!

(*Game Show Audience stands and cheers, and Franklin Roosevelt exits.*)

(*Kara, Justin, Lee gather around and congratulate Tallia Why.*)

Luckee Chanse: (*pulls Tallia aside*) And now, Tallia, here's our announcer, Rod Cast, to tell you a little bit about what you've won on . . . (*points to audience*)

Game Show Audience: (*with energy*) Who Wants to Be President?

Rod Cast: (*enters*) Well, Tallia. As the winner of today's game, you get the chance to be sworn in as president of the United States for one whole day. You will begin by driving to the White House in another prize you've won on our show today, a new car! (*Game Show Audience cheers*)

Tallia Why: But I'm not old enough to drive.

Game Show Audience: Ohhhhhhh . . .

Rod Cast: Oh. You're not? How old are you?

Tallia Why: Nine and a half.

Rod Cast: Hmmm. I'm afraid you'll have to wait a few years to be president, because you have to be at least 35 years old. That's the law!

Tallia Why: Uh-oh. Really?

Luckee Chanse: Wait a minute. I've got an idea! (*whispers in the ear of Rod Cast*)

Rod Cast: Oh, okay! Tallia, since you're not old enough to be president, your prize will be to write and deliver a speech for the president!

Tallia Why: (*jumping up and down*) Yippee! That's the best prize ever! I mean I can hardly even wait to get started, because, you know, I really like talking. (*continues talking as the other contestants crowd around her to congratulate her*) I could talk about schools and the environment and I suppose I could even talk about . . .

Luckee Chanse: (*to Game Show Audience*) And that ends another game of . . . (*points to the audience*)

Game Show Audience: Who Wants to Be President? (*cheering*)

Curtain Call

Presidents' Day

FOLLOW-UP ACTIVITIES

Presidential Trivia Game

Purpose: Learn interesting facts about presidents and hone research skills.

How to: Place students in small groups and assign each group one president to research. Groups will be responsible for finding three to five facts about their assigned president and recording each fact with the name of the president on an index card (facts can be serious, such as the date of Lincoln's Gettysburg Address, or fun, such as the number of pigs in Roosevelt's pig collection). Students may wish to look for facts on the Internet, in encyclopedias or almanacs, or in one of the many tidbit fact books about presidents, such as *Lives of the Presidents: Fame, Shame (and What the Neighbors Thought)* by Kathleen Krull and Kathryn Hewitt (Harcourt Children's Books, 1998). Once they have completed the fact cards, have groups share their facts with the class. Then collect the cards and shuffle. For whole-group work, quiz the class on the facts they've just learned. For small-group work, divide the cards evenly among the groups and let an assigned student serve as "trivia master" and quiz the others in his or her group. Have groups swap card sets and appoint a new trivia master for the next round.

Mock Presidential Candidates

Purpose: Create a presidential candidate with a personal history and opinions on issues that students can relate to.

How to: Place students in pairs or small groups. Ask each group to create a mock presidential candidate that includes the candidate's name, job history, and a campaign platform consisting of three to five issues that are important to students. Students' lists may include such issues as school uniforms, cafeteria food, homework policies, busing, and length and structure of the school year. Have students organize their ideas on the Our Candidate sheet (page 20).

Invite students to create pamphlets or posters for their candidates and write newspaper interviews about them. You may wish to have one student from each group represent a candidate in a mock presidential debate. As a culminating activity, host a class-wide election and ask students to vote for the candidate of their choice.

Our Candidate

NAME

PLACE OF BIRTH

DATE OF BIRTH

Job History

✓

✓

✓

✓

Important Issues	*Candidate's Stand*

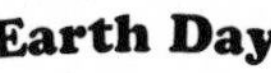

"All of Us One"

A read-aloud play for Earth Day, celebrated April 22

In "All of Us One," students come to better understand the history of Earth Day as well as the environmental gains that have been made as a result of this civic holiday.

History

The idea for the celebration of Earth Day began in the 1960s as a grassroots effort by Senator Gaylord Nelson of Wisconsin to raise national awareness about the importance of the environment. This idea culminated on April 22, 1970, when 20 million people nationwide celebrated the first Earth Day. No one, including Senator Nelson, had any idea of how huge the environmental movement would become, or the amount of legislation that would arise directly from it, including the creation of the Environmental Protection Agency.

For his work on Earth Day and his passion for the environment, Senator Nelson was awarded the Presidential Medal of Freedom in 1995, the highest honor a civilian can receive from the U.S. Government. In his own words, Senator Nelson tells us: "We are not free to decide about whether or not our environment 'matters.' It does matter, apart from any political exigencies. We disregard the needs of our ecosystem at our mortal peril. That was the great lesson of Earth Day. It must never be forgotten."

If You Stage the Play . . .

Set: Give students the opportunity to create a "newsroom" with a table and two chairs for the news anchors, as well as a separate section for Della Vine's studio. Props may include a "Planet Green Earth News" banner hung above the table, charts and weather graphs, papers and coffee cups for the anchors, and pretend microphones.

Costumes: Students may wish to brainstorm ideas for specific costume pieces to match their characters. Costume ideas include professional-looking clothes for reporters, green or brown clothes for Ima Leaf, paper leaves taped on Ever Green (who may stand carefully on a chair), camouflage marks and antennae for the Army Ants, sunglasses and yellow clothes for Sun, and watering cans for Rainclouds.

The Cast
(in order of reading level)

Nonspeaking

CREWMEMBER #1

CREWMEMBER #2

Grade 2

ARMY ANT #1

ARMY ANT #2

ARMY ANT #3

RAINCLOUDS

Grade 3/Low 4

PROLOGUE READER

Grade 4

ARMY ANT CAPTAIN

FLIT

KID #1

KID #2

IMA LEAF

DELLA VINE/DEL LA VINE

SONNIE SHINE

EVER GREEN

Grade 5/High 4

MARA SKY

SUN

Vocabulary

anchor *noun* the lead reporter in a team of television news reporters.

federal *noun* having to do with the national government.

grassroots *adjective* starting with a few people and then growing.

legislators *noun* people who make laws.

literally *adverb* actually, without stretching the truth.

nationwide *adjective* taking place in many parts of the country.

ozone *noun* a type of oxygen that surrounds the earth and helps protect it from the sun's harmful effects; air pollution can destroy the ozone layer that protects the earth.

scrimmage *noun* a practice battle or game.

tireless *adjective* determined.

All of Us One!

HONORING EARTH DAY, CELEBRATED APRIL 22

THE CAST

(in order of appearance)

PROLOGUE READER (optional)

SONNIE SHINE (anchor #1) • MARA SKY (anchor #2)

DELLA VINE (Del LaVine for boys)

IMA LEAF

ARMY ANT CAPTAIN

ARMY ANT #1 • ARMY ANT #2 • ARMY ANT #3

KID #1 • KID #2

FLIT

EVER GREEN

CREWMEMBER #1 • CREWMEMBER #2

SUN

RAINCLOUDS (three to five people)

PROLOGUE (optional): Senator Gaylord Nelson, from Wisconsin, was the man who helped create the first Earth Day on April 22, 1970. What began as a simple idea grew into a national understanding about the importance of our environment. Because of his tireless work on Earth Day and for the environment, Senator Nelson was awarded the Presidential Medal of Freedom in 1995. This is the highest honor a civilian can receive from the U.S. Government.

News Segment #1

Sonnie Shine: (*to audience*) Hello and welcome to this special edition of *Planet Green Earth News*. I'm your host, Sonnie Shine, and this is my co-host, Mara Sky.

Mara Sky: (*to audience*) Thank you, Sonnie. As you know, today is Earth Day and for this occasion, our special feature reporter, Della Vine, has prepared a unique interview.

Sonnie Shine: That's right, Mara. Let's turn now to Della Vine, who is in her studio getting ready for some very special guests. Della?

Della Vine: (*in studio, holding microphone and addressing audience with great energy; Ima Leaf is seated next to her*) Thanks, Sonnie, and hello to all of our viewers. We are lucky today to visit with a number of very special guests who have made the trip to our studio to tell us about Earth Day. First, I'd like our viewers to meet Ima Leaf, who was actually present on the very first Earth Day. Ima?

Ima Leaf: Thanks, Della! My, oh, my, what an event that was! Did you know that over 20 million people celebrated that first Earth Day, way back in 1970?

Della Vine: 20 million? That's a lot of people.

Ima Leaf: That sure is. And in Washington, D.C., there were so many legislators outside celebrating Earth Day that they actually had to close Congress for the day.

Della Vine: My goodness. And where were you on that first Earth Day?

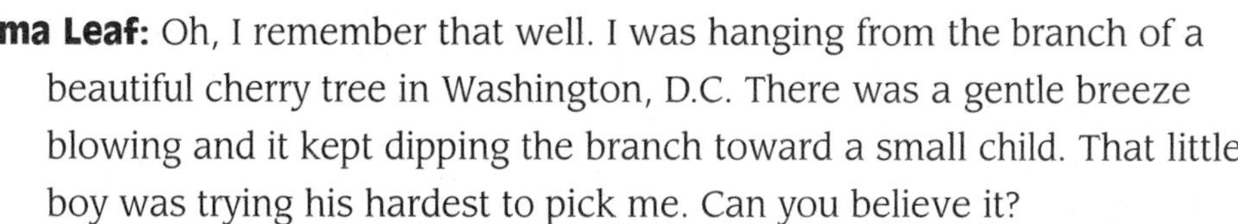

Ima Leaf: Oh, I remember that well. I was hanging from the branch of a beautiful cherry tree in Washington, D.C. There was a gentle breeze blowing and it kept dipping the branch toward a small child. That little boy was trying his hardest to pick me. Can you believe it?

Della Vine: Oh, my, what did you do?

Ima Leaf: Well, I said to that child, "Child, you just leaf me alone." Get it? *Leaf* me alone? Ha-ha-ha. And just as that pesky little boy almost had me, the breeze blew me out his reach.

Della Vine: Ha-ha. Very clever. Well, Ima, thanks for stopping in and telling us a little about that first Earth Day. Now, I believe our next guest is waiting to speak with us. (*Ima exits and Army Ants enter*)

Army Ants: (*together*) March! March! March!

Army Ant Captain: (*loudly*) Company, halt! (*Army Ants stop; Captain sits*)

Della Vine: Well, hello, and thank you for coming to *Planet Green Earth News* to talk about Earth Day. As our audience may have guessed, you are a troupe of Army Ants, correct?

Army Ants: (*together, loudly*) Yes, ma'am!

Della Vine: And what thoughts would you like to share with us about Earth Day?

Army Ants: (*together, loudly*) Graaass, ma'am!

Della Vine: Grass? Did you say "grass"?

Army Ants: (*together, loudly*) Yes, ma'am!

Della Vine: Grass. Okay. . . . Perhaps your captain could explain—by himself?

Army Ant Captain: Well, ma'am, we'd like your viewers to know that Earth Day was a grassroots effort.

Della Vine: Oh, I understand. That's the "grass" part.

Army Ant Captain: Yes, ma'am. You see, a grassroots effort is something that starts small but then grows, just like grass. A grassroots idea just kind of takes over in people's minds and hearts and that's exactly what happened with Senator Nelson's idea for Earth Day. It began very small and spread as fast as grass to become a huge nationwide celebration. And so we call it a grassroots effort.

Della Vine: Absolutely. I don't know if anyone had any idea how strong the environmental movement would become as a result of that first Earth Day.

Army Ants: (*together, loudly*) No, ma'am!

Army Ant Captain: As a matter of fact, did you know that the EPA was created because of Earth Day?

Della Vine: EPA? What does that stand for?

Army Ant Captain: The Environmental Protection Agency. It is a federal agency that helps to protect our environment and keep the earth safe.

Della Vine: Well, that's certainly important.

Army Ants: (*together, loudly*) Yes, ma'am!

Army Ant Captain: Well, ma'am, we need to get back into the field to practice for our scrimmage with the crickets next week. It's been a pleasure. Company, march!

Army Ants: (*together, loudly*) March, march, march! (*they exit*)

Della Vine: Well, viewers, it's time for a commercial break. We here at *Planet Green Earth News* would like to extend a special thanks to Ima Leaf and to the army ants for taking the time out of their busy day to speak to us. We'll be back in a few minutes.

(*News actors exit. Kid #1 and Kid #2 enter and stand next to each other. Kid #1 holds a box. Kid #2 holds a sneaker.*)

Commercial Segment

Kid #1: Hey, there. I haven't seen you for a while! How've you been?

Kid #2: (*sadly*) Oh, hi. Not so good.

Kid #1: What's wrong?

Kid #2: (*sighs*) Well, my mom told me I have to . . . I have to . . . No, I just can't say it.

Kid #1: (*gently*) It's okay. You can tell me.

Kid #2: (*holding up sneaker*) I have to throw away my favorite sneakers!

Kid #1: (*holding nose*) I can see why! But don't worry. I've got great news! I just got back from buying the brand-new handy dandy automatic recyclo-sneaker. (*holds up box*)

Kid #2: You did? What's that?

Kid #1: Well, you take your favorite old, smelly sneakers and put them in the automatic recyclo-sneaker, like this. (*puts one old sneaker in box*) Then you shake it, like this. (*shakes box*) And presto! Out comes a brand new shoe, ready for you to wear. (*pulls out new shoe that was hidden in the box*)

Kid #2: Wow! That's amazing! I have to get my own automatic recyclo-sneaker right away!

Kid #1: (*smiling at audience, holding box*) That's right! The automatic recyclo-sneaker. Yours for only $19.95 at select stores. Helps reduce waste and lets you keep that old pair of shoes without stinking out your friends and family.

Kid #2: And it comes fully guaranteed!

News Segment #2

(*Commercial actors exit; news actors enter.*)

Sonnie Shine:(*to audience*) Hello and welcome back to *Planet Green Earth News* and our continued coverage of Earth Day. I'm Sonnie Shine, your anchor.

Mara Sky: (*to audience*) And I'm Mara Sky. Before the commercial break, our special feature reporter, Della Vine, was in the studio interviewing various guests about Earth Day. We now return to her.

Della Vine: (*back in studio, facing audience*) Thank you, Mara and Sonnie. Welcome to this segment on Earth Day. Joining me in our studio next is a special hummingbird named Flit. Good afternoon, Flit, and welcome.

Flit: (*enters, speaking rapidly*) Thank you. Thank you. Oh, thank you so much. I love talking about Earth Day, you know!

Della Vine: Yes, Flit, please tell our viewers exactly why Earth Day is so special to you.

Flit: Oh, yes, yes, yes, it is special indeed! Because of Earth Day, we now have over 642 parks in the United States that we didn't have before!

Della Vine: That's a lot of parks.

Flit: Yes, yes, yes, it is! And even more important than that, because of Earth Day, we have the Endangered Species Act, which protects animals from becoming extinct and lost forever.

Della Vine: So we don't have to worry about losing little creatures like you.

Flit: Oh, no, no, no! Not as long as the Endangered Species Act stays in place. Uh-uh, no way—not going to happen! All of the animals are going to be around for a long time, thanks to Earth Day!

Della Vine: And we're so glad, Flit. Is there anything else you'd like to say about Earth Day?

Flit: Well, yes, yes, yes! I hope everyone gets outside this Earth Day and enjoys some of those beautiful parks we have! As for me, I must be off, off, off. There are nests to build, babies to feed, nectar to drink. Busy, busy, busy. Happy Earth Day to you and your viewers! (*exits*)

Della Vine: Thank you, Flit. And now, viewers, for our next interview we need to travel outside, because our next guest is literally stuck in the ground. (*walks to Ever Green*) Hello, Ever Green, and welcome to this special edition of *Planet Green Earth News*. We're so glad you're able to join us!

Ever Green: (*very slowly*) Thank you, Della, and hello to all of your viewers. Not only is it Earth Day, but today also happens to be my birthday!

Della Vine: Well, happy birthday!

Ever Green: (*slowly*) Thank you. I'm 175 years old today.

Della Vine: Amazing, Ever Green. I must say you don't look a day over 75.

Ever Green: (*slowly*) Yes, well, it's all in the sap.

Della Vine: Now, Ever Green, you had something important that you wanted to tell our viewers about Earth Day.

Ever Green: (*slowly*) Yes, Della, I did. Some people get confused about the differences between Earth Day and Arbor Day. Do you know about Arbor Day?

Della Vine: Well, I know that the word *arbor* is Latin for "tree."

Ever Green: Very good. And Arbor Day, also known as Tree Day, was started in 1872 to encourage people to plant trees.

Della Vine: And didn't it become a national holiday in 1970, about the same time as the first Earth Day?

Ever Green: Yes. But what people don't always understand is that Arbor Day is about planting and caring for trees, which, of course, is very important.

Della Vine: Of course. I'm sure you have a special interest in the care of trees.

Ever Green: Yes, trees provide a home for animals, as well as adding oxygen to the air. We also act as protection against harsh natural elements, such as snow and heavy rain.

Della Vine: Trees are an important part of our environment.

Ever Green: Yes, but remember: We are all interconnected with the rest of nature. Earth Day was created to help people become aware of our *whole* environment and not just its individual pieces. Aaaaah, look, the sun is coming out. I've been waiting for a good sunbath.

Della Vine: Well, we'll leave you to that sunbath, Ever Green. Thank you so much for talking with us. (*walks back towards studio; Crewmember #1 hands her a note*) Oh, this just in! We have arranged for an interview with the sun! (*she enters studio; Crewmember #2 hands her sunglasses; Sun enters*) I believe the sun is here now. Hello and welcome. You're live with *Planet Green Earth News*.

Sun: (*loud, excited*) Hello, hello! Isn't it a glorious day today! I hope you're wearing sunscreen, Della, because I'm big and bright and hot, hot, hot!

Della Vine: Well, hello, Sun. I was hoping . . .

Sun: (*interrupts*) I hope the camera is getting my good side. I'd like to say hello to all my friends. Hi to Jupiter and Mars, and of course, I can't forget Saturn. Hello, Saturn! I do hope you're keeping those planetary rings straight, dear.

Della Vine: Every side is your good side, Sun. Now, I was wondering if . . .

Sun: I am, after all, one of the shining stars of Earth Day. Literally. I am a shining star. Get it?

Della Vine: Yes, Sun. Ha-ha. Good joke. Now, about Earth Day.

Sun: Earth Day? Is that today? Oh, my, there's so much to do to get ready.

Della Vine: Well, if you could just take a moment to share your thoughts about Earth Day with us, that would be . . .

Sun: (*interrupts*) Well, the ozone layer, of course.

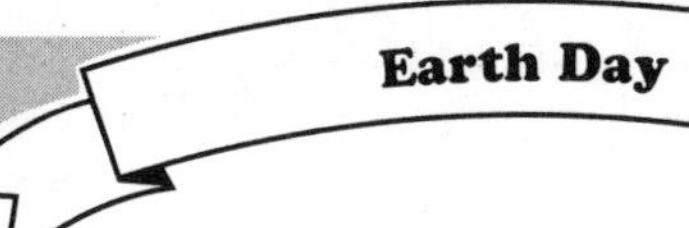

Della Vine: Excuse me? The ozone layer?

Sun: Yes. The ozone layer. It's the protective covering around the atmosphere of the earth. Because I am so big and powerful, the ozone layer keeps me from scorching all of you down here to smithereens. I wouldn't want to burn you lovely people and plants on Earth with my amazingly powerful rays!

Della Vine: Oh, yes, the ozone layer is important. But what does that have to do with Earth Day?

Sun: (*laughing*) Oh, my dear! Because of Earth Day, people are aware of how important—and how fragile—the ozone layer is. They have been working hard to protect it by driving cars that give off less pollution and passing laws to keep factories from overpolluting the air.

Della Vine: So, if we're not careful, pollution can destroy our natural sun-screen!

Sun: Right. And Earth Day has inspired people to do other things to help the earth, like recycling, turning off lights, and using less water. These are all things that will keep the earth around for a long time, so I can add my big, beautiful brilliance to everything living on it! And now, I must be off. There are trees to grow and things to do for Earth Day, you know. Ta-ta!

Della Vine: (*to audience*) Well, that wraps up another feature segment of *Planet Green Earth News*. This is . . . (*Crewmember #1 enters with a note*) Wait. It appears there are . . . Does this say "rain clouds"?

(*Rainclouds enter with empty watering cans.*)

Rainclouds: (*together*) Swish, Swish. (*"raining" on Della Vine*)

Della Vine: Oh, dear. This is not quite what I expected today. I forgot my umbrella! (*trying to stay dry as more Rainclouds appear*) Well, this is Della Vine with *Planet Green Earth News*, coming to you live on this very special Earth Day. Back to you, Sonnie and Mara!

Mara Sky: Thank you, Della, for that report. I do hope you stay dry! This is Mara Sky . . .

Sonnie Shine: . . . and Sonnie Shine with another edition of *Planet Green Earth News*. Make sure to tune in next week for Della's special feature segment on the fine art of making mud pies.

Mara Sky: And our undercover investigation "When Bugs Go Bad." Have a nice evening and a happy Earth Day!

Curtain Call

Earth Day

FOLLOW-UP ACTIVITIES

Environmental Commercials

Purpose: Create an environmentally helpful product and a commercial to promote it.

How to: Ask students to decide whether they will create an imaginary product, such as the Recyclo-Sneaker, or promote an environmentally friendly action, such as planting trees or turning off unnecessary lights. Place students in small groups. Invite groups to select an idea for a product or service and then write a collaborative script highlighting it. Distribute copies of the Bright Ideas for a Green Planet organizer on page 34 to help them develop their ideas. Encourage students to include both persuasive and descriptive language to help promote their message or product. After students have practiced, their commercials may be videotaped or performed live; the ad may be incorporated into a reading or performance of the play.

Extend it! Ask students to create persuasive pamphlets or signs to accompany their commercials. Signs can be posted in the schools and pamphlets can be distributed to other classes.

Environmental Picture Book Study

Purpose: Raise environmental awareness and support reading skills through a comparative book study.

How to: Select four or more environmentally focused picture books for a short theme study. Such picture books provide an excellent opportunity for brief comparative literature studies with older students. Gather picture books that carry environmental themes, such as *Just a Dream* by Chris Van Allsburg (Houghton Mifflin, 1990), *Someday a Tree* by Eve Bunting (Clarion, 1993), or *The Great Kapok Tree: A Tale of the Amazon Rain Forest* by Lynn Cherry (Gulliver Green, 1990). You may wish to read a different picture book to the entire class daily for a period of days or have students read several picture books together in small groups. Ask students to compare the themes and authors' messages, using the discussion points below.

Discussion points:

- What is the author's message?
- How is the message delivered—through pictures, text, or a combination of both?
- What do you think is most effective?
- Do you agree with the author's message?
- Describe how you could deliver the same message in another way.

Bright Ideas for a Green Planet

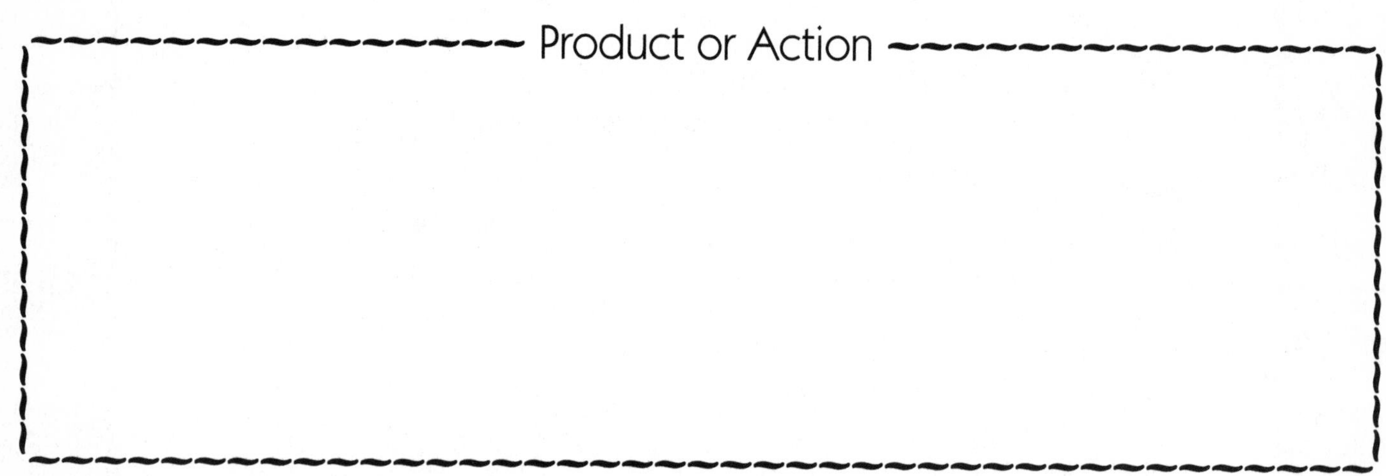

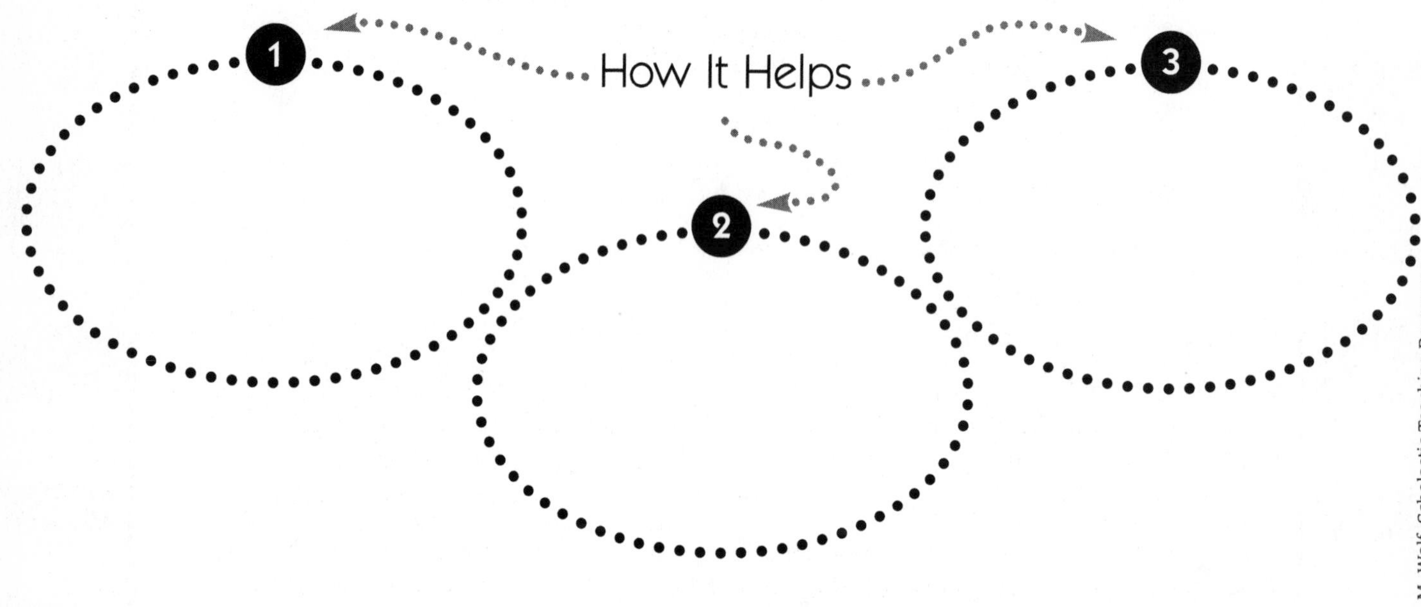

Slogan
(Persuade your buyer or participant!)

"Remember Not to Forget"

A read-aloud play for Memorial Day, celebrated the last Monday in May

In the play, "Remember Not to Forget," students learn about the history and origins of Memorial Day, as well as a number of common traditions we observe to commemorate this national holiday.

History

Originally called "Decoration Day," Memorial Day began in 1868 as a way to honor soldiers who had died fighting in the Civil War. Although there are many legends about its origin (more than two dozen states claim to have originated the holiday), it was first declared a national holiday on May 5, 1868. After World War I, Memorial Day observances began to include the remembrance of all American soldiers who have died in war. In 1971, a congressional act made it an official national holiday, to be celebrated the last Monday in May.

Americans commemorate this holiday in a number of ways, including the Boy and Girl Scout Luminaria program and the VFW (Veterans of Foreign Wars) Buddy Poppy program. The VFW program, which supports veterans and their families in need through the sale of poppies, was inspired by the poem "In Flanders Fields" (page 48). Canadian doctor John McCrae wrote this poem during the First World War. As Dr. McCrae tended to the wounded in France, he noticed a field of red poppies blooming over the graves of dead soldiers and was inspired to create what would become one of the most recognized war poems ever written.

If You Stage the Play . . .

Set: While this play calls for a simple set, students may wish to include props that suggest the setting of a park or a field. This might include paper bushes and trees that are propped against chairs as well as gardens made from recycled materials or pretend playground equipment. For those scenes that take place in a cemetery, students may use cardboard boxes to create simple headstones or commemorative plaques that match the time period of the scene.

Costumes: Costumes should reflect the time period and occupations of the characters in the scenes. For example, the elderly guide may have a cane or graying hair. Soldiers may wear appropriately dark colors or military-style uniforms or hats. Scouts may wear a sash or medals, and state characters may simply carry a sign with the state name.

The Cast

(in order of reading level)

Grade 2

VIRGINIA • GEORGIA

SOLDIER #1 • SOLDIER #2 • SOLDIER #3

Grade 3/Low 4

VOLUNTEER #1

MISSISSIPPI • PENNSYLVANIA • NEW YORK

WOMAN #1 • WOMAN #2 • VOLUNTEER #2

KID #1 • KID #2 • GIRL SCOUT

Grade 4

BYSTANDER #1 • BYSTANDER #2

BYSTANDER #3 • VOLUNTEER #3

BOY SCOUT • YOUNG SOLDIER

MOINA MICHAEL

Grade 5/High 4

PROLOGUE READER (optional)

GENERAL JOHN LOGAN • ELDERLY GUIDE

Vocabulary

civil *adjective* having to do with a nation's people.

ideal *noun* something that is considered perfect.

infantry *noun* a unit of soldiers who fight on foot, rather than on ships or in airplanes.

legend *noun* a story that is often told as if it were true, but cannot be proved.

memorial *adjective* honoring the memory of people or events.

observe *verb* to respect or pay attention to.

poppy *noun* a type of brightly colored flower.

pursue *verb* to try to reach or achieve.

remembrance *noun* action taken to honor a memory or person.

***Casting Note:** To reduce the number of characters in this play, you may want to create a single United States character who reads all the individual states' lines.

Remember Not to Forget

HONORING MEMORIAL DAY,
CELEBRATED THE LAST MONDAY IN MAY

THE CAST
(in order of appearance)

PROLOGUE READER (optional)
KID #1 • KID #2
ELDERLY GUIDE • YOUNG SOLDIER • WOMAN #1 • WOMAN #2
NEW YORK • MISSISSIPPI • PENNSYLVANIA • GEORGIA
VIRGINIA • GENERAL JOHN LOGAN
BYSTANDER #1 • BYSTANDER #2 • BYSTANDER #3
SOLDIER #1 • SOLDIER #2 • SOLDIER #3 • MOINA MICHAEL
VOLUNTEER #1 • VOLUNTEER #2 • VOLUNTEER #3
GIRL SCOUT • BOY SCOUT

PROLOGUE (optional): The conclusion of the Civil War in 1865 was both an ending and a beginning for our country. It marked the end of slavery and the beginning of a country that pursued freedom for its people. After all, this country was founded on ideals of freedom. Memorial Day began one year later, in 1866, a day to remember those who died fighting in the Civil War.

Memorial Day has become a day for us to remember any man or woman who has died while serving in wartime, a day to remember those who gave the ultimate sacrifice for their country.

(*Kids #1 and #2 enter*)

Kid #1: So what are you going to do this weekend? It's Memorial Day on Monday and that means . . .

Kid #2: We get a day off from school!

Elderly Guide: (*enters*) Well, hello, young'uns. Did I hear you talking about Memorial Day? (*Kids nod*)

Kid #1: We were just trying to figure out what we were going to day with our day off.

Elderly Guide: A day off, huh? Do you know why we celebrate Memorial Day?

Kid #2: I'm not sure, but I think it has to do with war.

Kid #1: And we always get a day off from school.

Elderly Guide: Well, did you know that the first Memorial Day took place right after the Civil War, way back in 1868?

Kid #1: Really?

Kid #2: No, I didn't know that.

Elderly Guide: To truly understand this holiday, you have to start at the beginning. Look over there. (*points offstage*) Do you see that young soldier?

Kid #1: (*hands up to eyes, looking offstage*) Where?

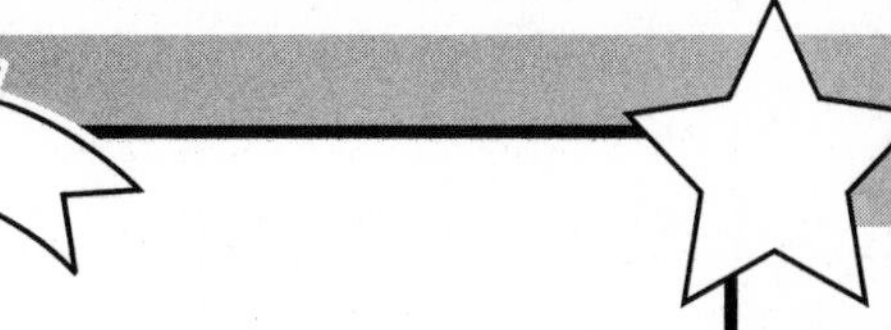

Kid #2: (*hands up to eyes*) I don't see anything.

(*Young Soldier, Woman #1 and Woman #2 enter from the direction Elderly Guide is pointing.*)

Elderly Guide: There—over there.

Kid #1: Oh, yeah. I see him!

Elderly Guide: You two go on over there and he'll tell you more.

(*Kid #1 and Kid #2 approach Young Soldier and women. Elderly Guide exits. The two women kneel at a grave and gesture to show that they are tending to the grave. The Young Soldier watches.*)

Kid #2: (*to Young Soldier*) Sir, excuse us, sir?

Young Soldier: Yes?

Kid #1: What are you watching?

Young Soldier: Well, this here is the year 1866, only one year after the end of the Civil War. I came to this cemetery to remember one of my friends who was killed in the war.

Woman #1: And he found us here.

Young Soldier: And I was amazed and surprised by their kindness.

Kid #2: What kindness?

Woman #2: We came to take care of the graves of soldiers from the South who were killed.

Young Soldier: But they were also taking care of my friend's grave, and he was from the North.

Woman #1: His friend's grave was neglected and needed tending to. North or South, all these boys died fighting for what they believed in.

Woman #2: And they all deserve to be remembered.

(*Elderly Guide enters quietly.*)

Young Soldier: Now, if you'll excuse me, I need to help these kind women take care of these graves. (*Young Soldier and Women #1 and #2 exit*)

Elderly Guide: That is one legend about how Memorial Day began.

Kid #1: Really?

Elderly Guide: Yes. The story goes that in 1866, a soldier from the North came upon two Southern women taking care of a Northern soldier's grave.

Kid #2: Even though people from the South disagreed with people from the North?

Elderly Guide: Exactly. Seeing the two sides come together helped people realize that both sides were grieving for their fallen young men. But as I said, this is just one legend about how Memorial Day began. There are actually many legends about its start. More than two dozen states claim to have helped it begin. States like . . .

(*New York enters, followed by Mississippi, Pennsylvania, Georgia, and Virginia.*)

New York: New York played an important part in starting this holiday. In 1873, we were the first state to officially recognize Memorial Day as a holiday. (*exits*)

Mississippi: Mississippi was also important in the first Memorial Day celebrations. (*exits*)

Pennsylvania: Pennsylvania helped begin Memorial Day. (*exits*)

Georgia: So did Georgia! (*exits*)

Virginia: Hey, don't forget about Virginia! We helped, too! (*exits*)

Elderly Guide: And there were many others states involved as well.

Kid #1: But when did it become an official holiday?

Elderly Guide: Ahh. If you head on over in that direction, to the year 1868, that general standing there will tell you more.

(*Enter General John Logan, Bystanders #1, #2, and #3. Kid #1 and Kid #2 approach as Elderly Guide watches from afar.*)

Kid #1: Hello, sir, we were wondering . . .

Bystander #1: (*to Kid #1*) Shhh.

Kid #2: (*to Bystander #1, pointing at General John Logan*) But we were told that he could tell us about Memorial Day.

Bystander #2:(*to Kid #2 in a stage whisper*) That's General John Logan. He's about to make an important announcement.

Kid #1: That's who?

Bystander #3: General John Logan. He's the commander of the Grand Army of the Republic in the year of 1868.

Kid #2: The Grand Army of the what?

Bystander #1: The Grand Army of the Republic. It's a group of veteran soldiers who fought in the Civil War. General John Logan is their leader.

Bystander #2: Hush, now. He's about to speak.

General John Logan: (*addressing the crowd*) On this day, the fifth of May, 1868, we do declare the observance of Decoration Day. We establish this day to help remember those soldiers who died in the Civil War. Let this show forever that we have not forgotten the cost of a free and undivided country. (*Bystanders, Kid #1, Kid #2 clap*)

Kid #1: (*to Bystander #1*) So was this the first Memorial Day?

Bystander #1: This was the first official Memorial Day.

Bystander #2: And it took place right here, at the Arlington National Cemetery in Arlington, Virginia.

General John Logan: Let us now place flags on the graves of both the Southern and Northern soldiers who died fighting for their beliefs. (*General John Logan exits, followed by Bystanders; Soldiers #1, #2, and #3 enter*)

Soldier #1: (*walking past Elderly Guide and Kids, carrying a small American flag on a stick*) Good afternoon. (*exits*)

Soldier #2: (*follows #1*) Thank you for observing Decoration Day. (*exits*)

Soldier #3: (*follows #2*) Excuse me, please. (*exits*)

Kid #1: (*to Elderly Guide*) Who are they?

Elderly Guide: This is the 1950s. Those young soldiers are members of the Third United States Infantry. Every Memorial Day weekend, they put small United States flags on all of the graves at the Arlington National Cemetery. Then they patrol 24 hours a day to make sure the flags stay put. They're still doing this every Memorial Day, even now.

Kid #2: That's a lot of flags!

Elderly Guide: Absolutely. Over 260,000 flags in all.

Kid #1: Whoa. But everyone's been calling it Decoration Day. When did it become Memorial Day?

Elderly Guide: Well, after the Civil War it took a great while before our United States really became united. Even though people had been celebrating Decoration Day for one hundred years, it wasn't until 1971 that Congress declared it a national holiday, officially calling it Memorial Day. (*enter Moina Michaels, Volunteers #1, #2, and #3, with red flowers*)

Kid #1: (*pointing*) Hey, look! All those people have red flowers.

Kid #2: (*to Elderly Guide*) Do you think it has to do with Memorial Day?

Elderly Guide: Why don't you find out? (*Kids #1 and #2 approach Volunteers*)

Kid #1: Excuse me, why do you have a red flower?

Volunteer #1: It's a poppy. Moina Michael gave it to me.

Kid #2: Who?

Volunteer #2: You don't know who Moina Michael is?

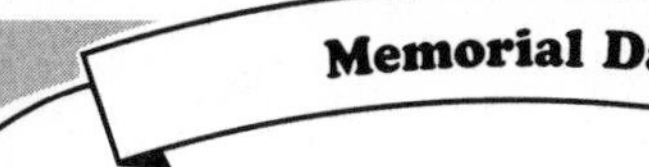

Volunteer #3: Or why we're wearing poppies on Memorial Day?

Kid #1: Uh, no. Sorry.

Volunteer #1: There's Moina, there. She'll explain it.

Kid #2: Excuse us, are you Moina?

Moina Michael: Why, yes, dear, I am. Would you like a poppy? (*hands one to Kid #2*)

Kid #2: Thank you.

Kid #1: (*also accepts a poppy from Moina*) Thank you. Can you tell us about these poppies?

Moina Michael: Of course, dear. In 1915, I read a lovely poem called "In Flanders Fields" by John McCrae. The poem talked about poppies growing over a field of buried soldiers. It inspired me to do something to help remember those who have died in war. I liked the idea of the poppies, so I decided to make some of my own that people could wear to remember.

Kid #2: So the red poppy became a sort of symbol—that's a great way to remember!

Moina Michael: Thank you, dear. Now, before I rush off to get some more red poppies for the rest of the day, I'll leave you with this poem:

We cherish too, the Poppy red
That grows on fields where valor led,
It seems to signal to the skies
That blood of heroes never dies. (*exits*)

Kid #1: (*to Volunteer #1*) So she was the one who thought of the idea to wear poppies on Memorial Day.

Volunteer #1: That's right. And her idea got so big that a group of veteran soldiers took on the project as their own.

Volunteer #2: It's called the Buddy Poppy program and all the money made goes to help veterans and their families.

Volunteer #3: And it's been so successful that in 1948, the United States Postal Service even made a stamp to honor Moina Michael for her efforts.

Kid #1: Really?

Kid #2: Wow. That's a pretty big deal.

Volunteer #1: Yes, well, Moina's idea was a pretty good one. And it keeps us volunteers busy. Please excuse us—we must help Moina with the poppies.

Volunteer #2: See you later! (*Volunteers #1, #2, and #3 exit; Elderly Guide approaches*)

Kid #1: (*to Elderly Guide*) Did you hear that?

Kid #2: Yeah. The idea for the red poppies that are sold on Memorial Day was started by Moina Michael.

Elderly Guide: Yes. It's a tradition that's been around a long while. And after World War I, about the same time Moina was creating her poppies, it was decided that Memorial Day should be a time to remember those who have died in *all* United States wars.

Kid #1: That's right: Memorial Day really is about more than just the Civil War now.

Kid #2: That makes sense. (*enter Girl Scout and Boy Scout*)

Girl Scout: (*to Kid #2*) Hello, can you help us, please?

Kid #2: Sure. What do you need?

Boy Scout: We're looking for the Fredericksburg National Cemetery.

Girl Scout: The one on Marye's Heights.

Kid #1: Gosh, I'm not sure if I know where that is.

Kid #2: Why are you going there?

Boy Scout: Well, I'm a Boy Scout and she's a Girl Scout.

Girl Scout: And every year before Memorial Day, we put candle lanterns on each of the graves at the Fredericksburg National Cemetery.

Boy Scout: To commemorate Memorial Day.

Kid #1: That sounds like a big job!

Girl Scout: Well, we do light over 15,000 candles every year.

Boy Scout: It's called the Luminaria Program.

Girl Scout: And even though there's a lot of candles to light, it's a really good way to remember those who have died fighting in war.

Kid #2: Yes. It really is.

Boy Scout: But we have to find the cemetery first.

Elderly Guide: I can help you there. (*pointing*) If you keep going that way for another few blocks and then turn right, you can't miss it.

Girl Scout: Gosh, thanks!

Boy Scout: Yeah, thanks. Let's go! (*Boy Scout and Girl Scout exit*)

Kid #1: (*to Elderly Guide*) I had no idea there was so many things that have to do with Memorial Day.

Kid #2: Yeah, and I didn't know how the holiday started.

Elderly Guide: In fact, it's such an important holiday that in the year 2000, President Clinton declared a National Moment of Remembrance to take place at 3:00 p.m. every Memorial Day. That means everyone is supposed to stop for one minute and think about those people who have died fighting in war.

Kid #1: (*looking at watch*) I'm going to set my watch for Monday at three.

Kid #2: I'm going to go home to tell my brother about this.

Kid #1: Me, too! (*shakes Elderly Guide's hand*) Thanks! It was nice talking to you.

Kid #2: (*shakes Elderly Guide's hand*) Yeah, thanks for all the information!

Elderly Guide: Absolutely. Just remember in the future not to forget.

Curtain Call

Memorial Day

FOLLOW-UP ACTIVITIES

Memorial Day Writing Prompts

Purpose: Extend ideas about remembrance, service, and symbolism.

How to: In journals or during free writing time, invite students to write about any of the following (note that students will need copies of "In Flanders Field" (page 48) to respond to the last prompt):

- What are three events in your life that you think are important to remember? What do you do to remember these events? Why is it important to remember these events?
- What are some of the ways people remember soldiers who died in war on Memorial Day?
- Think of and write about at least three ways you can help your fellow citizens, neighborhood, or country. Describe how you can help someone who is your age, someone who is younger, and someone who is older.
- Make a list of at least five things from your bedroom at home that are symbols of important things in your life. Be sure to include where these items came from.
- Read the poem "In Flanders Fields" and write your own remembrance poem for Memorial Day.

The Importance of Symbols

Purpose: Understand symbolism by creating a meaningful class symbol.

How to: Remind students that the red poppy has become a symbol strongly associated with Memorial Day. Brainstorm a list of familiar items that serve as symbols, such as the U.S. flag, yellow ribbons, or colored bracelets. As a class, create a list of items that might symbolize something about the class, such as a pen (if students enjoy writing) or a globe (if students enjoy geography or traveling). Let students vote for one item to become the class symbol. In small groups, invite students to create posters of this symbol.

Extend it! You may wish to have students create individual symbols that represent an aspect of themselves or interview their families and create a family symbol. Andrew Clements's *Frindle* (Simon and Schuster, 1986) offers students an interesting look at symbols and word meanings.

In Flanders Fields

by Lieutenant Colonel John McCrae, M.D. (1872–1918), Canadian army

In Flanders Fields the poppies blow
Between the crosses row on row,
That mark our place; and in the sky
The larks, still bravely singing, fly
Scarce heard amid the guns below.

We are the Dead. Short days ago
We lived, felt dawn, saw sunset glow,
Loved and were loved, and now we lie
    In Flanders fields.

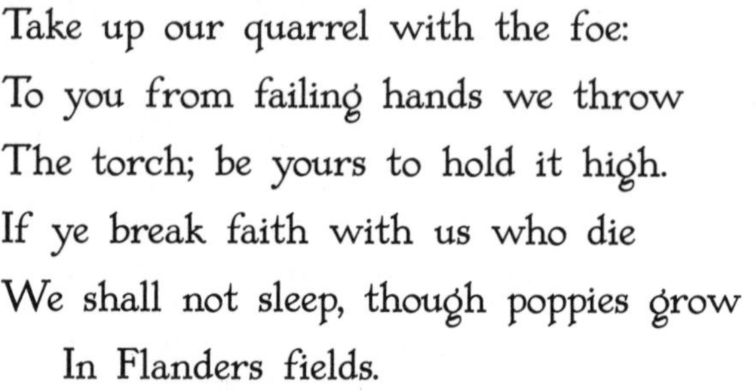

Take up our quarrel with the foe:
To you from failing hands we throw
The torch; be yours to hold it high.
If ye break faith with us who die
We shall not sleep, though poppies grow
    In Flanders fields.

Canadian doctor John McCrae wrote this poem in 1915 as he helped wounded soldiers during World War I. He noticed that a field of red poppies had begun to grow on the recently dug graves of young soldiers. This sight inspired him to write about the war in the voice of the soldiers who had died.

"Along the Path to Independence"

A read-aloud play for Independence Day, celebrated July 4

In this spoofy play about the origins of Independence Day, taxation without representation and independence become characters whose actions clearly explain to students these challenging concepts.

History

Although we celebrate our country's independence on only one day, many events over the course of many years led the original 13 colonies of the United States to fight for their independence from England in the late 1700s. Most of these events centered around unfair taxes and fees levied by the English parliament, King George, and other English officials. These led the colonists from quiet discontent to boycotts, protests, and finally to the Revolutionary War.

The Declaration of Independence was formally adopted on July 4, 1776, and signed on August 2, 1776.

If You Stage the Play . . .

Set: For a historically accurate set, give students the chance to create facades for a house for the Thirteen Colonies, as well as for a small town or storefront. Narrators may wish to sit on either side of the stage and Warren Peace may be seated in various parts of each scene, even if he doesn't have lines. Although they are from the present day, props such as a calculator, cell phone, and business card will add a humorous note.

Costumes: Students may enjoy dressing in traditional colonial costumes for this play, such as full skirts, knickers, and fancy jackets. Mr. Tax may dress in black and wear a traditional "bad guy" black hat to match. Newspaper Kids may wear vests and carry large fabric sacks to hold newspapers.

The Cast

(in order of reading level)

Nonspeaking parts

SHOPPERS (three to five)

Grade 2

SOLDIERS #1, #2, #3, #4

MERCHANT

PAUL REVERE

SON OF LIBERTY #4

Grade 3

FRIENDS #1, #2, #3

GEORGE WASHINGTON

JOHN HANCOCK

SONS OF LIBERTY #1, #2, #5, #6

Grade 4

SAMUEL ADAMS

NEWSPAPER KIDS #1, #2, #3, #4, #5, #6

WARREN PEACE

SON OF LIBERTY #3

INDIE PENDENCE (low 5)

Grade 5

PROLOGUE READER (optional)

MR. TAX

THIRTEEN COLONIES (T.C.)

NARRATOR #1

NARRATOR #2

Vocabulary

colony *noun* a land or group of people ruled by another country.

congress *noun* meeting where people make laws for governing.

declaration *noun* announcement; a paper or speech that says something important.

delegate *noun* a person acting or speaking for himself and his neighbors.

intolerable *adjective* too unfair to live with.

independence *noun* self-rule; freedom from the rule of another country.

liberty *noun* freedom to do as you please.

Parliament *noun* group of people who make laws in England.

protest *noun* an event where people complain to their government; *verb* to complain publicly about government actions.

quartering *noun* giving someone food and a place to live or to stay.

taxation *noun* charging people money to pay for government.

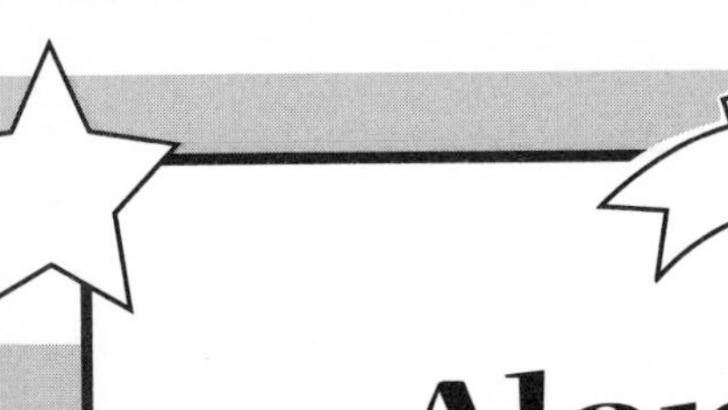

Along the Path to Independence

HONORING INDEPENDENCE DAY, CELEBRATED JULY 4

THE CAST

(in order of appearance)

PROLOGUE READER (optional)

NEWSPAPER KID #1 • NARRATOR #1 • NARRATOR #2

THIRTEEN COLONIES (T.C.) • MR. TAX

SON OF LIBERTY #1 • SON OF LIBERTY #2 • SON OF LIBERTY #3

NEWSPAPER KID #2 • MERCHANT • WARREN PEACE

SHOPPERS (three to five nonspeaking parts) • INDIE PENDENCE

NEWSPAPER KID #3 • FRIEND #1 • FRIEND #2 • FRIEND #3

SON OF LIBERTY #4 • SON OF LIBERTY #5 • SON OF LIBERTY #6

NEWSPAPER KID #4 • SOLDIER #1 • SOLDIER #2

SOLDIER #3 • SOLDIER #4 • NEWSPAPER KID #5

GEORGE WASHINGTON • SAMUEL ADAMS • PAUL REVERE

NEWSPAPER KID #6 • JOHN HANCOCK

PROLOGUE (optional): There were many reasons the original 13 colonies wanted independence from England. One big reason had to do with taxes. Colonists were becoming more and more self-sufficient. They wanted a voice in how the tax money they sent to England would be spent. They wanted more say in how that money would be collected. Yet their taxes continued to go up and they still had no say about it. This is called taxation without representation. After many protests, meetings, and finally war, the colonies officially adopted the Declaration of Independence on July 4, 1776, declaring their freedom from England.

Scene One—House of Thirteen Colonies

Newspaper Kid #1: Hear ye! Hear ye! Get the latest issue of *The Troubled Times*! The 13 colonies have to pay taxes without being asked! (*gives copies of* The Troubled Times *to each of the Narrators, exits*)

Narrator #1: (*reads headline of newspaper*) Yes, troubled times they were in the year 1764. Our heroine, the Thirteen Colonies (known as T.C. to her friends), was facing great difficulty with her mother country, England.

Narrator #2: (*holding newspaper*) You see, T.C. was just beginning to grow and develop as a country in her own right.

Narrator #1: But the colonies were still ruled by England and the English parliament had decided to pass some laws that would keep T.C. in her place.

Narrator #2: The English parliament was a group of wealthy people who made laws in England. They decided to collect more money from the colonies to help their own businesses in England by putting a tax on things the people used.

Narrator #1: And they never asked the colonies if they could afford this or if they wanted it. So that's where the problems began.

Narrator #2: And that's where we join our heroine, T.C., to see what these troubled times will bring for her.

(*T.C. enters.*)

T.C.: Oh, It's a beautiful day! The cows are milked, the chickens are plucked and I'm feeling like a bit of coffee with some sugar. *(goes to the cupboard to get coffee and sugar)*

Mr. Tax: (*knocks on the door*) Hello?

T.C.: (*opens door*) Yes? May I help you?

Mr. Tax: I'm Mr. Tax, ma'am. Here's my business card. (*hands her a card*)

T.C.: (*looks at card*) Oh, you must be new here. I was just about to sit down for some coffee and a spot of sugar. Would you like to join me?

Mr. Tax: Actually, I'm here to collect money on both of those items.

T.C.: What? What do you mean collect money?

Mr. Tax: (*Unrolls scroll and reads aloud*) As per the Sugar Act of 1764, passed by Parliament, all colonists will pay taxes on sugar and coffee, as well as other items they buy.

T.C.: But I already pay taxes to help keep the government running.

Mr. Tax: (*ignoring her*) That'll be (*takes out a calculator and punches numbers*) this much, please. (*shows her the number on the calculator and holds out hand*)

T.C.: (*angrily*) But this isn't fair!! I told you I already pay money to help the government run! No one asked me if I could afford to pay taxes on sugar and coffee, too!

Mr. Tax: Well, ma'am, I'm just doing my job. What you've got here is a little situation known as taxation without adequate representation. I hear it's happening everywhere these days. I need the money, please.

T.C.: Oh, all right. (*gets money from pocket; gives it to Mr. Tax*) Here. Send this back to England. And tell them I'm not happy!

Mr. Tax: Thank you, ma'am. Try to have a nice day. (*exits*)

T.C.: Well, I'm going for a walk. (*walking toward town and the merchant's shop, mumbling to self*) Taxation without representation, huh? Take my money without asking me, will they! Hmph.

Son of Liberty #1: (*bumping into T.C.*) Excuse me! (*hurries past*)

Son of Liberty #2: (*passing T.C.*) Pardon me! (*hurries past*)

Son of Liberty #3: (*nearly knocking T.C. over*) Oops, sorry! (*stops to help T.C.*) Are you okay?

T.C.: I think so. (*dusting herself off*) You wouldn't believe the kind of a day I've had! Did you know that England is taxing us on sugar and coffee? Did anyone ask you about this? Because I don't remember them asking me if this was okay!

Son of Liberty #3: No, ma'am. (*stage whispers*) And actually, I'm one of the Sons of Liberty, and we're going to fight these new taxes. Here's a pamphlet. There's going to be a protest. Gotta run!

(*Sons of Liberty exit. T.C. exits while reading the pamphlet.*)

Scene Two—The Merchant's Shop

Newspaper Kid #2: (*enters*) Hear ye! Hear ye! Get your copy of *The Troubled Times*! England repeals the Sugar Act and passes the Stamp Act! (*gives copies to each narrator*)

Narrator #2: It didn't take long for the colonists to convince England to lift the Sugar Act of 1764.

Narrator #1: The Sons of Liberty helped organize boycotts and marches to protest this act.

Narrator #2: However, just one year later, in 1765, England passed a new law, known as the Stamp Act.

Narrator #1: This act said that all official documents had to be stamped with a special English mark that the 13 colonies had to pay for every time it was used.

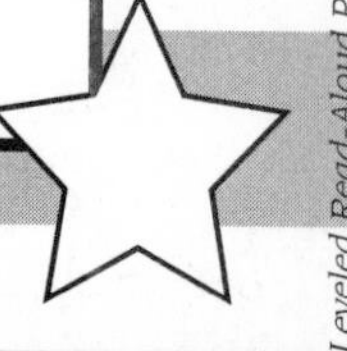

Narrator #1: And that was the beginning of a whole new set of problems for T.C.

T.C.: (*looking at a copy of* The Troubled Times) Well, that's that! I'm glad that whole Sugar Act tax thing is over. Now maybe things will get back to normal. Let's see what I've got to do today. (*looks at a list*) Feed the kids, pay for the chickens, drink some *tax-free* coffee, and oh, yes, I need to get a copy of my uncle's will from the merchant's shop. (*walks to Merchant's shop; shoppers pretend to shop*)

Merchant: Well, good morning, Thirteen Colonies.

T.C.: Oh, please, call me T.C. All my friends do.

Merchant: Okay, T.C., how may I help you?

T.C.: I need a copy of my uncle's will, please.

Merchant: Oh, yes. I have that copy in my files. Just let me go find it. (*exits*)

Mr. Tax: (*enters*) Well, hello, T.C.

T.C.: Oh, you again. It's Thirteen Colonies to you. I thought we got rid of you.

Mr. Tax: Well, I'm afraid it won't be that easy! You owe me (*figures on calculator, shows T.C.*) this much, please. (*holds out hand*)

T.C.: For what? I'm not buying sugar or coffee. What do I have to pay taxes on now?

Mr. Tax: Well, according to (*pulls out and reads from scroll*) the Stamp Act, recently passed in 1765, you must pay taxes on all papers that have the English stamp. And that includes your uncle's will.

T.C.: What? Give me a break! This is ridiculous. Nobody asked me about this new law!

Mr. Tax: (*shrugs*) Sorry—just doing my job.

Merchant: (*enters, holding will*) Here you go, T.C. (*notices Mr. Tax*) Oh, it's *you*.

Mr. Tax: (*waves at merchant*) Hello!

T.C.: (*hands Mr. Tax the money*) Here. Just . . . Just take your tax money and go away. (*Mr. Tax exits, counting the money; T.C. leaves the store as Merchant and Shoppers exit; Warren Peace enters*) Well, that does it! This has to stop.

Warren Peace: Hey, there, T.C. You look troubled. Can Warren Peace help at all?

T.C.: Oh, Warren! This is all so ridiculous. Things were going just fine until England decided to start imposing all these taxes. First it was the sugar tax and now it's the Stamp Act. I just don't know what to do. (*sighs*)

Warren Peace: (*with sympathy*) There, there. It's hard being a colony. But you know, T.C., I might be able to help.

T.C.: Really?

Warren Peace: I'd like you to meet my brother. (*stands up and calls out*) Indie?

Indie Pendence: (*enters*) Hey, Warren, how are you doing?

Warren Peace: Great! Indie Pendence, I'd like you to meet my friend, Thirteen Colonies, known as T.C. around these parts. I think she might want to hear what you have to say.

T.C.: Pleased to meet you, Indie.

Indie Pendence: Likewise. Do you know what independence means?

T.C.: I think so. But tell me more about it.

Indie Pendence: Independence means being able to run your own government the way you see fit—imposing your own taxes, using the money for things that matter to you, and setting your own laws.

T.C.: Wow! That sounds liberating!

Indie Pendence: Yes, indeed. But independence may come at a high price. Let me give you my business card, and you think about things for a while. Just call me if you want to talk some more. (*all exit*)

Scene Three—The House of T.C.

Newspaper Kid #3: (*enters*) Hear ye! Hear ye! The latest copy of *The Troubled Times* just out! England repeals the Stamp Act and passes The Townshend Acts! (*gives copies to each narrator*)

Narrator #1: Once again, the colonies managed to convince England to repeal an unfair tax.

Narrator #2: But after repealing the Stamp Act of 1765, the British Prime Minister, Charles Townshend, passed a new set of taxes in 1767, known as the Townshend Acts. These laws placed tariffs on items brought into the colonies, such as lead, paint, paper, and . . . once again, tea.

Narrator #1: This time, anger over the Townshend Acts led to a protest that ended in violence, known as the Boston Massacre, in 1770.

Narrator #2: Five colonists were killed in the Boston Massacre, which led England to repeal the Townshend Acts.

Narrator #1: This repeal took away all of the previous taxes.

Narrator #2: Except the tax on tea. That one continued.

Narrator #1: And this tea tax led the colonists to get creative and do things such as grow their own tea so they wouldn't have to buy it from England.

Narrator #2: It also led the Sons of Liberty to organize a big protest event in 1773 known as the Boston Tea Party.

(*Enter T.C., followed by Friends #1, #2, and #3.*)

Friend #1: Here you go, T.C. Here are some tea plants that you can start growing in your garden.

T.C.: Oh, thank you. I'll get these planted right away. I can't believe we're only allowed to purchase England's tea.

Friend #2: And pay taxes on it!

Friend #3: Well, we'll show them. We'll just plant our own tea. Ha!

T.C.: This worries me, though. Things just keep getting worse and worse.

Friend #1: Yes, but I've heard there's someone new in town. Someone named Indie Pendence.

T.C.: I've met him. And I've met his brother too, Warren Peace.

Friend #2: I've heard Indie Pendence might be able to help us.

T.C.: But what if it involves war?

Friend #3: Well, it could end in peace, and liberty from England!

Friend #1: Independence sounds pretty good to me! Hey, look (*pointing*), it's the Sons of Liberty!

Son of Liberty #4: (*enters quickly*) Hey, did you hear? (*exits*)

Son of Liberty #5: (*enters quickly*) There's going to be a party! (*exits*)

Son of Liberty #6: (*enters quickly*) And you're invited! (*leaves pamphlet; T.C. and Friends #1, #2, and #3 gather around*)

Friend #3: (*looking at pamphlet*) The Sons of Liberty are calling it the Boston Tea Party!

Friend #1: They're going to dump all the tea from England into the water of the Boston Harbor.

Friend #2: Whoa!

Friend #3: Let's go watch. It says we're invited! (*all exit*)

Scene Four—The House of T.C.

Newspaper Kid #4: (*enters*) Hear ye! Hear ye! Get your copy of *The Troubled Times*! England vows to make the colonists pay for all of the lost tea in the Boston Tea Party. England also passes new laws—even harsher than before! (*gives one copy to each Narrator*)

Narrator #1: (*reads headline to self*) Oh, boy. Things were going from bad to worse for the colonists.

Narrator #2: No kidding! These new laws—the colonists called them the Intolerable Acts of 1774—were pretty tough, especially the one called the Quartering Act.

Narrator #1: Yes. This act said that the colonists had to let British soldiers come live with them in their houses.

Narrator #2: And the colonists had to take care of them and feed them using the food they were already being taxed on by England.

Narrator #1: Things were not good for T.C. as she stood in her garden one day, taking care of her new plants.

T.C.: (*looking at the plants*) Oh, these little tea plants are coming along nicely. (*to plants*) I'm going to need you after the Boston Tea Party. England is still pretty upset about all the tea they lost. We're not going to be getting any tea from them for a while.

Mr. Tax: (*enters*) Hello, Thirteen Colonies. How've you been?

T.C: Oh, it's you. (*with sarcasm*) How lovely.

Mr. Tax: Oh, don't worry. I'm not here to . . .

T.C.: (*holds up hand, interrupting*) Wait. I know, I know. You're just doing you're job, right?

Mr. Tax: Actually, I'm not here to collect taxes. I'm here to tell you about the Quartering Act. (*unrolls scroll; reads*) According to the newest version of the Quartering Act of 1774, all colonists must willingly house and feed British soldiers who arrive at their door.

T.C.: (*slowly*) You have got to be kidding.

Mr. Tax: Oh, I am so not kidding. Guys? (*Soldiers enter, each carrying luggage*)

Soldier #1: (*cutting in front of T.C. and Mr. Tax*) Excuse me!

Soldier #2: Pardon me!

Soldier #3: Outta my way!

Soldier #4: Got anything to eat?

T.C.: Hey, watch it! You're stepping on my plants.

Mr. Tax: I think you'd better show them the kitchen.

Soldiers #1, #2, #3, #4: (*together*) We're hungry, hungry, hungry, hungry!

T.C.: That's it! I'm calling Indie Pendence! (*takes out cell phone*) He told me he could be reached at J-U-L-Y-4-1-7-7-6. (*talks into phone*) Hello, Indie Pendence? This is Thirteen Colonies and we need to talk . . . (*all exit*)

Scene Five—Really Troubled Times

Newspaper Kid #5: (*enters*) Hear ye! Hear ye! Hot off the presses! It's *The Really Troubled Times*. Get your copy now! (*gives one copy to each narrator*)

Narrator #1: (*reading over paper*) Well, the Intolerable Acts were the final straw for the colonists.

Narrator #2: They were ready to fight for their independence from England.

Narrator #1: And they decided they would do whatever it took, including going to war.

Narrator #2: T.C. met with Indie Pendence to discuss how to be free from England. (*T.C. and Indie Pendence enter and walk across stage, talking*)

Indie Pendence: You know, T.C., independence is wonderful. But like I said before, it may come at a high price. It will probably involve my brother, Warren Peace.

T.C.: I know. But I've really thought about this and I've decided we have to be our own country. We have to be independent. Hopefully, if we have to start with war, we will end with peace. (*both exit*)

Narrator #1: The first step toward independence was the formation of the First Continental Congress, in the fall of 1774.

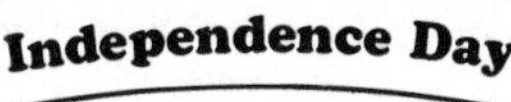

Narrator #2: This was a group of representatives from all of the colonies except Georgia. They met in September and October in 1774 to decide what to do about the Intolerable Acts and to begin preparing for independence.

Narrator #1: Many well-known people attended this congress, including Samuel Adams, George Washington, John Adams, and Patrick Henry.

(*Samuel Adams and George Washington enter and walk across stage, talking.*)

Samuel Adams: So what you're saying, Mr. Washington, is that we need to tell England what we think our rights are.

George Washington: Yes, Mr. Adams, and then we won't buy anything from England until they recognize our rights.

Samuel Adams: And if they still won't let us have our rights, then in six months we will hold another Continental Congress to decide what to do next.

Narrator #2: And that is exactly what happened.

Narrator #1: The Second Continental Congress met in May of 1775 and included new people, such as Benjamin Franklin and Thomas Jefferson.

Narrator #2: At this congress, delegates began to prepare for a war to gain their independence. They made one last try to work peacefully with the king of England.

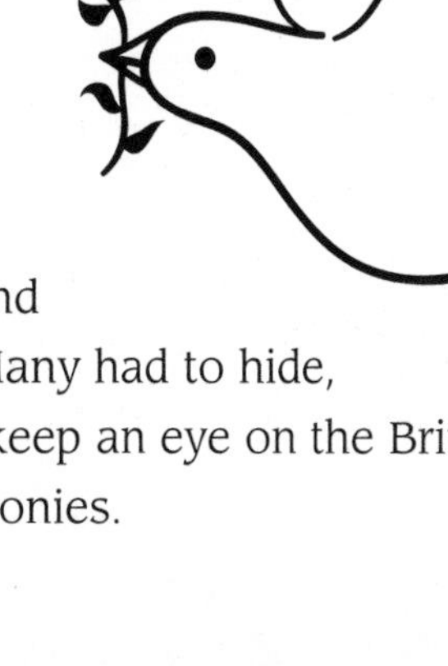

Narrator #1: And they sent something called the Olive Branch Petition to the king, telling him that they felt loyalty to him but disapproved of what his governors were doing.

Narrator #2: But King George declared that the colonies were officially in rebellion, and it became dangerous for Washington, Adams, and their fellow delegates to stay in their towns. Many had to hide, although they left one trusted man behind to keep an eye on the British soldiers who were already stationed in the colonies.

Narrator #1: This trusted man's name was Paul Revere and in April of 1775 . . .

Paul Revere: (*interrupting, runs across stage*) The British are coming! The British are coming! The British are coming!

Narrator #2: He warned the colonists that more British soldiers were coming, so they had to be ready for war.

Narrator #1: That same night, the first gunshot of the Revolutionary War was fired.

Narrator #2: It is not known whether the colonists or the British fired the first shot, but this became known as "the shot heard 'round the world."

Narrator #1: And the long battle for independence between the colonies and England officially began.

Scene Six—Hopeful Times

Newspaper Kid #6: (*enters*) Hear ye! Hear ye! Get your copy of *The Hopeful Times*! The colonies adopt the Declaration of Independence! (*gives one copy to each Narrator*)

Narrator #1: (*reads headline to self, then addresses audience*) Even though the Revolutionary War was still being fought, the colony delegates met again in 1776 to write the Declaration of Independence.

Narrator #2: This important document was officially accepted on July 4, 1776, and signed on August 2, 1776.

(*T.C., Indie Pendence, Warren Peace, John Hancock, and Samuel Adams enter*)

John Hancock: Here's a pen. I'll sign the Declaration of Independence first and then everyone else can sign, too. (*Indie Pendence leans over so John Hancock can sign on his back*)

Indie Pendence: (*laughing*) Hey, that tickles! (*others continue signing as the Narrators talk*)

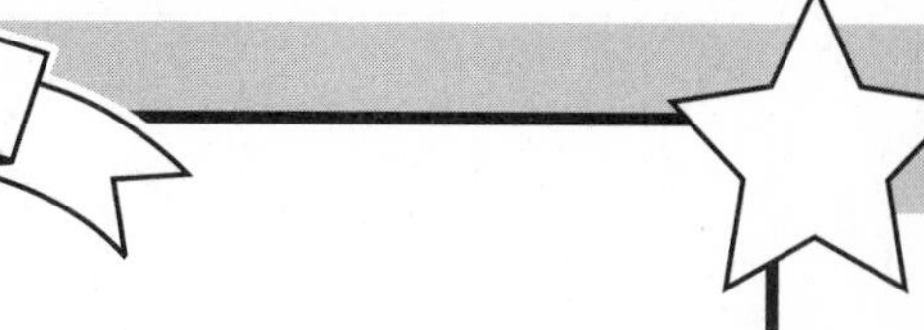

Narrator #1: The war continued with England for another seven years. Afterward many of the same delegates began to write the U.S. Constitution, which they signed on September 17, 1787.

Narrator #2: And in 1789, George Washington was unanimously chosen to be the country's first president.

Narrator #1: The colonists were able to ship Mr. Tax back to England. (*enter Mr. Tax*)

Mr. Tax: Hello, is anybody here?

T.C.: Get him boys! Send him back where he belongs! (*Warren Peace and Indie Pendence help Mr. Tax off-stage*)

Mr. Tax: (*as he's exiting*) Hey, wait! I like this place! Hey!

Narrator #2: And the rest, as they say . . .

Narrator #1: . . . is history.

Curtain Call

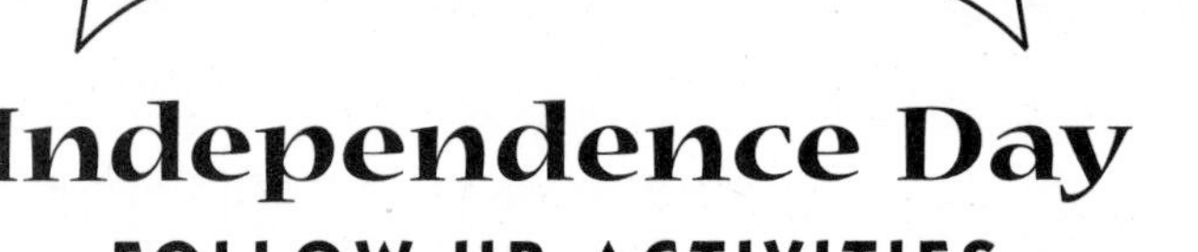

Independence Day

FOLLOW-UP ACTIVITIES

Creating a New State

Purpose: Explore concepts of democracy and independence by creating a new state government.

How to: Place students in heterogeneous groups of three to five students. Tell them to imagine that an uninhabited island has been discovered and their groups have a chance to create a new state on the island. Instruct each group to create a list of at least five things all group members have in common, such as a food they all enjoy, a sport they all play, or a place they all have visited. Using this list as a guide, invite the group to create a state that has a name and common theme; for example, "the Soccer State." In addition, each group should draw a map for their state, a common system of currency, and a set of three to five laws that will govern their state. Encourage students to copy their laws onto a copy of the Constitution-frame paper on page 65. Let students create a poster of their state displaying this information, and have groups share them with the class. Discuss the challenges, responsibilities, and benefits of all of their states coming together to live as one country.

Extend it! Ask students to research and compare different forms of government, such as democracy, monarchy, and socialism.

Independence Day Writing Prompts

Purpose: Build understanding of these concepts: freedom, independence, and government.

How to: In journals or during free writing time, invite students to write about any of the following:

- What do the words *freedom*, *justice*, and *liberty* mean? Do they mean different things to different people? Do you think they have meant different things at different times in our nation's history?
- List three freedoms you can't imagine living without. To what lengths would you go to defend these freedoms?
- Imagine you were in charge of creating a constitution for a new country. What five things would you include in this constitution? (Have students rewrite their ideas on copies of the Constitution-frame paper, to share and display.)

Constitution

"The Museum of Labor and Industry"

**A read-aloud play for
Labor Day, celebrated the first Monday in September**

"The Museum of Labor and Industry" helps students learn about the history of Labor Day and appreciate the struggles that industrial workers have engaged in throughout America's history to achieve fair working conditions and pay.

History

In the early years of our country, industrial workers faced dangerous working conditions, unbearably long workdays, and low pay. In response, a movement slowly grew during the early 1800s to improve working conditions in mills and factories across the country. This movement took the form of strikes and labor walkouts, some of which ended in great violence, but all of which ultimately helped create fairer working conditions for laborers. Consequently, the idea for a day to celebrate the contributions of American workers was also born. The first unofficial Labor Day took place in New York City in 1882. This was followed by a presidential declaration in 1894 by President Grover Cleveland establishing an annual national Labor Day.

If You Stage the Play . . .

Set: This play takes place through a "living museum" format, in which exhibits and statues come to life when they are turned on. You may wish to have students in the exhibits remain motionless onstage throughout the play, or have them enter and exit for their specific parts.

Costumes: Let students brainstorm distinctive costumes that reflect their characters or exhibits. For example, the textile worker may have a pair of scissors or hold a bundle of cloth, miners may wear hard hats and carry buckets, and the sailor may carry a fishing net or fishing pole. For the exhibits, encourage students to think of costumes that reflect both the occupations of the characters and the time period they inhabit.

The Cast

(in order of reading level)

Grade 2

STRIKERS #1, #2, #3

Grade 3

SPECTATORS #1, #2, #3

TEACHER

PRINTER

COAL MINER

TEXTILE MILL WORKER

JONATHAN

EMILY

MOLLY MAE

STUDENT #1

High Grade 3/Low 4

STUDENTS #2, #3, #4

NEWSIE

Grade 4

GROVER CLEVELAND

SAILOR

REPORTER

WORKERS #1, #2, #3

STEELWORKER

Grade 5

TOUR GUIDE

PROLOGUE READER

Vocabulary

accomplishment *noun* a task completed successfully.

cause *noun* goal or purpose.

employer *noun* a person or a business that hires workers.

exhibit *noun* a display, such as at a museum.

industry *noun* 1. businesses that make or sell things; 2. making or selling products.

mill *noun* a factory where paper, cloth, or steel is made.

mine *noun* underground tunnels where workers dig for metal or minerals.

slogan *noun* a saying used by a group of people to make their ideas known.

textiles *noun* cloth.

The Museum of Labor and Industry

HONORING LABOR DAY,
CELEBRATED THE FIRST MONDAY IN SEPTEMBER

THE CAST

(in order of appearance)

PROLOGUE READER (optional)

TOUR GUIDE

STUDENT #1 • STUDENT #2 • STUDENT #3 • STUDENT #4

TEXTILE MILL WORKER • COAL MINER • STEELWORKER

SAILOR • PRINTER • EMILY • JONATHAN • REPORTER

MOLLY MAE • NEWSIE • STRIKER #1 • STRIKER #2 • STRIKER #3

WORKER #1 • WORKER #2 • WORKER #3

SPECTATOR #1 • SPECTATOR #2 • SPECTATOR #3

GROVER CLEVELAND • TEACHER

* Note: Exhibits and statues may stay "frozen" on stage during the entire play or they may move on and off the stage as needed.

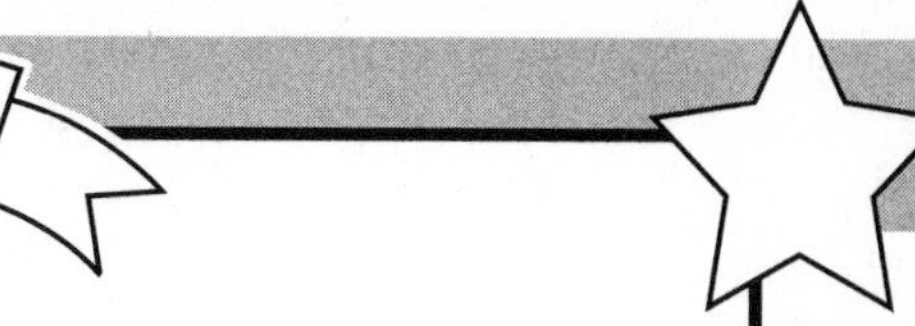

PROLOGUE READER: (optional) Labor Day is a holiday that began in 1882. It celebrates the accomplishments of people who make the products we depend on—our clothes, our school buses, and even the chairs we sit on. This holiday grew out of people's unhappiness with very poor working conditions. Today, we celebrate Labor Day to recognize positive changes in industry and to honor the courage, hard work, and leadership of American workers.

Tour Guide: Good morning, class. Welcome to your field trip through the Museum of Labor and Industry. My name is Ms. Turry and I will be your tour guide through the museum.

Students: (*together*) Hi, Ms. Turry.

Tour Guide: I'm so glad you could join us, because today you are going to learn some very interesting things about work and Labor Day. Before we begin our tour, I want to make sure that everyone knows what the word *labor* means.

Student #1: Is labor like something you pull?

Tour Guide: No, that's a lever. Does anyone else know?

Student #2: (*raising hand*) Yeah, I think I know!

Tour Guide: Yes?

Student #2: I think it means work.

Tour Guide: Exactly. It does mean work. But it means a certain kind of work. Let's go into the Hall of Statues so we can understand more about what kind of work a laborer does.

Student #3: Look at all these statues!

Student #4: Cool! What do they do?

Tour Guide: These are all statues of people who work as laborers. When you press their buttons, they will turn on and explain what kind of work they are involved in.

Student #2: Oh! I want to press a button!

Student #3: Hey, yeah. That sounds cool!

Tour Guide: Each of you will have the chance to push the button of one statue and turn it on. (*to Student #1*) Why don't you start?

Student #1: Uh, okay. It's not going to hurt, is it?

Tour Guide: No, not at all. Go ahead. (*Student #1 presses Textile Worker button*)

Textile Mill Worker: (*turns "on," smiling*) Hello! Now, don't you all have some fine, pretty clothes. I know all about that because I work in a textile mill. I have a very important job, because I help make the cloth that will be turned into the clothes that you wear. The next time you go shopping for clothes, don't forget that I helped get them there. (*turns "off"*)

Student #2: Cool! It's my turn! (*pushes Coal Miner button*)

Coal Miner: (*turns "on," smiling*) Hello. I bet everyone is feeling nice and warm. That's thanks to me. I am a miner and I work deep inside a coal mine to bring coal up for you to use to heat your buildings. And . . . (*points to Steelworker, who stands next to him*)

Steelworker: (*turns "on," smiling*) . . . and I bet you arrived here today in a car or bus or train that had metal in it. You can thank me for that. I work in the steel industry. I got some of his coal, burned it, and used it to melt steel so it could be shaped into buildings and cars and other important things that people use. (*turns "off"*)

Student #3: I wonder what this one will be? (*pushes Sailor button*)

Sailor: (*turns "on," smiling*) Ahoy, there, mates! This is your local sailor here. I help to catch the fish you ate for dinner last night. Thanks to me, you're getting a healthy delicious meal without ever having to go to the ocean to catch it yourself. Eat up and enjoy! (*turns "off"*)

Student #4: Finally, it's my turn! Here we go. (*pushes Printer button*)

Printer: (*turns "on," smiling*) Well, look at this fine group of young people! You look like you know all about world events. I bet that's because you read one of the newspapers that I helped print. Yup, I'm a printer, and I help to get you information in newspapers and magazines. I'm in charge of cutting huge rolls of paper into the size you can read and making sure

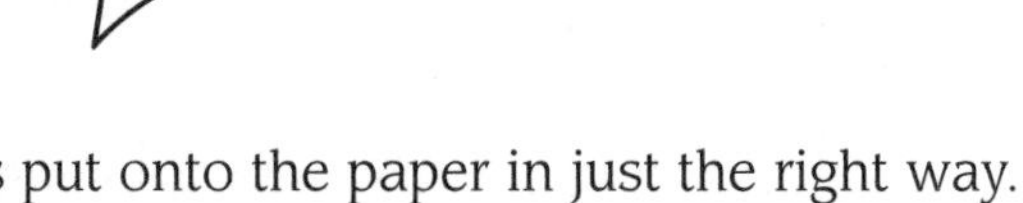

the ink gets put onto the paper in just the right way. It's a big job and I'm proud to do it! (*turns "off"*)

Tour Guide: So after hearing from our statues, does anyone have a better idea about what a laborer is?

Student #2: I think I get it.

Tour Guide: Go ahead. What do you think?

Student #2: Well, none of those people sits at a desk all day.

Tour Guide: You're right. Any other thoughts?

Student #4: Hey, that's right. None of those workers have jobs where they sit a lot during the day or sell stuff or . . .

Student #1: Yeah, and all of them do some kind of work where they have to use their hands or arms or legs for a big part of their job.

Tour Guide: That's right.

Student #3: So, are laborers people who have jobs where they have to use their hands or bodies to make something?

Tour Guide: Precisely.

Student #3: Wow. They have some pretty important jobs.

Tour Guide: Yes, and don't forget that all jobs are important, just different. They are all a necessary part of life in our country. Well, now that you understand a little bit more about these kinds of jobs, let's move to the Hall of Labor History. Gather around now so you can see our first exhibit. (*Students stand off to the side as if they are watching, but also so the audience can see*) This exhibit takes place in 1870 and will show you what kind of conditions many people in industry used to work in. (*pushes exhibit button "on"*)

Jonathan: Good morning, Emily. You're a bit late this morning. The sun has been up for five minutes already.

Emily: I know, Jonathan. But our workdays are so much longer now that it is summer and the sun stays out longer. I hate working from sunup to sundown. Yesterday, we worked 16 hours! And even in the winter, we still have to work at least 12 hours.

Jonathan: Well, at least we have jobs. And we don't have to work in the mines, where people die from accidents all the time.

Emily: I suppose. And tomorrow is payday. We get paid for the whole week. What are you going to do with your 25 cents?

Jonathan: I'm saving up! I'm going to put five whole cents in the bank, so someday I can buy my own horse.

Emily: Good for you, Jonathan. Good for you. (*exhibit turns "off"*)

Student #2: A quarter? Did she say they got paid 25 cents for the whole week?

Tour Guide: Yes. In the 1800s, employers could pay as little as they wanted. And many industrial workers were forced to live in terrible houses that their employers built for them, houses that had leaky roofs and rats living in them.

Student #1: Rats, gross!

Tour Guide: And did anyone hear how many hours they worked?

Student #3: I thought she said they worked from sunup to sundown.

Student #4: That's a lot of hours.

Tour Guide: Yes, at that time, people in industry worked at least 12 hours every day and usually more. And as you noticed, they didn't get paid much, either.

Student #2: Wow.

Tour Guide: But what was even worse than that was child labor.

Student #4: Child labor?

Tour Guide: Yes, until around 1915 or so, hundreds of thousands of young children worked in industry in this country instead of going to school.

Student #3: Cool!

Student #1: Yeah. I think I'd rather work instead of go to school. Then you'd get money and not have any homework!

Tour Guide: Well, let's find out how a child laborer felt about it at the next exhibit. (*presses "on" button of child labor exhibit*)

Reporter: (*to Molly Mae*) Hello, there, young lady. I'm a newspaper reporter writing about American children who are working in the year 1905. Can you tell me how you old you are and where you work?

Molly Mae: Why, yes, sir. My name is Molly Mae and I'm 9 years old. I been workin' this mill for a year. I run the cotton machine.

Reporter: So you started when you were 8?

Molly Mae: Yes, sir.

Reporter: And do you like working in the textile mill with cotton?

Molly Mae: Oh, it's fine. I get paid almost five whole cents a day so I can feed my sisters at home.

Newsie: (*interrupting*) Newspapers! Newspapers for sale!

Reporter: (*to Newsie*) Excuse me. I'm a newspaper reporter and . . .

Newsie: Get outta here, Mister. This is where *I* sell newspapers! Go find someplace else to sell yours. I'll get a beating if I don't sell all my newspapers tonight!

Reporter: No, no. I'm not selling papers. I'm writing a story about children who work in the year of 1905. Can you tell me how old you are?

Newsie: Well, as long as you're not gonna sell no papers.

Reporter: No. I just write for them.

Newsie: Well, sir, I am 10 years old, yes I am, and I been selling these papers for five years. I am the best there is!

Reporter: Well, I'd be happy to buy one from you. Here's a penny.

Newsie: Thanks, Mister.

Reporter: What's your best story today? I bet you know all the news in this paper.

Newsie: Oh, no, sir. I memorize the headlines, but I can't read. I can't go to school, 'cause I work instead.

Reporter: Well, would you like to go to school?

Newsie: Sure, but I can't. Gotta sell papers. (*exits*) Newspapers! Newspapers! (*exhibit turns "off"*)

Tour Guide: Well, what did you think?

Student #2: Wow. I didn't know that kids worked like that when they were so young.

Student #1: I thought you'd make more money if you worked, but they sure didn't make much money.

Tour Guide: No, hardly enough to live on. Thankfully, by 1920, people began to realize that it was more important for all children to be educated instead of working all day.

Student #3: Yeah, I bet those kids never got to be very smart.

Tour Guide: Well, now there are laws that make it illegal for children to work full-time. And children under a certain age can't work at all.

Student #3: Yeah, well, I still wish we didn't have homework.

Student #1: I think I'll take homework over selling newspapers out on the street all day!

Tour Guide: Okay. Let's move along to our next exhibit. This is a brand-new exhibit that our museum just received. It takes place in 1880 and you will actually be the first people to see it. (*pushes "on" button of the Strike exhibit*)

Strikers #1, #2, #3: (*together, loudly*) Strike! Strike! Strike!

Student #2: (*covers ears*) They're so loud!

Strikers #1, #2, #3: (*together, loudly*) Strike! Strike! Strike!

Student #1: (*covers ears*) What are they saying?

Strikers #1, #2, #3: (*together, loudly*) Strike! Strike! Strike!

Student #3: (*covers ears*) I don't get it!

Strikers #1, #2, #3: (*together, loudly*) Strike! Strike! Strike!

Student #4: (*covers ears*) Turn it off!

Tour Guide: (*presses "off" button*) Oh, dear. I don't think this exhibit is working properly. They're supposed to do more than just yell all the time.

Student #1: What were they talking about?

Student #2: Yeah, what's a strike?

Tour Guide: You see, workers began to grow more frustrated with long hours, little pay, and dangerous working conditions. To try to make things better, many workers decided to group together and refuse to show up for work.

Student #3: Oh, is that called a strike?

Tour Guide: Yes. And if all of the workers of a company refuse to work, and go on strike, it can cause that company to lose money, which might help them see how important the workers are.

Student #2: And then would the companies make things easier, like shorter hours and more pay?

Tour Guide: Yes, and in the early 1880s, one of the first things workers asked for was to work just eight hours a day, instead of from sunup to sundown. They even wrote a slogan for what they wanted. The slogan is written on that last exhibit. Will you read it?

Student #4: (*reading slogan*) It says, "Eight hours for work, eight hours for rest, and eight hours for what you will."

Tour Guide: This meant that workers wanted to work only eight hours every day, instead of 12 or more hours. The next exhibit will explain more about strikes and the dangers that striking workers faced.

Student #1: Is this one going to be loud?

Tour Guide: No, I know this exhibit is working properly. Let's give it a try. (*pushes "on" button of Haymarket Affair exhibit*)

Worker #1: So how long have we been on strike now?

Worker #2: What's the date?

Worker #3: It's May 12, 1886.

Worker #2: Well, then, we've been on strike for 12 days. Have faith. We're striking for an eight-hour day, remember?

Worker #1: I remember. I'm just afraid. Did you hear what happened last week in the Haymarket Square in Chicago?

Worker #2: No, what happened?

Worker #3: Oh, it was a terrible thing. There was a group of workers striking for the eight-hour day, just like us. The police came and a bomb went off . . .

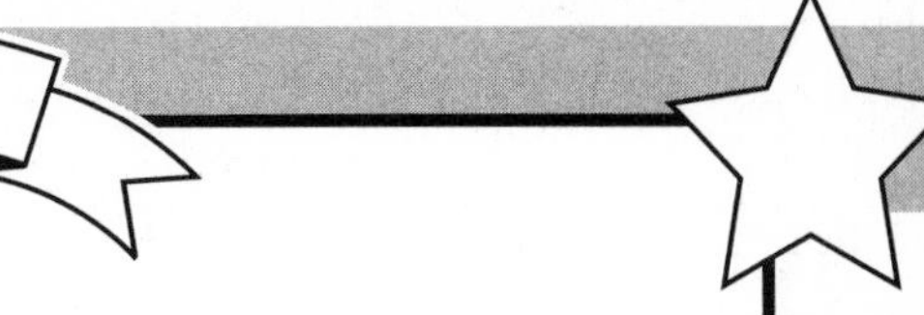

Worker #2: What happened?

Worker #1: Several people were killed, both police officers and workers. They arrested some of the workers. But some people think the workers weren't the ones who started the violence. There are people with money and power who don't want us to succeed.

Worker #2: Just remember that our cause is a good one.

Worker #1: I'll try. (*exhibit turns "off"*)

Student #2: So what did happen?

Student #3: Did they find the people who set off the bomb?

Tour Guide: Well, unfortunately, no one was ever really sure who started the violence at Haymarket Square. They did arrest eight workers, but later, the governor of Illinois decided their trial had been unfair. Unfortunately, by that time, four of the workers had already been punished by the courts and hanged. It was a very sad situation.

Student #4: But what does this have to do with Labor Day?

Tour Guide: Well, because of the efforts—and sacrifices—of many workers like these, over more than a hundred years, laborers were granted many more rights, including an eight-hour workday and better pay. As for Labor Day, let's watch our final exhibit in the hall of history to find out how this all fits together. (*pushes "on" button*)

Spectator #1: Isn't this exciting!

Spectator #2: Yes, I can't wait!

Spectator #3: What? What's happening? What's going on?

Spectator #1: Our president, Grover Cleveland, is going to make an announcement.

Spectator #3: An announcement? What kind of announcement?

Spectator #2: Hush, now. President Cleveland is speaking!

President Cleveland: On this day, the first Monday in September, 1894, I declare a national holiday to honor the working man and woman. Let us spend this day eating, resting, and celebrating the accomplishments such people have made to this great country of ours.

Spectators #1, #2, #3: (*together*) Hurray! (*exhibit turns "off"*)

Tour Guide: So now we celebrate Labor Day on the first Monday in September. And we celebrate this day to help us remember what rights workers have fought for and the accomplishments they provide our country. (*Teacher enters*) Oh, here's your teacher.

Teacher: Hello, class. How was your field trip?

Student #1: We learned so much!

Student #2: Yeah, did you know that people in industry used to have to work for 12 or more hours?

Student #3: And children as young as 6 or 7 worked in mills?

Student #1: And also sold newspapers?

Student #4: And workers risked a lot of accidents and even death because they had to work in unsafe conditions?

Teacher: Well, it sounds like you learned a lot. It will be easy for each of you to write a 500-page report about your trip through the Museum of Labor and Industry.

Students #1, #2, #3, #4: (*together*) What? (*sounds of protest*)

Teacher: No, I'm just kidding! But when we get back to school, I do want to hear more about what you learned.

Student #2: Whew! That's a relief!

Student #3: Yeah. I was afraid we might have to go on strike or something.

Curtain Call

Labor Day

FOLLOW-UP ACTIVITIES

The Museum of Living Jobs and Careers

Purpose: Create a living museum and teach others about aspects of labor and industry.

How to: Begin by brainstorming a list of careers and jobs in today's industry. You may wish to place careers into categories such as automobile production, food processing, textiles, mining, and logging. Invite students to choose one career or job they find interesting and research its elements, such as uniform or style of dress, required tools, typical workday, and reasons why people might choose this job. Instruct students to use this research to create a 30- to 60-second monologue. Have them set up exhibits around the room to create a living museum. Invite another class to visit the museum and allow visitors to press the "on" buttons (small red adhesive dots) of the statues. When turned "on," students, in costume, perform their monologue, and then they freeze to turn "off."

A Job Walk Through Time

Purpose: Research how various jobs have changed in the past one hundred years.

How to: Choose four or five types of jobs for students to research, such as auto mechanics, teachers, physicians, firefighters, or sailors. Place students in small groups or pairs. Challenge students to research aspects of one of these jobs as it was conducted a hundred years ago. Research points may include pay, workday, specific rules that applied to the job, required uniform or clothing, and necessary tools or equipment. To culminate their research, have them complete copies of the Jobs Then and Now Chart (page 80) to show the differences between the jobs as they were and as they are today. Ask students to use the information they've gathered to create a comparative poster or graph comparing aspects of the jobs today with the same aspects one hundred years ago.

Extend it! Invite students to create a timeline for the future of jobs and careers. Ask students to imagine how various aspects of a job will change over the next hundred or two hundred years.

JOBS THEN AND NOW CHART

TYPE OF JOB ______________________

Then YEAR: _____	**Now** YEAR: 20___